Audit Cultures

If cultures are always in the making, this book catches one kind of culture on the make. Academics will be familiar with audit in the form of research and teaching assessments – they may not be aware how pervasive practices of 'accountability' are or of the diversity of political regimes under which they flourish. Twelve social anthropologists from across Europe and the Commonwealth chart an influential and controversial cultural phenomenon.

The challenge is that these new accountabilities are at once obstructive and enabling of good practice. Through accountability the financial and the moral meet in the twinned precepts of economic efficiency and ethical practice. Audit practices have direct consequences, and, in the view of many, dire ones for intellectual production. Yet audit is almost impossible to critique in principle – after all, it advances values that academics generally hold dear, such as responsibility, openness of enquiry and widening of access. The volume also therefore examines some of the parameters of professional ethics.

Audit Cultures provides an excellent opening for future debate on the 'culture' of management and accountability. It will be an essential resource for students of culture and relevant to academics everywhere.

Marilyn Strathern is Professor of Social Anthropology at Cambridge University and Mistress of Girton College.

European Association of Social Anthropologists

Series facilitator: Jon P. Mitchell
University of Sussex

The European Association of Social Anthropologists (EASA) was inaugurated in January 1989, in response to a widely felt need for a professional association which would represent social anthropologists in Europe and foster cooperation and interchange in teaching and research. As Europe transforms itself, the EASA is dedicated to the renewal of the distinctive European tradition in social anthropology.

Other titles in the series:

Conceptualizing Society
Adam Kuper

Other Histories
Kristen Hastrup

Alcohol, Gender and Culture
Dimitra Gefou-Madianou

Understanding Rituals
Daniel de Coppet

Gendered Anthropology
Teresa del Valle

Social Experience and Anthropological Knowledge
Kirsten Hastrup and Peter Hervik

Fieldwork and Footnotes
Han F. Vermeulen and Arturo Alvarez Roldan

Syncretism/Anti-Syncretism
Charles Stewart and Rosalind Shaw

Grasping the Changing World
Václav Hubinger

Civil Society
Chris Hann and Elizabeth Dunn

Anthropology of Policy
Cris Shore and Susan Wright

Nature and Society
Philippe Descola and Gisli Pálsson

The Ethnography of Moralities
Signe Howell

Inside and Outside the Law
Olivia Harris

Locality and Belonging
Nadia Lovell

Recasting Ritual
Felicia Hughes-Freeland and Mary M. Crain

Anthropological Perspectives on Local Development
Simone Abram and Jacqueline Waldren

Dividends of Kinship: Meanings and Uses of Social Relatedness
Peter Schweitzer

Constructing the Field: Ethnographic Fieldwork in the Contemporary World
Vered Amit

Gender, Agency and Change: Anthropological Perspectives
Edited by Victoria Ana Goddard

Audit Cultures

Anthropological studies in
accountability, ethics and
the academy

Edited by Marilyn Strathern

London and New York

First published 2000
by Routledge
2 Park Square, Milton Park, Abingdon, Oxon, OX14 4RN

Simultaneously published in the USA and Canada
by Routledge
270 Madison Ave, New York NY 10016

Routledge is an imprint of the Taylor & Francis Group

Transferred to Digital Printing 2005

Typeset in Galliard and Gill Sans by
Exe Valley Dataset Ltd, Exeter, Devon

British Library Cataloguing in Publication Data
A catalogue record for this book is availabe from the British Library

Library of Congress Cataloging in Publication Data
Audit cultures: anthropological studies in accountability, ethics, and
the academy/edited by Marilyn Strathern.
    p.   cm.—(European Association of Social Anthropologists)
Includes bibliographical references and index.
    1. Education, Higher—Evaluation—Social aspects. 2. Educational
anthropology. 3. Educational accountability—Social aspects.
4. Education, Higher—Moral and ethical aspects. I. Strathern, Marilyn.
II. European Association of Social Anthropologists (Series)

LB2324.A87 2000
306.43—dc21   00-028073

ISBN 0-415-23326-7 (hbk)
ISBN 0-415-23327-5 (pbk)

Contents

Contributors

Vered Amit is Associate Professor at the Department of Sociology and Anthropology, Concordia University, Montreal, Canada. She has conducted fieldwork in London (UK), Quebec, the Cayman Islands and Vancouver. She is presently conducting a study of transnational consultants. She is the author of *Armenians in London: The Management of Social Boundaries* (1989), co-editor of three books and editor of a recent volume in the EASA series entitled *Constructing the Field: Ethnographic Fieldwork in the Contemporary World*.

Vassos Argyrou is Associate Professor of Social Science at Inter-college, Nicosia, Cyprus. Among his publications are *Tradition and Modernity in the Mediterranean* (1996), 'Is "Closer and Closer" Ever Close Enough? De-reification, Diacritical Power, and the Specter of Evolutionism' (*Anthropological Quarterly*), and ' "Keep Cyprus Clean": Littering, Pollution, and Otherness' (*Cultural Anthropology*).

Thomas Fillitz is Assistant Professor at the Institute of Social and Cultural Anthropology, University of Vienna, and Lecturer at the Institute of Volkskunde (Folklore Studies), University of Graz. Research and teaching: theoretical anthropology, consumerism and anthropology of art. Field researches: northern Nigeria (1991) on political movements; Ivory Coast and Benin (1997) on contemporary art in Africa. He is preparing a book on *The Construction of Cultural Space: Thirteen Contemporary African Artists*; and directs a research project on 'Intercultural teaching and learning: a case study of eighteen schools in Vienna and Upper Austria'.

Dimitra Gefou-Madianou is Professor of Social Anthropology at Panteion University, Athens, Greece. She studied at Athens and New York (Columbia). Fieldwork has been conducted in various parts of Greece and she has published in the fields of alcohol, gender, 'anthropology at home', ethnicity and identity formation, drugs, anthropological theory, culture and ethnography. She is currently Head of the Section of Social Anthropology and Vice-Head of the Department of Social Policy and Social Anthropology at Panteion. Recent publications include *Current Trends in Anthropological Theory and Ethnography* (ed.) (1998), 'Cultural polyphony and identity formation: negotiating tradition in Attica' (*Amer. Ethnologist*, 1999), and *Culture and Ethnography: From Ethnographic Realism to Cultural Critique* (1999).

Ananta Kumar Giri is on the faculty of the Madras Institute of Development Studies, Chennai, India. Dr Giri has an abiding interest in alternative movements and alternative ideas for social reconstruction and cultural renewal. He is the author of *Global Transformations: Postmodernity and Beyond* (1998), *Values, Ethics and Business: Challenges for Education and Management* (1998), and (in Oriya) *Sameekhya o Purodrusti (Criticism and the Vision of the Future)* (1999).

Richard Harper is Director of the Digital World Research Centre, at the University of Surrey, UK. He has been at the forefront of research into the use of sociological and interdisciplinary techniques for understanding the digital technologies in organizational life, and is a regular public speaker on this theme. Published and forthcoming work includes *The Myth of the Paperless Office*, with A. J. Sellen (forthcoming); *Organizational Change and Retail Finance: an Ethnographic Perspective*, with D. Randall and M. Rouncefield (2000) and *Inside the IMF: An Ethnography of Documents, Technology and Organisational Action* (1998).

Maryon McDonald was formerly Reader in Social Anthropology at Brunel University and is now Fellow and Director of Studies in Anthropology at Robinson College, Cambridge, UK. Her work includes '*We are not French!*' *Language, Culture and Identity in Brittany* (1989), *History and Ethnicity* (with E. Tonkin and M. Chapman, 1989), *Gender, Drink and Drugs* (1994) and several articles, reports and a forthcoming book on European Union institutions, which she has been researching since 1992.

Peter Pels (University of Amsterdam/University of Leiden) currently works on the historical ethnography of elections in 1950s Tanganyika, and a history of occultism in relation to 19th- and 20th-century anthropology. He edited (with L. Nencel) *Constructing Knowledge* (1991) and (with O. Salemink) *Colonial Subjects: Essays in the Practical History of Anthropology* (1999). He wrote *A Politics of Presence: Contacts between Missionaries and Waluguru in Late Colonial Tanganyika* (1999), and is an advisory editor of *Current Anthropology*. He has been active on the EASA Ethics Network.

Eleanor Rimoldi is Senior Lecturer in Social Anthropology at Massey University, Albany Campus, Auckland, New Zealand. Research interests currently focus on civic life in urban New Zealand ('Culture: the Private, the Public and the Popular', *Social Analysis*, 1997), the history of social anthropology (forthcoming special issue of *Social Analysis* on New Zealand social anthropology, eds E. and M. Rimoldi), and on comparative education ('Education in Bougainville-Buka: Site of Struggle' in *Critical Perspectives on Education Policy, ACCESS*, 1992). A Rotary Grant for University Teachers will enable her to teach in Bougainville in the year 2000 and follow up her interest in the re-establishment of education systems on the island after nine years of civil war.

Cris Shore is Senior Lecturer and Head of the Anthropology Department at Goldsmiths College, University of London, UK. His first research was an ethnographic study of the Italian communist party, and his most recent work has explored the cultural politics and organizational cultures of the European Union. Recent books include *The Future of Anthropology* (with A. Ahmed, 1995), *Anthropology and Cultural Studies* (with S. Nugent, 1997), *Anthropology of Policy* (with S. Wright, 1997), and *Building Europe: the Cultural Politics of European Integration* (2000).

Marilyn Strathern is Professor of Social Anthropology at the University of Cambridge and Mistress of Girton College, Cambridge, UK. Her interests are divided between Melanesian (*Women in Between*, 1972) and British (*Kinship at the Core*, 1981) ethnography. *The Gender of the Gift* (1988) is a critique of anthropological theories of society and gender relations as they have been applied to Melanesia, while *After Nature* (1992) comments on the cultural revolution at home. The co-authored *Technologies of Procreation* was reissued in 1998, a collection of essays *Property, Substance and Effect* published in 1999.

Susan Wright (DPhil Oxford) is Senior Lecturer at the Department of Cultural Studies and Sociology, University of Birmingham, UK. Her first research area is Iran, where before and after the Islamic Revolution she has studied tribespeople's responses to changes in the state. She has continued her research on changing ideas of citizenship and forms of governance in Britain. She established the National Network for Teaching and Learning Anthropology, and has managed a discipline-specific educational development programme funded by HEFCE. Recent books include *Anthropology of Organizations* (1994), *Power and Participatory Development* (with N. Nelson, 1995), and *Anthropology of Policy* (with C. Shore, 1997).

Preface

This volume is based on materials and ideas first presented to the 1998 meetings of the European Association of Social Anthropologists in Frankfurt, at a plenary session under the title *Conditions Of Work, Conditions For Thought* and at an associated workshop, *Auditing Anthropology: the New Accountabilities*. Those contributors who have published a version elsewhere (Vassos Argyrou, Peter Pels, and Cris Shore and Susan Wright) have here written afresh. The plenary and workshop had the benefit of commentaries from Dr Jean-Claude Galey and Professor Richard Werbner: we are grateful to them both for their interest and insights. Thanks are also due to Jon Mitchell not just for the substantial work which he has devoted to this volume – along with several other EASA volumes – but for his own intellectual contribution.

Marilyn Strathern
Cambridge, August 1999

Introduction

New accountabilities

Anthropological studies in audit, ethics and the academy

Marilyn Strathern

If cultures are always in the making, the contributors to this book have caught one kind of culture on the make. It is informed by practices confined to no single set of institutions and to no one part of the world. Recognizable in the most diverse places, these practices also drive very local concerns. They determine the allocation of resources and can seem crucial to the credibility of enterprises; people become devoted to their implementation; they evoke a common language of aspiration. They also evoke anxiety and small resistances, are held to be deleterious to certain goals, and as overdemanding if not outright damaging. An old name is used for the new phenomenon: accountability. Its dual credentials in moral reasoning and in the methods and precepts of financial accounting go back a long way. But over the last two decades, and in numerous contexts, it has acquired a social presence of a new kind.

Close to home, often overlooked, or (thankfully) shut out from the 'real' tasks of productive work, a new league of expectations has mushroomed in the white-collar and professional workplace. For many anthropologists the workplace is the university, and here higher education is being moulded and managed according to what seems an almost ubiquitous consensus about aims, objectives and procedures. The emergent consensus is one which endorses government through the twin passage points of economic efficiency and good practice.

This is how the financial and the moral meet in one turn of the century rendering of accountability. That there is culture on the make here is evident from the concomitant emergence, and dominance, of what are deemed acceptable forms. Only certain social practices take a form which will convince, one which will persuade those to whom accountability is to be rendered – whether it is 'the goverment' or the taxpayer/public – that accountability has indeed been rendered. Only certain operations will count. Hence, as far as higher education is concerned, some rather specific procedures have come to carry the cultural stamp of accountability, notably assessments which are likened to audit. The concept of audit in turn has broken loose from its moorings in finance and accounting; its own expanded presence gives it the power of a descriptor seemingly applicable to all kinds of reckonings, evaluations and measurements. In this volume, audit (in its expanded sense) is the immediate starting point for an anthropological enquiry into some of the impacts of new ways of practising, or performing, 'accountability'.

An audit culture?

Procedures for assessment have social consequences, locking up time, personnel and resources, as well as locking into the moralities of public management. Yet by themselves audit practices often seem mundane, inevitable parts of a bureaucratic process. It is when one starts putting together a larger picture that they take on the contours of a distinct cultural artefact.

What we see in academic practice is part of a global pheno-menon.[1] Audit regimes accompany a specific epoch in Western international affairs, a period when governance has become recon-figured through a veritable army of 'moral fieldworkers' (NGOs), when environmental liability has been made an issue of global concern (after the Rio convention), when the ethics of appropriation has been acknowledged to an unprecedented scale in respect of indigenous rights, and when transparency of operation is everywhere endorsed as the outward sign of integrity. At the same time the apparently neutral 'market' provides a ubiquitous platform for individual interest and national politics alike, while 'management' is heard everywhere as an idiom of regulation and organization.

But what does such ubiquity imply? Here this volume makes its anthropological contribution. Through exemplification across differ-ent domains, it begins to delineate something of the scale and pervasiveness of the way in which the twinnned precepts of economic efficiency and good practice are being pursued. It is not intended as a survey; rather, it is intended to demonstrate the multiplex, cross-cutting character of values and practices promul-gated in the name of accountability. So it opens out a range of social situations. These are confined to no one population or type of state apparatus but compose a field of institutionalized expectations and instruments. To draw particularly from the lived experience of academia, a kind of local ethnography, as several of the contributions do, is to draw on the insights and frustrations of familiarity. The practices in question bear on academics in their everyday lives. They thus have direct consequences, and in the view of many dire ones, for intellectual production. Yet as an instrument of accountability, holding out the possibilities of a globalizing professional consensus, audit is almost impossible to criticize in principle – after all, it advances values that academics generally hold dear, such as responsibility, openness about outcomes and widening of access.

The contributors to this volume assume that anyone interested in the future of anthropology as a discipline should be interested in the kind of institution which reproduces it. However far afield socio-cultural (hereafter social) anthropologists go, throughout the twentieth century perpetuating what they do as 'anthropology' has invariably required their looping back into higher education and specifically into a university system.[2] The conditions of reproduction are also the daily conditions of work for its academic practitioners. These recent developments, especially those where production is subject to rituals of verification from outside, impinge in new and important ways. Indeed, as these chapters make evident, 'change' seems to impinge from every side. When one is in the midst of it, the recognition of change is always of course the moment at which reproduction seems to be suspended, and the moment thus always appears to be on the brink of a new epoch. This is the sense in which the 'new' in 'new accountabilities' is to be understood. An anthropologist's question might be just how one recognizes epochal change.

The phrase, 'rituals of verification', comes from a study by a university teacher of finance and accounting which opens with a quotation from a social anthropologist (Power 1997: 1, quoting Douglas 1992). Its subject is an exploration of those new management practices which in English go under the name of audit, derived as I have said in the first place from protocols of financial accountability but extended to become a now taken-for-granted process of neo-liberal government and contributing substantially to its ethos. Where audit is applied to public institutions – medical, legal, educational – the state's overt concern may be less to impose day-to-day direction than to ensure that internal controls, in the form of monitoring techniques, are in place. That may require the setting up of mechanisms where none existed before, but the accompanying rhetoric is likely to be that of helping (monitoring) people help (monitor) themselves, including helping people get used to this new 'culture'.

In case the term culture still seems out of place, let me add that the new practices concern more than style and presentation. The quotation from Douglas is to the effect that accountability is part of the general fabric of human interchange, which should make us interested in the forms it takes. She adds that checking only becomes necessary in situations of mistrust. Checking up on people can thus carry sinister overtones. But some governments[3] (and the UK is an example) have discovered that if they make explicit the practices whereby people check themselves, they can ostensibly withdraw[4] to the position of simply checking the resultant indicators of per-fomance. Their intervention has already taken place: in the social adjustment which corporations, public bodies and individual persons have already made to those self-checking practices now re-described as evidence of their accountability to the state.[5]

Power's field is the United Kingdom, a focus made explicit in chapters 2 and 6 of this volume, and again in the Afterword. However these accounting-derived protocols are not confined to the UK, any more than the culture of an international community is tied to specific political regimes. The language of audit[6] fuels cultural debate within the European Commission (Chapter 4), and within Europe has for example taken root with almost revolution-ary force in Greece (Chapter 10). Audit flourishes in the explicit traffic of policy ideas which flow between countries, as between Britain and New Zealand, the example given in Chapter 3.[7] It has all the momentum of a cultural movement, and one which is also going to generate resistance (Chapters 4 and 9). Of course while auditing in this expanded sense – or resistance to it – is found worldwide, as a Westerner would see it, it is not found everywhere in the world. The cases detailed reduce the sense of ubiquity in another way. They are meant to be exemplary, not representative; however, in one respect they are fortuitously clustered. If an obvious axis to these contributions is European experience (Austria, Cyprus, Greece, the EC), another is that of the old British Commonwealth (Canada, India, New Zealand) – with the UK in both (and the comment from India is a comment on the situation in the UK). As a result, the contributors are familiar with a specific range of governmental regimes, which reflect among other things the Anglo-Saxon bias made evident in Chapter 4.

For these regimes one may take the expectations created by audit as part of the phenomenon of bureaucratic 'indifference' which Herzfeld (1992) has described, part of the machinery by which the state itself evades accountability.[8] If we accept the argument of evasion,[9] then the turn of the century twist is that what conceals the state's evasion of accountability includes a call to account of those institutions which it funds. Now Herzfeld argues that any enlightened analysis of such systems must not in turn hide behind institutions but put social agency back into the picture. Readers will encounter human agents of all kinds in the following chapers. However, the centre stage is given to an agent of a non-human kind: we can think of audit as an actant [10] to which all kind of powers are attributed. The principal other character to which this book refers is 'ethics'. Ethics is a social actor frequently enrolled to justify auditing practices, yet as frequently seen as betrayed by or in resistance to them.

Contexts

This is the context of this volume. Were one to focus on the way the papers have been written, and the considerations they take up, several theoretical and topical antecedents suggest themselves. The ground for making 'accountability' an object of study as such has already been well laid in the discipline: by the anthropology of the state, by an anthropology at home which has included the study of organizations and institutions, by a flourishing European anthropology, by energetic debate on reflexive writing, not to speak of interest in those translocal discourses which obviate some of the excesses of globalization theory. Then there is the small burgeoning literature on universities and university education to which anthropologists are beginning to contribute, as well as their attention to policy in government and interest in areas such as management studies. Indeed it would be fascinating to see what genealogies could be constructed for the topic. At the same time, my hunch is that these would turn out to be purification exercises (Latour 1993),[11] unlikely to be commensurate with the hybrid interests most readers will bring to this topic. Individual anthropologists these days will have read or touched on many of these 'contexts'.

None of these arenas of study has led directly to the present topic although several of them have indeed prepared the ground for anthropologists' receptivity to it. Closer cousins could even be claimed from outside anthropology, for example in some of the new writing in the fields of financial management and accounting, and from sympathetic sociologists. 'Critical accounting' is of particular interest to social anthropology. This is partly because it blows away academic prejuduce about stale and rigid bureaucracies (under certain circumstances, they can be all too creative). And it is partly because social anthropologists would probably recognize their own interests among the new interests of the discipline. Some work in this area is touched on briefly in the Afterword. One cannot claim this field as though it had led to the present volume, although it is importantly in background of Chapter 4, for instance,[12] but one could perhaps call it a resource which anthropologists might find profitable in the future.

If I were to choose a 'context' it would have less the character of a genealogy than of a network.[13] I have been struck by certain criss-crossing observations, by the way in which social commentators (including anthropologists contributing to this volume) have seen similar epochal implications not just in 'audit' but in other con-temporary practices, of which the fields of 'ethics' and 'policy' are examples taken in these essays. As a result these domains seem to intersect. It is the simultaneity that is compelling here: similar implications for how we describe society and culture are being drawn, quite independently in the cases I am thinking of, from apparently independent fields. That is an ethnographic observation, if you like, on how we may observe current cultural changes – with appropriate limitations depending as always on the instances which happen to command attention. A network of descriptions per-taining to audit, ethics and policy, then, carries the comments I offer in the Afterword.

But that is to speak largely for myself. What is common perhaps to the contributors of *Audit Cultures* is a context of a more immediate kind: their working lives as university academics. Perhaps it is less interesting *how* they write their chapters than *why* they write them.[14] I suspect that in several cases that 'why' has come directly out of their conditions of work. It will have come out of a shared concern with the future of academic practice, and (as some of them would add) with the future of the type of open enquiry which anthropological ethnography in particular promotes.

Thus, while some of the contributions which follow include extended academic arguments, others have more the character of position papers.

It goes along with this that important antecedents lie not just in the literature but in other forms of communication. Aspects of many of the issues presented in the volume have been discussed in public forums; in Europe, the European Association of Social Anthropologists has played a key role.[15] One could always trace a genealogy of sorts through EASA's first decade of conferences and publications. If the 1998 conference at Frankfurt brought forward some of the spirit of the very first meeting at Coimbra with its emphasis on reconceptualization, these essays pick up on the interest in historical traditions within European anthropology voiced at Prague in 1992 (cf. the volume *Fieldwork and Footnotes*); the questioning of *Civil Society* (after the volume of that name), and a critical approach to governance (e.g. *The Anthropology of Policy*) voiced at Oslo in 1994. In addition, they capitalize on some unfinished business from Barcelona (1996): the EASA Workshop on Teaching Anthropology had raised questions about the multiple placement of anthropology vis-à-vis other disciplines and the diverse forms this takes across Europe. However, none of these took up the new practices of accountability in quite the way envisaged here.

The volume

Part I comprises a single ethnographic study. It describes the public presentation of a technique at the heart of financial auditing, performance statistics, and offers observations from a viewpoint outside both anthropology and the academy. The author himself is best described as an interdisciplinarist.

Power quickly followed his citation about checking being necessary in situations of mistrust (see above, p. 4) by the well-established point that checking itself requires trust – trust in measures used, trust in sources of information – since it simply would not be humanly possible to check everything. There also has to be a level of operational consensus (1996: 299). Chapter 1 shows us both the places where trust has to precede verification, and how an accumulative process of 'agreeing' to the data in hand builds up a picture to which both sides must assent. In the auditing of a country's gross economic performance, the figures over which there is debate and which have to be 'agreed' present the country's evidence of its own self-checking apparatus. The question is whether the financial statement of an enterprise gives a true and fair view.[16] The set of operations which Harper observed (the IMF on Mission) thus prefaces this volume as a reminder of the origins of 'audit' in financial accounting – although there is of course much more to accountability in everyday financial management than audit itself (Munro and Mouritsen 1996).[17] The reminder is salutory because an aura has come to surround numbers and, despite the caveats of professional auditors, it is those unfamiliar with financial auditing who tend to sanctify them. However, it should be added, when it comes to the performance indicators of public institutions, checking tends to be at a remove and agreements over outcomes do not get negotiatated in the kind of face-to-face encounters described here; much regular auditing of books also allows little room for negotiation. But when Harper stresses the 'uniqueness' of one particular IMF mission, he does so as an ethnographer conscious of the roles of personalities and the unfolding nature of relationships. The chapter thus works as a comment upon the indeterminacy of social practice.[18]

Part II takes us straight into academia, and current arguments in the UK. Chapter 2 lays out factual information about auditing in higher education to which the reader is referred as a source of some of the concerns lying behind this collection as a whole. Procedures of accountability which came into higher education from elsewhere also leak out of it and into 'the community' (Chapter 3). The final chapter in this section is a reminder of other histories of account-ability, and in a situation where it is contested as an 'Anglo-Saxon' assault on the spirit of 'European' governance.

The audit process replicates certain forms of organizational behaviour which Munro (1999: 619) identifies as cultural perfor-mance. Organization participants, in his words, may construct their cultural performances in ways that make themselves visible to one another, both as members of a group and as individual managers who are identifiably 'in' control. Chapter 2 asks what the emphasis on visible performance conceals. Strongly informed by a Foucauldian approach to 'political technology' (and see Chapters 5 and 8), its concern is with a sequence of government policies and their reception, indeed absorption, by an academic community whose 'autonomy' is allowed only certain prescribed forms of expression (only certain performances of empowerment, and not others, count). Devoted to a specific case study (universities in the UK), it thus lays out the development of a set of what can only be called cultural policies which has profoundly altered expectations in the higher education sector over the last two decades. It takes further some of the points on which the authors have already written together (see for instance Shore and Wright 1997, 1999). Here I add that the authors' forthright position, and their sad tale of how anthropology got its hand slapped, anticipates the contributions in Part IV.

Compiled from government documents, the press and discussion papers, Chapter 3 is a report on the way in which quality control measures are flooding across several areas of life in New Zealand. The apparent need for universal assessment of all kinds of skills flows from educational institutions into 'the community' – once, that is, education itself has been redefined as skills-based. Part of a radical upheaval of the country's whole educational system, the insight that learning does not stop at the school or university gate is taken as a bureaucratic truth, a piece of expert knowledge to be pressed into professional service. Whether as a teacher or an anthropologist, Rimoldi does not conceal her own stance, and clearly regards the extension of assessment procedures into areas of (previously) informal learning as a gross misapplication of social knowledge. The hairdresser's subsequent insights are chastening. They also give one pause; issues surrounding the 'democratization' of qualifications are not at all straightforward, and contain challenges which many colleagues welcome.[19] A subplot is the would-be ethnographer's own thwarted enterprise. But it was, so to speak, thwarted even before she failed to obtain funds: the chapter is also a brief case study in false opportunities (to be policy relevant) and the potential dilemma of collusion.

Like Chapter 1, Chapter 4 is based on an extended field study and gives historical depth to a crisis of public confidence which was interpreted by many as a crisis in accountability. Although elsewhere the European Commission may appear monolithic in its auditing demands (cf. Chapters 9 and 10), inside the EC – with its policy interests in how 'Europe' gets defined – the apostatization of audit regimes is seen as the invention of some Member States rather than of all of them. National origin divides those who take the new accountability/audit as a crucial matter of organizational rationality, without which colleagues could not work together, from those who see it as an assault on the very mechanisms of trust, honour and and personal relations by which colleagues do indeed have to work together. Either side may fear for institutional survival. McDonald's study holds up to the light arguments of a kind also found in higher education, but in a context where they become pinned onto perceived national and cultural differences.

Part III raises something of an internal debate, both between the three chapters and with the rest of the book. Together they shift accountability from its role as an instrument of policy to its place in more general ethical concerns. They thereby problematize the work of criticism. In a contribution that lies athwart many of the others in the volume, Giri (Chapter 6) argues that the first step is to problematize the work of politics. So whereas Chapter 5 suggests that 'ethics' can be aligned with audit as part of a continuing tradition of neo-liberal governance, and one which demands of the critic enhanced political sensitivities, Chapter 6 offers ethics as a route to bypass what is seen as the shortfall of a political response. In direct dialogue with both contributions, Argyrou (Chapter 7) argues that the metaphysical stance by which the discipline has already defined itself means that it cannot help constantly calling itself to account.

At the start of Part III, then, Pels (Chapter 5) lays out the extent to which Foucault's concept of technologies of the self might illuminate the recent resurgence of interest in ethics. The resurgence he has in mind is to be found in renewed discussion about professional codes of ethics. While for anthropologists much debate is attributed to dilemmas inherent in the ethnographic enterprise, he points out that these are also dilemmas of the neo-liberal self. In that sense they cannot be divorced from politics. Pels (1999) had earlier argued that ethics talk often conceals political strategy, and one can certainly ask what policy directions lie behind the apparently neutral invocation of good practices. Here he suggests that the ethical code which attends to the ethos of self-auditing – aligned in some cases with marketable selves – serves different 'technologies of self' from those addressed to professional duties oriented towards a public domain. Running throughout the account is his elucidation of a duplex or split self, the 'ethical double-self' which Hoskin (1996; cf. 1995) from his vantage point in management accounting first finds in the eighteenth-century enlightenment, and which in turn Pels finds deep in ethnographic practice. He argues that there is a specific history to be written here, of which the recent confessional mode in anthropological writings is only a part. In the course of his argument, he reminds us of an important element in the humanist tradition, the concept of an ideal towards which every person would strive, which is missing from contemporary ethics. This is a point which the next chapter, albeit in a contest of a kind, then takes up.

Chapter 6 is a call to academics to examine themselves, their ideals, and their own self-closing creations – including political critiques of academic self-closure. Giri thus takes up self-examination as an issue which lies behind many of these chapters, but recasts it in terms of how it is to be recovered as an imperative. He deliberately writes in an emotive tenor. For the issue is the degree of conviction with which self-criticism can be extended to the academic's own practices, and thus the kinds of cultivation of the self that can become the subject of such criticism. Written in large terms, this offers an approach to the problem that comes from the academy's relationship to the state (Hart 1998). It is the academy's dependency on the state rather than its responsiveness to 'society' which leads to the kind of political reactions, to the practices of accountability, that is, which Giri finds so insufficient. Of course we might want to ask what kind of society is imagined here. (Or what segment of society; the academy has no problem in being responsive to 'the market'.) But that imagining is presumably part of the academic task. As he says in another context, the central question is the mode of *self*-engagement: it may be important 'to think of ourselves as pilgrims or seekers rather than professionals' (1998: 395).

If Giri criticizes arguments which some of the contributors (Pels, Shore and Wright, Strathern) have made elsewhere, and develop further here, Argyrou (Chapter 7) examines arguments found in the other two chapters in Part III. His comments on the place of self-criticism in anthropology, *ethnology* as he calls it,[20] act to some degree as a summation of the preceding chapters, and extend them with insights of a philosophical kind. Rather than adding to his own points, however, I draw attention to the role he offers ethnography. Two ethnographic commentaries illuminate his argument about the basic metaphysics of the discipline. One draws on Cypriot observations about the relationship between being a creator and being the object of another's creation; the other comes from a synthesis of ideas on 'the gift'. He uses the gift to point to the paradox which Western thinkers (including ethnologists) create when they try to act at once as creators (constructing or describing the world) and as creations within it (part of the 'real world' they describe). This engenders the same kind of 'impossibility' that time introduces into the gift, for both a return and a failure to return compromise the gift's original status. The aptness of his analogy lies in the fact that it is very much a Western type of 'free gift' which he has in mind, one where at the moment of giving the donor goes, culturally speaking, into denial about expectations of return. It is because of all the other ways in which ethnologists have encountered what they describe as 'gifts' that the starkness of the ('Western') dilemma is revealed. And what is so productive about basing an analogy on ethnographic realities is the truism that such realities are always larger that what is imagined for them at the outset – and often unexpectedly so.

Finally, the concluding section (Part IV) turns specifically to universities. Each case (Chapter 8, Canada; Chapter 9, Austria; Chapter 10, Greece) is obviously unique. The point of these particular instances – exemplars of practices, components of which readers of this book may recognize as bearing in on their own circumstances – is to bring some of the earlier issues home in a concrete way. And because the arguments come directly, so to speak, from the mouths of practitioners, they are quietly but frankly partisan. As university academics, these contributors are concerned with how things might be taken forward in certain particular versions of the daily and everyday milieu in which many practising anthropologists find themselves.

Amit introduces the case studies (Chapter 8). She describes a particular historical juncture in the unfolding of events at a single Canadian university. Here we see how an auditing system combines with other instruments of university governance – each instrument applies its own pressures; the combination magnifies their effects. She dwells especially on the new 'ethical' injunctions imposed on research and how ethics (including taking others into account) is co-opted, as the slogan of academic freedom is, in the service of regulation. It is important to register the way in which regulations chop off debate in mid-stream, ignoring the necessarily heterogeneous nature of open discussion, its diverse strands. She herself joins several arguments. The background is an on-going debate about acountability both within and outside anthropology. She thus invokes the conversation between D'Andrade and Scheper-Hughes, as she does the stand-off between those Canadian academics (including anthropologists) who promote the new regulations and those who are opposed; she also offers a further viewpoint to other positions taken in this volume. It is salutory, for instance, that she finds no panacea in ethnography. To be better informed about the intricacies of the bureaucratic machinery will not necessarily help. In the end she very simply states her stance in the name of independence of scholarship.

Fillitz's chapter (9) returns us to Chapter 2 (the academy at the historical moment of moving into an audit regime) and Chapter 3 (the role of the media in debate), as well as reminding us of the cultural presence of the EU (Chapter 4). From Austria, it gives a retrospective view, so to speak, of measures being taken in the UK in the early 1980s, but against a quite different history of student access. It depicts in detail, and the detail is important, the diverse reactions of the media: issues relate on the one hand to mass education and on the other to the crucial though often unspoken question of state funding which runs through other contributions. What kind of public mandate does the university have? Here we see a spectrum of reactions. Fillitz also draws attention to the wider context of university governance and the way in which certain of the values and processes of audit have been pressed into contemporary political service. Whereas Amit points to the failure of the academic to equip him or herself with information, yet ends on a sceptical note about that very enterprise, Fillitz points to accusations from outside about the failure of the academy to scrutinize itself – and half agrees with them.

In Chapter 10 Gefou-Madianou also takes a historical moment, the three decades of development in Greece when the university system was opened up at the very moment anthropology became a discipline on the curriculum. Amit has just described the cumulative effect of changes seemingly gathering at an ever progressive rate, while Fillitz pointed to academic conservatism at the heart of much of that has happened recently – in Gefou-Madianou's case, however, it seems a matter of moving forwards only to move backwards again. The chapter gives the sense of a zigzagging, non-linear, trajectory. Greek institutions poised to enter a liberal world suddenly found it shrinking around them, and within a decade a new mood began altering what it was that Greek institutions were 'learning' from elsewhere in Europe, with the EC as a particular source of ideas and direction. Gefou-Madianou claims that one of the virtues of the Greek case is that the rest of Europe may be able to 'learn back' from colleagues working in Greece, insofar as the

Greek academy has, so to speak, long lived under an audit regime. The focus of the chapter is on the implications for anthropologists caught up in such a milieu, and she addresses herself frankly to what anthropologists in Greece should now be doing.

So how do these issues bear on the kind of discipline social anthropologists would wish to see flourish? The contributors to this volume acknowledge the need for accountability while being critical of the kind of social processes it often seems to put in train. They thereby bring an important question back to anthropological practice. If the anthropologist cannot avoid what is happening in their own workplace, in their wider relationships with others as ethnographers and practitioners they cannot avoid the ethics of accountability either. The question – and it reaches well beyond anthropology – is how to deal with challenges that are at once obstructive, destructive even, *and* vitalizing.

Notes

1 To those who subscribe to the notion of 'the global', that is. I am thinking less of academic debate over globalization than of the fact that it was a concept captured in the first place by Western capitalism.

2 Through training, qualification, the tying of research awards to tertiary institutions.

3 And it is also a manager's dream: 'If only people would be acountable, the argument [of chief executive officers] goes, then the company could turn away from the dead hand of command and control . . . where people wait to be told what to do' (Munro 1996: 3).

4 On the concomitant increase of control through 'self-management', see Grey 1996 after Du Gay 1994.

5 Self-checking is checked in various ways. Higher education institutions in the UK may be required to demonstrate that their own monitoring protocols are in place. The direct checking of performance (in research, teaching) can then point to the relevant quality controls (peer refereeing, student evaluation).

6 While to an outsider the key words and modes of discourse encountered in audit practices may appear to make up a coherent entity, to an insider audit talk may seem to have been, in the words of Rolland Munro (pers. comm.), 'not only bootstrapping itself from its financial accounting roots but re-incorporating into itself much of the discourse of the new managerialism – ahead of the latter ever clarifying itself'.

7 Much more could be said about internationalization. In other areas of education, international bodies monitor 'global educational effectiveness' (cross-country indicators) (Stronach 1999).

8 Bureaucracy mobilizes values or practices that lie beyond the competences of any particular individual bureaucrat, a situation which can lead to individuals adopting the stance of indifference which is largely

the subject of Herzfeld's work. It becomes theoretically pointless therefore to ask who audits the auditors. Power (1997: 113) gives an apparently pragmatic reason as to why the outcome of audit practices cannot be audited (all that can be audited is the due process under which they are conducted), then adds, 'the outcome of the audit process, the production of assurance, is obscure and defies measurement'. It is a truism that 'obscurity' will not go away, however many onion layers of auditors auditing auditors are removed.

9 In contesting this point, Cris Shore (pers. comm.) suggests that current practices of audit and surveillance are far from 'indifferent'; on the contrary they present the face of obsessive concern (care/ interference). This raises a question about the unit of analysis to which the epithet might apply. It seems to me there is a profound indifference to the (social) complexity of outcomes in favour of the devising and implementing of management and policy strategies which can be measured by performance indicators.

10 As in Actor Network Theory (e.g. Law 1999).

11 So to locate the present study in, say, 'the anthropology of politics', would be overdetermining for the kind of account it is (any [lineal] delineation of ancestors presumes a degree of independent reproduction).

12 I am grateful to Maryon McDonald for most generously assisting my introduction to the field.

13 Whether Latourian (1993) or Rilesian (2000). Latour is interested in the way linkages between material, social, circumstantial and other elements/moments yield diverse kinds of entities available to knowledge, including apparently new entities altogether – new epistemological objects. He calls these chains of connections 'networks', and the work of the network is 'translation' (across domains). (It is one half of his view of the modernist project, the other being the work of separation [of categories from one another] and the corresponding boundary maintenance performed by 'purification'). Riles takes Network as an embracing term for a particular, if pervasive, epistemological condition. It derives from the double ubiquity of self-examination (reflexivity) and information flow. These combine in ways that make it seem there is no 'inside' or 'outside' to knowledge, a situation which becomes obvious to the ethnographer, for instance, when analysis and phenomena become the 'same thing' (the analytical and reflexive aptitude of the subject races ahead of that of the observer; cf. Berglund 1998). She thus uses 'Network' to refer to informational connections, and specifically to a set of institutions, knowledge practices and artefacts which internally generate the effects of their own reality by reflecting on themselves.

14 We can derive a formal reason from Riles's (2000) discussion of Network. If she describes a phenomenon which has no inside or outside – no stabilization of the relationship between text and context – then it obviates the very concept of 'context' itself. (An example is given in the Afterword concerning policy and audit: each appears now to be outside the other, and now be folded within it, but once seen as

internal can never quite regain externality.) So it is true, I think, that it would not actually, in this instance, matter *which* genealogy fuelled the means of writing; motivation comes from a position which needs to be stated.

15 In Britain, some of these issues have already been the subject of debate through the National Network for Teaching and Learning Anthropology. This is a consortium of UK departments which provides a forum for discussing anthropological, educational and policy issues related to teaching and learning in the discipline, funded by HEFCE (see Chapter 2) on a fixed-term basis. It has contributed to academic productions germane to the present enterprise. I am thinking, for instance, of the teaching materials prepared at the Department of Human Sciences at Brunel University (Gellner and Hirsch 1999) which bring together debates and research on the ethography of organizations. Their Introduction offers an excellent overview of anthropological writing in this still relatively new field, its axis being an intersection between the three areas 'science', 'family, health and welfare', and 'development and politics'. It concludes with an 'ethical' case study.

16 Power 1997: 17; selective testing dates to the 1930s, when auditors found that instead of checking every arithmetical step it was more efficient to evaluate the strength of internal control (1997: 20). The converse was the development of internal checks to see whether a system is suitable for quality checking (1996: 303).

17 And Harper points out the way in which financial audit (assessing past performance) may shade into management accounting (seeking directions for the future).

18 As Tsoukas observes (1996: 20), social practices are infinitely concrete and infinitely particular, for 'a social practice is inherently indeterminate. One can indefinitely go on describing it'. The point is taken up in the Afterword.

19 New Zealand has taken things to interesting extremes. Apropos speed of change, Weber (1948: 225) pointed to the fact that modern business management rests on speed of operations, and that means of communication was then, in the early twentieth century, leading to an 'extraordinary' increase in the tempo of administrative reactions. Quick reactions to situations is optimized by bureaucratic organization. Much earlier (1868), Miss Buss, promoter of day school education for girls, wrote 'to a lady in Otago': 'I have read with much pleasure your interesting account of the progress of education in your colony [New Zealand]. You will soon leave the old country behind if you go so rapidly. There is much to be done before it can be said that England has a great national system of education' (Ridley 1896: 201).

20 He keeps to the designation 'ethnology' for reasons he sets out. Although this departs from usage elsewhere in the book, the departure serves a more important editorial function than homogeneity would: the chapter itself opens with a commentary which presumes his distance from colleagues.

References

Berglund, E. 1998 *Knowing Nature, Knowing Science: an Ethnography of Local Environmental Activism*, Cambridge: Whitehorse Press.

Douglas, M. (1992) 'The Normative Debate and the Origins of Culture', in M. Douglas (ed.) *Risk and Blame: Essays in Cultural Theory*, London: Routledge.

Du Gay, P. (1994) 'Making up Managers: Bureaucracy, Enterprise and the Liberal Art of Separation', *British Journal of Sociology*, 45: 655–74.

Gellner, D. and Hirsch, E. (eds) (1999) *The Ethnography of Organizations: A Reader*, under auspices of National Network for Teaching and Learning Anthropology, MSS, Brunel University.

Giri, A. (1998) 'Transcending Disciplinary Boundaries: Creative Experiments and Critiques of Modernity', *Critique of Anthropology*, 18: 379–404.

Grey, C. (1996) 'Towards a Critique of Managerialism: the Contribution of Simone Weil', *Journal of Management Studies*, 33: 591–611.

Hart, K. (1998) 'The Politics of Anthropology: Conditions for Thought and Practice', *Anthropology Today*, 14: 20–22.

Herzfeld, M. (1992) *The Social Production of Indifference: Exploring the Symbolic Roots of Western Bureaucracy*, Chicago: Chicago University Press.

Hoskin, K. (1995) 'The Viewing Self and World We View: Beyond Perspectival Illusion', *Organization*, 2: 141–62.

—— (1996) 'The "Awful Idea of Accountability": Inscribing People into the Measurement of Objects', in R. Munro and J. Mouritsen (eds) *Accountability: Power, Ethos and the Technologies of Managing*, London: International Thomson Business Press.

Latour, B. 1993 *We Have Never Been Modern* (trans. C. Porter), London: Harvester Wheatsheaf.

Law, J. (ed.) (1999) *Actor Network Theory and After*, Oxford: Blackwell.

Munro, R. (1996) 'Alignment and Identity Work: the Study of Accounts and Accountability', in R. Munro and Mouritsen, J. (eds) *Accountability: Power, Ethos and the Technologies of Managing*, London: International Thomson Business Press.

—— (1999) 'The Cultural Performance of Control', *Organization Studies*, 20: 619–40.

Munro, R. and Mouritsen, J. (eds) (1996) *Accountability: Power, Ethos and the Technologies of Managing*, London: International Thomson Business Press.

Pels, Peter (1999) 'Professions of duplexity: a prehistory of ethical codes in anthropology', *Current Anthropology* (with comments) 40: 101–36.

Power, M. (1996) 'Making Things Auditable', *Accounting, Organizations and Society*, 21: 289–315.

—— (1997) *The Audit Society: Rituals of Verification*, Oxford: Oxford University Press.

Ridley, A. E. (1896) *Frances Mary Buss and her Work for Education*, London: Longmans, Green & Co [2nd ed.].

Riles, A. (2000) *The Network Inside Out*, Ann Arbor: Michigan University Press.

Shore, C. and Wright, S. (eds) (1997) *Anthropology of Policy: Critical Perspectives on Governance and Power*, EASA series, London: Routledge.

—— (1999) 'Audit Culture and Anthropology: Neo-liberalism in British Higher Education', *Journal of the Royal Anthropological Institute*, 5(4): 557–75.

Stronach, I. (1999) 'Shouting Theatre in a Crowded Fire: "Educational Effectiveness" as Cultural Performance', *Evaluation* 5(2): 173–93.

Tsoukas, H. (1996) 'The Firm as a Distributed Knowledge System: a Constructionist Approach', *Strategic Managment Journal*, 17: 11–25.

Weber, M. (1948) 'Bureaucracy', Part III chapter 6 of *Wirtschaft und Gesselschaft*, in H. H. Gerth and C. W. Mills (trans. and ed.), *From Max Weber: Essays in Sociology*, London: Routledge and Kegan Paul Ltd.

Part I

Chapter 1

The social organization of the IMF's mission work

An examination of international auditing

Richard Harper

Auditing is increasingly showing its face to professional ethnographers whether they be working within the traditional domains of their trade, anthropology and sociology, or in those new domains in which ethnographers find themselves, as in my own case, within the corporate research world. Auditing may be used, albeit indirectly, to assess the 'productivity' of ethnographers, the 'value' of their findings and the allocation of resources for ethnographic projects. As a response to this new way of looking at their work, ethnographers have been revisiting the organizational history of their trade – the institutional processes for training, dissemination of results and so forth. This is enabling them to determine just how auditing may categorize and cut up the ethnographic enterprise.

Ethnographers have also been looking outside their own practices to those who undertake audits. Here the scope of enquiries is enormous. There are both the practices of those academics who find themselves auditing their colleagues – anthropologists on anthropologists as it were – and also those trades traditionally associated with auditing and whose institutional practices have been bound up with it. Chartered accountancy is perhaps the most obvious, and over the past fifteen years or so a substantial body of ethnographic research has begun to show itself in journals such as *Accounting, Organisations and Society*. In addition, there are those institutions which have been practising enormously influential forms of auditing without the title. These have been the focus of much less attention.

The International Monetary Fund ('the Fund') provides a case in point. Though this organization is of great consequence, and though its work can be conceived of as a kind of auditing of national economies, it has remained beyond the scope of ethnographic enquiry. This is all the more surprising given how the IMF is often invoked in anthropological ethnographies of underdeveloped communities as the single organization that has caused more strife than any other. Such accusations (irrespective of whether they are right or wrong) are made with little knowledge of how the Fund does its business. As Gardner and Lewis (1996) remark, macro-economics – the stuff of the IMF's work – has remained uninvestigated territory for anthropology.

One may ask why this is. It may be that the view anthropological ethnographers have of the Fund has been so negative that any entreaty they may have made for access has been unacceptable to the Fund itself. I certainly heard numerous stories to that effect when undertaking my study. (It needs to be remembered that I do not present myself as an anthropologist.) Another reason may be that anthropologists have wanted to examine both the Fund and one of the governments it works with. Doing so would enable the anthropologist to examine what one might call, following Power, the 'audit loop'. Such requests are likely to be spurned for the simple fact that they would require agreement from too many people.

In any event, my own view is that ethnographic research should commence with step-by-step investigations, rather than with encompassing activities. As I observe in my account of the Fund (Harper 1998), even confining myself to the processes of the one institution streched my capacites and I had a team to help me.

An ethnography of the IMF

It is in this context that I present my own study of the inner workings of the IMF as illustrative of a particular empirical tradition of ethnographic organizational research. My focus inevitably feeds into and is in turn fed by the already mentioned spurt of interest into the role of auditing in society in general (Power 1997; Harper 1987, 1988, 1989). For the Fund's business involves a kind of auditing: large scale, dealing with numbers that are vast and representing activities at an incredibly gross level, but nonetheless auditing.

Specifically, I focus on one of the main activities of the Fund, namely the point when it gathers its auditing data. This primarily occurs during what are called Fund missions. A description of one of these forms the centrepiece of this chapter. I describe how this mission, and by example all missions (at least the common sort, known as an article IV), consist of a division of labour which supports an iterative process whereby a mixture of arithmetical, econometric and meeting skills are used to create data that are reconciled and measured against the data collected by others within the mission. This process results in an overall picture – an audit – of an economy. This is then used as a basis for discussion with the local (or member) authorities, and ultimately is used to create various documents, the most important of which is called a staff report. These documents, or textual devices to given them a fashionable sociological name, are the vehicles through which the Fund presents and justifies its auditing work.

This chapter does not so much focus on the way in which these devices are used by the Fund itself (i.e. after a mission) as on their production during missions, and in particular, on certain aspects of missions which, it is suggested, are fundamental to the social organization of international auditing, at least of the kind the Fund undertakes. What I have in mind are those phenomena which Fund staff themselves call the facts of life. It is these they have to contend with, orient toward and work around. These 'facts of life' are interesting ethnographically because they consist of the matters of practical relevance constitutive of the rationalities deployed by Fund staff. Following Anderson *et al.* (1989), Harper *et al.* (2000), Lynch *et al.* (1983) and Lynch (1985), I view these 'local rationalities' as the bedrock of socially organized behaviour. A concern with them will ensure that the analysis remains empirical.

Amongst the facts of life I will consider is how data work on missions is a deeply social process and not just one that involves economic analysis. For, although data may be found in a variety of different places (namely, different offices within the various institutions of the member authority government agencies), only certain persons within those offices have the rank to sanction the relevant interpretations and associated numbers. These people provide the stamp of approval. A Fund mission must seek these out. On the mission described here, one individual had a particularly important role in this. For though this individual was not able to give official sanction to every single number, his data, his views on that data, his explanations and accounts of policy were treated as absolutely essential and vital to the mission's ability to comprehend the situation. Trust in this individual was crucial to the mission's work. The mission was not unusual in having a close relationship with one person in the member authorities. This is the norm in mission work (though it does not occur in every case).

Rituals too are part of the facts of life on missions – though Fund staff would not use the term themselves to describe the events I have in mind. One important aspect of ritual has to do with getting numbers and associated interpretations 'signed off' by the right person (usually senior officials). Another has to do with the process of agreeing a basis for policy concerns in discussions between the mission and the authorities. Here a mission chief will make fairly ritualized orations to the local authorities; these commence and sometimes terminate the discussion of policy. I will not suggest that these orations are merely showpieces, or that they have no analytic value. Rather, I want to show that it is partly through ritual that the symbolic importance of the events are demonstrated and achieved. Further, it is through these same rituals that the symbolic status of the participants is also affirmed. Without ritual, the essential characteristics of the events – in this case policy discussions – would be changed. This character ensures that the outcome of these meetings is treated as consequential; or, put another way, ensures that these are meetings that *count*.

Of course in this setting, the word 'count' has at least two relevant meanings, the first implying the significance of the meetings, the second pointing towards the fact that these events are in crucial respects about counting numbers. I will show that such countings are not simply arithmetical (although they do involve a large amount of that), but are also the final stage of a social process which transforms 'speechless numbers' into ones having a 'voice'. This voice is communicating something very specific: it enables a mission to make warranted determinations of the present. In this sense, the Fund's business is essentially auditing; but I will go on to argue that this in turn enables determination of the future. For Fund missions are also very interested in divining what the future may be, and how to achieve that future through certain policies, through better understanding of the entrails of the present. Such grasping toward the future is not a kind of magic. It is undertaken on the basis of materials which can be demonstrated to be 'reasonable', 'warranted', 'accurate' and 'objective': in a phrase, that have been audited. This is not to say that the Fund missions always predict the future precisely. It is to say that missions get themselves into a position where making predictions is a reasonable thing to do. In this sense, the mission's predictions consist of a kind of *auditing science.* This is a practical, 'real world', hands-on skill. This is the heart of the matter. This is what Fund's auditing work is all about.

A sketch of the International Monetary Fund

The Fund, based in Washington DC, is a financial 'club' whose members consist of most of the countries of the world. Member countries contribute to a pool of resources which can then be used to provide low interest, multi-currency loans should a member find itself facing balance of payments problems. The Fund has some 3,000 staff, of whom 900 are professional economists. These economists analyse economic policies and developments – especially in the macroeconomic arena. They have particular interest in the circumstances surrounding the emergence of financial imbalances (including those that lead to a balance of payments crisis), the policies to overcome such imbalances, and the corrective policy criteria for making loans. This involves going on missions to the country in question.

The Fund is divided into a number of departments. The most important are 'area' departments responsible for particular member countries divided up into contiguous geographic blocks (Western Hemisphere, Middle Eastern). The area departments are divided into divisions, each with responsibility for certain countries. The divisions are populated by desk officers and chiefs. Desk officers are economists who develop and maintain expertise on any particular country. A chief will manage several countries and desk officers, and hence will be responsible for the information the Fund has about any particular set of member countries.

A case study of a fund mission

I confine my exposition to the main process of Fund missions and supplement this with three vignettes of particular events. The first, the team's first meeting, provides the opportunity to begin explaining how mission work is in large part a social process. It will also provide an opportunity to explain how members of a mission team assume that the materials they gather as part of this process have what one might call 'understandable' problems: numbers get added up incorrectly, miscategorization occurs, and spreadsheet tables get lost. These are part of the 'facts of life' in mission work and these are the things with which the team must deal, come what may. I will then characterize in general terms the data-gathering activities undertaken by this particular mission before providing a second vignette, this time of one of the meetings undertaken by two members of the mission with a key official in the authorities. Here I point towards how a mission needs to get a perspective that can enable it to distinguish between usable and unusable numbers. Some numbers are good for certain tasks, but not for others. I then discuss how the chosen numbers have to be 'socially validated'. In this case, the senior official could only sanction some and not all of the numbers of interest. Finally, in a third vignette, I will describe one of the policy meetings that occurred at the end of the mission. Here I draw attention to the ritualizing effects of these meetings (desired but not always achieved), important not only in giving those meetings the status they have but in transforming the numbers presented in those meetings into ones that count.

Before I start my exposition, two remarks need to be made. First, the mission team I describe consisted of a chief and his deputy, an administrative assistant, the desk officer responsible for the country in question, a fiscal economist, and a junior economist called an 'EP' (basically on trial through the Economists' Program). Second, for the sake of confidentiality, I call the country in question 'Arcadia'.

The first day: vignette one

The team left Washington together except for the chief and the administrative assistant who were to follow later. The departing team consisted of four economists, including the deputy chief, and myself. The first view we had of Arcadia came with a parting of clouds as we approached the airport: a blue sea, smooth coastline and ochre landscape pockmarked with little confusions of grey and white villages. In the distance, slowly emerging in the haze, was the great swathe of the capital city of Arcadia itself, a muddled warren of creamy white buildings at its heart, wide sweeping roads and modernist blocks in the suburbs, dusty olive green mountains behind.

On arrival, the team were the first to depart the plane. They were greeted with swoops and bows by a smiling official and a coterie of uniformed customs officers. The official directed customs officers to remove the team's luggage and lead them to passport control. There, he shooed the passport officials away, explaining to them that the team had diplomatic status and therefore didn't need visas. The desk officer pointed towards me. After some confusion, it was decided that I be given a tourist visa. Meanwhile, another smiling official arrived and presented the desk officer with a huge stack of documents. We were then introduced to two more individuals who would be our chauffeurs. Whilst negotiations were undertaken about how to load us and our luggage into the cars, the desk officer started to browse the papers he had been given. His head began to drop as he looked more closely, and he glanced at the rest of the team with an expression of glee and concern. 'Look', he said, 'Here are two copies of the budget, some other tables. I don't know what they are, but there are also four sets of the national accounts, all with the same bottom line. But look: they have different numbers. What is this?'

The rest of the team looked at each other and the deputy said: 'Don't worry just yet! We haven't even got to our hotel. Let's start work later!'

We were then driven down a broad avenue towards the centre of the city. There was a strong smell of eucalyptus and spice, mixed with the occasional waft of kerosene from the airport. After about 15 minutes, the drivers swerved off the road into a small lane leading up to a towering cement hotel set in its own formal gardens; a fountain trickled in front of the main entrance. This was to be the mission's home for the next two weeks. During check-in, the deputy announced that the team would be given half an hour to unpack before the first team meeting.

By the time I had arrived for the meeting, the deputy chief was already discussing with the desk officer the papers that he had been given at the airport. These had been spread out over the bed. The desk officer pointed towards them and was saying: 'Well these are what we want. I have sorted them out. I assume that they must have included some early drafts. It is not a problem. It is the bottom line that matters at this point. Besides, I can see from the way they have been working which is the most recent so I will use that. I can clarify things with officials later on. Still, here are some materials that each of you can use to help build up your tables.' At which point he started sorting out the tables and giving them to the rest of the team, explaining as he did so: 'These won't be completely right but you can use them to set up the spreadsheets. You can start entering them straight away. Here, use these numbers and these.'

The deputy then took over the meeting: 'Okay let's not worry about that at the moment. Let's try and plan out what we have to do.' She then outlined what meetings had been arranged, and a list was handed out. She pointed out who amongst the team would be meeting with which official and when. She turned to ask each economist: 'Do you know what you can get out of this person? What information will you still need after this meeting? Do you know who you will need to meet afterwards? Can I have those meetings arranged for you now?' She took particular pains to explain what the EP would be doing, listing the officials he would be seeing and explaining why he would see them: 'The first person you meet tomorrow at the central bank will give you the latest figures on (*the EP's concern*) but you should get a lot from her because she knows more or less everyone you will need to deal with. She will give you a lot of advice on what you need to find out. She is easy to get on with so don't worry, you will be all right.'

Meanwhile the desk officer kept interrupting with a kind of bubbly enthusiasm. He knew both the lady in question and most of the other officials that the EP would meet in the next few days: 'Yeah, don't worry, don't worry! They will tell you all you need to know. I'll help you also.'

The deputy then made a little speech. She explained that, in her opinion, the 'shift in credit towards the government' would be the crux of the staff report (by this she meant the question of how the government was financing itself, the mechanisms for this and the resulting influence on investment in the economy at large, including exports of manufactures). She wanted to reiterate that it was therefore going to be the main focus of the mission. She concluded by saying that she was expecting the Arcadians to supply most of the relevant facts in the next few days and that they would enable the team to get most of the materials 'into a fit condition for the chief's arrival'.

Once the meeting was over, the team met downstairs in the hotel restaurant. They knew that their rooms would be their main workplace for the next two weeks or so. They knew also that the work would increase as each day passed, and that they would become increasingly tired and irascible. The first evening was a chance to relax and be light-hearted, to renew friendships and, in the case of the EP and myself, to get to know some new 'colleagues'.

Comment

In many ways the first day was not consequential. But there are two telling aspects of the day's events on which I want to reflect: first, the attitude of the desk officer to the materials he was given at the airport, and, second, the deputy's concern with whom the mission members would be meeting.

As regards the first: the oddness of documents given the desk officer. Essentially what he found was that four sets of national accounts did not consist of the same individual numbers. It is extremely important to grasp his perspective on this. For example, a conspiratorial desk officer might have contended that the oddity was a reflection of deliberate obfuscation on the part of Arcadian officials. But this desk officer did not think this. Rather, his assumption was that the problem in the documents had to do with the nature of the material used in the Fund's work. To paraphrase, his view was that this material had to be worked up, crafted, and polished. Further, in this process mistakes can be made, sometimes simple and sometimes more complex. In this case, the oddness was actually the result of a clerical error: in his words, 'some early drafts of the tables had been picked up'. He did not view the numbers used in the Fund's work as existing in some tidy, clean and perfect world, a world, say, akin to a scientific laboratory. Instead, he assumed that these materials are produced in the ordinary world of offices, over-filled with paperwork and filing cabinets. In a phrase, these materials were produced in the mundane world where simple mistakes get made for all too ordinary reasons.

A lot turns on this. For when one is trying to understand a 'real world', practical activity such as the Fund's auditing work, it becomes all to easy to make misleading comparisons between what one might call the 'dirty facts' one finds in that real world and what one might call the clean, tidy facts one will find in the confines of, say, pure research. Such comparisons, wrong in my opinion, are commonplace, especially in relation to activities that involve numbers.

For example, it might be argued that there is a difference between the 'real', 'proper' economics undertaken in research settings (an economics which uses pure facts, unsullied by error or administrative mishaps), and those of the other, mundane world – the place of missions where facts are muddied by clerical errors, and where the problem is to clear away the 'noise'. And I think it important to view such a contrast as overexaggerating if not misrepresenting the issues in question. For this desk officer, and I would claim that this holds for all members of the mission, did not have a contrast of this order in mind. It was rather that they knew there would be practical difficulties in their work. They did not bemoan this. Their problem, if that is the right description for it, was not that these difficulties would arise, so much as they could not predict when these problems would show themselves. This was almost entirely contingent on circumstances. And as this first instance indicates, these contingencies did indeed show themselves at unexpected times, even before they had managed to unpack their bags.

The second issue to raise has to do with how and why the mission team displayed a concern with how its work involved a *social process*. The fact that the deputy wanted to talk about which meetings were arranged with whom, and therefore what would be the outcome of those meetings was not, I would argue, a reflection of the mere fact that data have to produced by someone. It is rather a recognition of the fact that in policy work, *numbers and persons go hand in hand*. There are a number of issues here, but of importance is that the team were recognizing and depending upon the relationship between an individual's role in an organization and the understanding that individual will have as a result of that position. This may seem a banal point, but it is fundamental to mission activity. For mission work is all about creating analysis through the social process of agreeing and determining the facts in question. What is of concern to members of a mission is not that this is so. It is rather what in practice this means: which people and in what ways can these things (agreement of the facts) be achieved in any particular instance.

Ordinary work

These arguments beg the question of exactly what members of a mission ask and of whom. In this case, the first few days of the mission were spent marching around the various buildings of the Arcadian authorities, gathering more numbers, and discussing with those responsible for their production issues to do with how to interpret those numbers, and on that basis, how to use them. Each member of the mission would have their own 'circuit' of meetings and officials to work around.

This data collection process consisted of various stages, akin to the peeling of an onion. First was collecting the first set of data.

This would supplement the data the desk officer had already collected over the year or via the questionnaire he had sent to the authorities prior to the mission.[1] These data would be collected in meetings at such places as the Central Bank for balance of payments and foreign currency holdings data, and the Ministry of Finance for fiscal figures. At the end of each day, each economist would add the figures to their increasingly extensive spreadsheets. The figures for one 'sector' would then be reconciled with the figures in the other sectors. When there was a problem of reconciliation between two or more sectors, the team would decide what might be the cause. They would conjecture, say, that the numbers collected for the fiscal sector were not up to date in comparison with figures from other sectors. To investigate this, the fiscal economist would be asked to enquire into when the figures were calculated in their next round of meetings. This may be thought of as a further stage of the mission, a further peeling of the onion.

Sorting out the facts in the facts

Key to the data-gathering tasks is not simply gathering the raw numbers but also gathering insight into how to understand or interpret those numbers. On the Arcadia mission, one official in the Ministry of Planning had an almost unique insight into the economic position of Arcadia. This was based in part on years of work in various ministries and in part on his current role in the Ministry of Planning. His connections with missions in the past had also resulted in the growth of considerable trust between him and Fund staff. The deputy chief and the desk officer wanted to talk with this individual not only to gather certain figures, but also to get some guidance on how to read and interpret the figures that the team as a whole were gathering. From this view he was the mission's 'chief informant'.

The deputy chief and desk officer were after two things. First, they wanted some advice on how to separate what they called the flotsam from the main body of economic fact, for the figures that would be collected consisted both of long-term trends or 'underlying movements' and elements reflecting one–off events. For instance, the Arcadians had bought two Airbuses in the previous year which had impacted on the current account and ultimately the Arcadian balance of payments. But the mission needed to separate out this fact since this was unique, or an exceptional item as it is sometimes called. It did not reflect the underlying trend. The mission was after this trend in the current account and in the balance of payments. The official in the Ministry of Planning could provide this 'inside information'. The second purpose of these meetings related to the fact that the official could share with them the authorities' own perspective on the current economic trends. Here concern was for the mission to understand the weight given to some issues and the indifference felt towards others. Ultimately there would be a good chance that these views would be shared with the team during the policy discussions that concluded the mission, but the team wanted to get an understanding before those events so as to tailor their investigations in such a way as to enable them to 'talk to those views'.

Trust between the official and the team was also such that the official could offer frank remarks which might be more difficult to make in the formalized and partly ritual events of policy discussion. For example, the official was quite willing to say that the authorities 'really didn't know' why some trend was manifesting itself in the figures whereas in the policy meetings such admissions would be difficult. It is important to realize that such frankness was not pointing towards failings on the part of the authorities. By and large they had a view of and considerable understanding about the matters at hand. It was just that there was a handful of issues that they were unsure about. This was a fact of life.

Essentially the process in question consisted of a series of meetings during which the numbers were briefly analysed and discussed. These meetings went on throughout the mission as the team gradually revised and built up its own knowledge. The process itself involved going through the individual numbers (or category of numbers) one by one, while the official simply outlined what he thought the team ought to know about that category and presented the Arcadians' view on those numbers. Sometimes the members of the mission raised their own concerns about a number, requesting the official to explain some issues there and then, or to investigate those numbers for discussion later on.

Discussing the facts among the facts: vignette two

I can illustrate this with the first of these meetings undertaken on the second day of the mission. The topic of this particular meeting was 'the macroeconomic framework and review of overall developments'. The official had already supplied some tables to the mission, and these formed the basis of the meeting. These tables consisted of consolidated balance of payments tables for the previous four years (including targets), as well as detailed tables of exports of goods, services and transfers, and the equivalent import tables. Much data on these tables would be very important at a later stage in the mission, but at the outset, these data could not be used. As the desk officer put it, they needed to learn 'how to read these tables'. Their concern was to know something about 'what lay behind the figures', to understand what they meant. It was through discussion with the official that they could learn this. Only in this way would the team be able to determine how to use the figures for their own purposes.

There were two components to this concern. The first was understanding what the figures for 'actuals' represented, and the second was understanding the relationship between the actuals and the related projections. The tables which had been supplied consisted of two columns for each year, one with the actuals and the other for the projected or estimated figures. So constructed, any contrast between the actuals and the projections was easy to see. Most of the meeting was conducted in reference to the contrast between these two orders of numbers.

To illustrate: once formalities had been completed, the desk officer said that the mission wanted to get some explanation as to why there had been a lowering of export volumes and an increase in imports over projections in the most recent quarterly figures. He pointed towards the relevant numbers in the tables. The official responded by saying the answer(s) lay not in the general but in the particular, and suggested that they go through each sub-category of exports and imports. This indeed was how they proceeded.

The first of these happened to be textiles. It also happened to be the case that this particular category bucked the general trend, since here had been an increase in textile exports over and above projections. The desk officer asked if the official could explain this: 'I suppose shirts are in demand!' He then smiled and said: 'I cannot fully say why textiles have been doing so well. The manufacturers are reporting that business has never been so good. They claim that their designs and quality makes for a good product. I don't think there is anything else I can say on that number.'

The desk officer made some notes, turned to his colleague to ask if she had any questions, and then they both agreed to move on. 'Mechanical and electrical goods: these are down on projections: why?'

'There is poor demand for these goods. It reflects the general weakening of demand in the world economy.'

'But if this is the case why has there been an increase in imports of raw materials given that there appears to be a slow down in the economy as a whole?'

'Well, because there has been an increase in investments in tourism. This has caused an increase in imports of raw materials – building goods. This is seasonal: it is the time when many buildings need rebuilding. It is not a trend.'

'Okay, whilst on the subject of tourism, let's move down the table to numbers for tourism: how is that there has been a decline? Or rather, how is it that there has been a reduction: receipts for tourism are down.'

'Tourism? There are more tourists this year but they spend less. I think it is that we went down-market a bit. The tourists who are coming this year spend less than those who came last year. This is a potential problem: if the hotels go down too far, the quality of the resorts goes down and the appeal to tourists reduces further. We are trying to ensure that we avoid that. We don't want to go through the crisis in [*a nearby country*]. They found that they went down so far that the market for tourism collapsed. They built so many cheap hotels that they destroyed the reason for going there.'

On certain categories of numbers the discussions became even more detailed. Partly this was a reflection of what numbers were available. For example, the imports numbers had the following categories which led the deputy chief and desk officer to ask for quite specific accounts: 'Why has there been such a large increase in agriculture and food stuffs? Look, this figure here: milk and yoghurt.'

'Well, it has become fashionable. I think it is to do with healthy eating.'

'But this is a huge increase, this is millions of litres. No, seriously!'

'Yes, what can I say? People in Arcadia didn't used to drink milk. It's not traditional. This year everyone is drinking it. I think young people think it will make them look like athletes.' The official then patted his stomach and said: 'I've not been drinking it!'

The desk officer and deputy chief looked at each other and laughed. 'Okay, let's not worry about that one, it won't show itself in the final total anyway.'

At other times the questions started out being rather more general but ended up being specific: 'Can we consider the totals for consumer imports for this period compared with the previous quarter. According to the tables you gave us there has been a large increase in demand . . .'

'No. Look, one problem is that the figures for the last quarter can't really be compared with the previous quarter because this quarter was Ramadan. So imports for consumer goods and agricultural goods will go up in Ramadan. It is a period of celebration.'

'I thought Ramadan was a period of fast.'

'Yes it is in [a *neighbouring country*] but not in Arcadia. It is like your Christmas here. Except that it lasts a month!'

'That's why it is such good place to live!'

'Okay. So anyway that is warning us about reading a trend into this.'

'Correct.'

Sanctioning numbers

As the week passed so the focus of concern changed in these meetings. Gradually, the team began to build up a higher-level picture where things such as oddities in the current accounts disappeared from view. Discussions were also undertaken on fairly complex problems such as how to determine the Arcadians' international competitiveness, and hence the optimum exchange rate for the Arcadian currency. A focus here was on the selection of the so-called 'basket of currencies' used to calculate these matters. The Arcadians opted for a different set from the mission team.

I do not describe these discussions, however, since the main point to draw from these meetings with the official in the Ministry of Planning is how he was able to give inside information – information that derived from his location within the government and at the centre of information production. Meetings with him comprised an informal nexus whereby the team were able to sort out the 'facts amongst the facts' and to learn about the authorities' perspectives. The many years of contact between members of the mission team and this official also gave the meeting an informal character, where matters of little importance were treated as an opportunity for jocularity. But this should not distract from the serious intent of these meetings nor the extent of professional understanding and expertise deployed in them.

It is important to note that as the team moved towards completion of the data-gathering stage of the mission, so they embarked on another cycle of activity. Here the role of this official changed. For though he was able to give very useful comment on many of the numbers in question, he was only able to *sanction* a sub-set. The team needed to get all of its figures sanctioned before they could start on the analysis of policy and prepare their efforts to discuss policy with the authorities.

By using the term 'sanction', I am pointing toward the fact that the Arcadian authorities had to agree to a number being used by the mission. To illustrate with the fiscal economist's activities: in one of the meetings he had with a senior member of the Ministry of Finance, he was directed to other, more junior officials. These individuals, the persons who had calculated the numbers in question, were then given an opportunity to explain their purposes in doing so. Thus one might characterize this part of the fiscal officer's activities as a process of going to the horse's mouth: getting to the person who was responsible for the production of the numbers in question. Now going to the horse's mouth is not all that the fiscal officer had to do. For once he had understood what the purposes were, once he had revised his own numbers, once he had worked up the picture as he understood it, he then had to go back to the more senior official to get that individual to 'sign off' the numbers.

There are a number of reasons why he had to do so. First, he had to make sure that the numbers he had got from the junior official would not be contradicted by numbers generated elsewhere. A senior official may be more likely to know if this were indeed so. Second, some of the figures he ended up using in his own work were the product of calculation prompted by his own questioning. Therefore the more senior official may not have seen these numbers beforehand. Since this official would ultimately be held responsible for these numbers, it was proper that *he or she* signed them off. Part of the protocol meant that the junior official showed the newly calculated numbers to his or her senior colleague before the fiscal economist did so. Another reason had to do with the fact that the view that the fiscal economist was constructing was slightly different from the one the Arcadians themselves constructed. Partly this was a reflection of the mission's concern with issues that bridged the concerns of the various ministries and institutions within Arcadia which generated the source materials for the mission.

Building up a picture

By combining the product of these meetings with the products of the data-gathering work, the team constructed a basis upon which they could start making some concrete determinations of current economic circumstances. More specifically, the team gradually aggregated the numbers, crosschecking and validating them, until they were confident enough to use the data to build integrated representations of those data. One of the most important of these representations was the *key economic indicators table*. Others were the *medium-term projection tables*. Ultimately the work undertaken with these tables enabled the team to embark on the last component of the mission – the policy discussions with the Arcadians. They still had to collect some data. The deputy chief was still awaiting some figures on external reserves, for example, and the fiscal economist was still making some final revisions to his tables. But they had enough to achieve their purpose: to gather and create sufficient materials to present persuasive and empirically warranted views on the economy, that is, views which had passed the test of audit.

The team's construction, built out of the residues of the hours they spent in meetings with various officials, deriving from their spreadsheets and elaborated in such things as the medium-term projections, was not 'merely' a description of the economy. The output of their work could not be measured on, say, the basis of completeness, comprehensiveness or accuracy alone. Rather, the product of their activities was a perspective about the present from which to reason through policy alternatives into the future.

This is a key feature of the Fund's auditing work. Whereas the kinds of auditing done in commercial enterprises is strictly limited to assessing the adequacy of the processes of number production, the Fund adds to that a concern with probing into the future: what it calls policy analysis. In this sense the Fund's auditing work looks more like management accounting in that it attempts to wrest from the routinely audited numbers sufficient materials to support policy analysis. Indeed, it is difficult to underestimate the importance attached to this future prognosis work. This is shown in the fact that the main event of all missions are the policy discussions which conclude them. As the deputy chief on Arcadia put it, these were: 'What it is all about. The thing that matters.'

Before I go on to the policy meetings themselves, it is important to understand that their character varies according to a number of factors. In some countries the meetings are held between the mission and a group of officials representing all the ministries and institutions concerned, while in other countries these meetings are fragmented. This was the case with Arcadia. Here, meetings were held with the Ministry of Finance, the Ministry of Planning and the Central Bank. Policy meetings are also affected by the extent of the information and expertise the authorities have available to them. Some members countries can find it difficult to keep abreast of their economic situation, simply lacking the institutional and human resources to do so. These members often depend upon the Fund to help them determine their situation and guide them in policy. Although Arcadia was rich in data, it was somewhat lacking in human resources, and so this was one of the roles of the mission.

These two factors, namely whom the meetings were with and the distribution of expertise within, had a number of consequences. Two are of concern. First, in Arcadia the mission would present a view on data collected from all the Arcadian sources, and not just to the individual ministry being presented to in any one meeting. It was likely that the mission's view would transcend the view of the ministry in question. Second, the team were able, to some extent, to determine aspects of the economic situation that would not have been perceived by the individual ministries. In this case, the mission had uncovered the fact that one part of the government was incurring expenses while another was receiving much less revenue than projected. Combined, this would have an impact upon government finance and ultimately on the take up of credit in the economy. From the mission's understanding, it appeared that the various ministries and institutions were not generally aware of this. The team knew this when they had been preparing for these meetings. Not only would they be presenting some news, but what they would present was not necessarily good news. This also played itself out in terms of the kinds of power relations displayed in the meeting. For in this case the mission would be *telling* the Arcadians something they needed to understand; the Arcadians would be obliged to *listen*.

Mindful of these matters, the team worked hard to prepare themselves. The tables upon which the discussions would be based were examined again and again. They attempted to determine what the figures still being crafted 'would turn out to be'. They spent a great deal of time considering how to express and articulate their views. It was particularly important that the team got the tenor and emphasis of this 'just right'. For they did not want to misrepresent the authorities' intentions and past policy motivations. Questions included whether they should *recommend* the authorities to pursue such things as restraint on credit to the government or should be *forcefully urged* to do so. Such distinctions were important in conveying the extent of understanding the team had of the Arcadian authorities' past conduct and current intentions. For example, to *forcefully urge* would give the impression that the team believed the authorities were unwilling to pursue this policy; *to recommend* would give the impression that the authorities were more willing to do so. The latter was deemed more appropriate since it reflected what the mission believed were the Arcadians' genuine attempts to keep government credit within practical limits. It also reflected the particular form of relations between the authorities and the mission. The mission had a role rather like that of external auditors: they enquired into how things were done, then offered correctives, encouragements and advice for the future. The Arcadians were in this sense the audited, the authorities on show.

The third vignette is of one these meetings. My concern is to highlight the ceremonial and ritual aspects of these meetings, and also draw attention once again to the kinds of practical ways the participants 'worked through the numbers'. But I will also draw attention to how, through the process of investigating future policies, the salient aspects of the current situation would come more clearly to the fore. Whereas I have been highlighting how the mission team's goal was to use the present to divine the future, I will now want to note that they also used reference to that future to further refine what the present may be.

Policy discussions: vignette three

When the team gathered early in the morning of the first day of the policy meetings, there was an atmosphere of relief – the worst was over. For, by this time, the economists had become exhausted. As each day of the mission had passed and the amount of data they had collected had increased, so they spent more and more time on data entry tasks and spreadsheet analysis. This work had reached such a fever pitch that in the days immediately prior to the policy discussions they had had little sleep, instead working late into the night keying in data, and finding the task taking ever longer as their minds and fingers became increasingly tired. But the atmosphere of relief was tinged with a degree of apprehension. For policy discussions can also be difficult occasions, not only in themselves – the local authorities being surprised and worried, for example, by issues the mission presents – but also because the upshot of these discussions can be that a mission team has to go back to revisit its calculations.[2] This was an outcome the team were loath to consider. It would mean more late nights, more exhaustion, and further delays before they could get home. Hence they loaded themselves into the official cars with a strange mix of smiles and weariness. The economists knew that they wouldn't be doing much during the discussions and that the chief would be the centre of attention. This was his day. But they knew also that the outcome of these meetings could either be the completion of the mission on schedule or the need for more work and delay.

On this particular day, there were to be two meetings: the first with the Ministry of Finance, the second with the Central Bank. I focus on the latter.

Meeting with the Central Bank

Officials were waiting for the delegation at the entrance to the bank, and led the team into a meeting room.The chief entered first, followed by his staff. Whilst waiting for the bank officials to arrive, the chief asked for his economists to sit either side of him. He took some spreadsheet tables from his briefcase and placed them on the desk in front. He began to move them around like a painter preparing his palette. He then asked the desk officer for one of the medium-term projections tables, which he added to his collection on the table. Finally, he took some handwritten notes from his jacket pocket and placed them in the centre of his documents. An official then burst in and announced the imminent arrival of the bank Governor. The team stood up. The Governor arrived with a flurry of officials and secretaries behind him. The Governor sat down directly opposite the chief, similarly surrounded by his cohorts.

After formalities, the chief stood up and commenced what can best be described as an oration. It was an oration in the sense that it had a formal structure, but more importantly it demanded a response or a reply, as we shall see. He began by complimenting the Arcadians on the work that had been achieved in the past year and the impressive performance in certain areas of the economy. He commented also on the continuing frailties in certain areas. He noted that there had been some practical difficulties in preparing the data during the mission as regard such things as the collection of the foreign debt figures and totals for credit to the government. But with the hard work of his team and the energies of the Arcadians themselves, the mission had been able to ascertain the basic features of the Arcadian economy. These were to be the basis of the discussions in the meeting.

The chief then started to run through the team's figures, explaining that these indicated that there would be a growth in the money supply of 6.5 per cent in the forthcoming year. Further, if government bonds were included in the figures, this would increase to 10.6 per cent. As he explained this, he moved his hands over the tables in front of him, occasionally lifting one to read, as if looking at an oracle. He then remarked on the fact that the team calculated certain figures differently from the Arcadians. For example, the Arcadians consolidated the figures for government credit from banks and other institutions, whereas the mission preferred to keep these banks and other institutions separated on their tables. One difficulty related to the fact that there had been virtually no borrowing from non-bank financial institutions in the past, so the team were not expecting to find any this year. In fact, there had been. Amongst the issues that the team believed lay behind this new development was a desire by the authorities to avoid liquidity problems in the banks whilst satisfying the government's need for credit.

The chief then came to what the mission believed was the heart of the matter. For it was the team's view that the authorities were clearly exceeding their projected credit levels to the government. There were a number of reasons, including lower than expected growth in some sectors and, most noticeably, an unexpected growth in expenditure in agricultural stocks, particularly for olives. Related to this, there was a reduction in the revenues from the sale of olives in export markets – all of this in a year where the harvest had been unusually good. The chief explained that, as a result of this situation, the Arcadian authorities would find their foreign reserves getting reduced to a very low level, little more than one week's imports, or even lower. This was, according to the chief, too little, and necessitated immediate corrective polices. Failure to adopt the correct policies could lead the Arcadians to seek assistance from the Fund in the near future.

When the chief finished his oration there was a long silence. Then the Governor turned to his officials and beckoned them to gather round his chair. For some minutes the Arcadians discussed matters quietly amongst themselves. All the mission could see was a wall of individuals with their backs facing outward. Gradually, officials started to peel off and return to their seats. Eventually, the Governor turned round to face the table again. There was some momentary discussions as to who should speak: the Governor instructed the official on his right to ask the first question. This individual, having looked either side, proceeded to say: 'We are not sure of all the figures you have presented. Could you go over them again and this time in a little more detail? We want to make sure we agree with them all.'

The chief preceded to reiterate the key figures. Several Arcadian officials had by this time taken their pocket calculators out and had placed them on the table. As the chief went through the numbers so they keyed the figures in. At last the chief finished. Again a pause. The officials with the calculators read out their totals. They confirmed the mission's calculations. It was suggested that the chief do a run through for a third time during which process each number would be 'checked' by the Arcadians. By this I mean that one of the bank officials had to agree or disagree with the numbers. The process involved calling out each number in turn and waiting for someone to accept it (or not). As with earlier stages, the numbers were all agreed to.

After this point the Governor and his staff formed a little group again and began to talk intensively amongst themselves. After a while, the officials turned round and asked the chief to explain where his team had received its figures. The chief responded by reporting on those individuals who had provided important numbers in institutions other than the bank. He asked his staff to help list these persons. The chief also explained how these figures had been consolidated with the figures his team had received from the Central Bank staff. The Arcadians then talked amongst themselves again. After a few more minutes had passed, the Governor explained that his staff did indeed agree with the figures that the chief had presented. They recognized the difficulties envisaged by the mission, and commented also on the fact that the team had been able 'to consolidate some figures that we were expecting to receive shortly.'

The chief then spoke up again and suggested that perhaps they should examine the olive and cereal stock figures in detail, and to begin to unpack the related issues. The desk officer quickly scribbled down the stock figures on a piece of paper and slid it in front of the chief who then read them out: the figures for the previous year had been 287.7 million for olives and 231 million for cereal (in the local currency denomination). This year the figures were 493 for olives and 214 for cereal. This meant there was a 71 per cent increase for olive stocks[3] since the past year. The chief then explained that, the question for the meeting was how the costs of this, combined with a reduction in revenues from the sale of olives, would impact upon the credit available in the economy. The chief explained that, in the mission's view, the situation would have a significant impact in the allocation of credit in the economy. It would mean that there would be a substantial growth in credit to the government, and this in turn would have an impact on growth and on the GDP. An increase in credit to the government would also result in continuing growth in money supply but without allowing a growth in investment and productivity. These would be 'squeezed out'. Accordingly, the chief went on, the authorities would need to revise their estimates for growth and reserves and revise their policy stance to achieve new projections. Otherwise, the government would take a larger share of credit in the economy, further adding pressures on the balance of payments.

Once this stage of the meeting was complete, participants started investigations of the detailed implications of the credit issue and its potential impact on other figures. The problem they had to solve was where exactly those connections between credit and other issues, such as growth, inflation and the balance of payments, would show themselves. This was to be found out in the process of working up the monetary tables. So the next stage of the meeting involved varying certain figures (or variables) in the tables to see 'just what' the impact would turn out to be in respect of other variables. In the first 'run through', the Arcadians suggested that their projections for inflation be slightly increased. The chief turned to his team and discussed what they would view as an acceptable alternative projection for inflation. Their concern was not to make up any inflation figure, but to determine what would be a 'reasonable variance' in the inflation rate. After some discussion, both sides agreed to a variation that increased inflation by 1.3 per cent. Once this had been determined, the impact of that variation upon other variables, such as government borrowing and balance of payments, could be calculated.

These investigations took some time. The meeting then proceeded to alter other variables to see what impact those changes might have on the economic situation. By the time they had done all this, they had spent nearly five hours together.

Comment

Obviously much more was involved in this meeting (and others I have ignored) than is conveyed in these brief remarks.[4] The investigative work, and the elaboration of the numbers and associated spreadsheets, all required considerable skill, not so much in the mathematics of these tasks but in the levels of expertise that were required to enable the participants to determine what levels of variation could be used. Ultimately this work led the team and the authorities to a position where they had produced a robust and well-reasoned account of the economy. It was not perfect, not 100 per cent accurate, but as best as it could be with the materials at hand.

There were a number of outcomes from these meetings. One was a finalized and jointly agreed set of key economic indicators. These would be presented in a Selected Economic Figures Table in the staff report. A second outcome was a specification of the salient factors in policy. For, once the basic figures had been agreed, investigations into the future were to be undertaken. These investigations involved making projections and varying different factors in these projections. The purpose of these investigations was not just to predict the future but also to enable better understanding of the present. In the meeting described, both sides came to an agreement as to what was of central concern to policy – namely, the current levels of government borrowing and the levels of growth in the economy and what this would mean for the future.

More specifically, these investigations of the future resulted in the realization that the current credit problems could lead the Arcadians to the Fund in the future. Alternatively, these current problems might be reduced by larger than expected revenues from export growth. Both possibilities looked plausible from the basic facts at hand. The team took this evidence to subsequent meetings on the last days of the mission, and used them to make persuasive arguments to the effect that the Arcadians should reduce structural impediments (manifest, for instance, in such things as complex and restrictive investment codes) to help ensure that the potential growth in the economy turned into a reality. These arguments were also presented in the staff report.

My concern here is to highlight features of these policy meetings that underscore the social organization of the work. In particular, I want to focus on the fact that these meetings were meetings that count, as I noted at the outset. There are two aspects to this. On the one hand, they were about adding numbers; on the other, these meetings had particular and crucially symbolic aspects. Both issues are intimately connected. But one has precedence over the other. Let me explain.

Meetings that count

The meeting described here consisted of two main parts, with a watershed in the middle. The chief's oration flowed across both stages. His oration commenced with a presentation not just of what the team had been working on, but what the team's view had become at that point in time. Given that the team was invested by the Fund to act on its behalf, this view was effectively the Fund's view. Moreover, the relationship between the mission and the authorities was one wherein the team was instructing the Arcadians as to what were the salient issues. In this respect, they were in a subordinate role as regards the mission. This was symbolized in the oration: the chief reported on the conduct of the authorities; he offered correctives; he gave guidance. This was more of a paternalistic relationship than one of equals. Accordingly, it was presented with all the solemnity it deserved. This was not an opportunity for the discussion of opinions or for jokes and levity.

Nonetheless, the Arcadians still had the power to reject the view offered by the chief. They had to respond to his oration. To this extent, this was paternalism without power. For though Arcadians had been involved in the development of this view – some more than others as we have seen – the Arcadian authorities had not officially accepted it and were under no obligation to do so. The period during which the Governor and his officials turned away and discussed the chief's remarks was the opportunity for them to decide whether to accept or reject it. It was therefore a moment pregnant with tension for the mission team. As it happens, in this process some of the figures could have been revised or amended, but none were in the meeting I described. Irrespective of that, the bottom line was that it was only once the Arcadians had announced acceptance that the next stage of the meeting could occur.

Before saying anything further about that second stage, I would like to argue that in accepting the numbers the Arcadians transformed the meeting into a ritual one, or rather one that had ritual effects. For their acceptance resulted in the numbers being ones that could be acted upon. They were transformed from being mere numbers into resources for policy. An important point to understand is that such ritual transformations cannot be guaranteed. If the Arcadians had rejected the numbers, this transformation would not have occurred. This is to reiterate the importance of the events and hence of the concern that participants had about them beforehand. After all, this was why the mission team were so apprehensive when they waited in the hotel lobby that morning: they knew the meetings could turn out to have the desired effect but they could also turn out quite otherwise.

This second stage also involved the chief standing up and making a speech – continuing his oration – but this time his remarks had a different character. If before they were descriptive, now they became an opportunity to outline issues to be investigated. It is in this respect that there was a watershed in the centre of the meeting. For after the Governor's acceptance, the chief's presentation became the common ground upon which both sides undertook subsequent analytical work. I shall say some more about that work in a moment, but before I do so, let me make some more remarks about how that transformation could occur.

In order for the 'acceptance of the numbers' to matter, these meetings were organized in such a way that all those persons whose views counted were there. Although, for example, the official in the Ministry of Planning might have been able to say 'Yes, these figures are right', his status was not sufficient to have his signing off represent the authorities as a whole. Rather, those in charge needed to have their say on matters. Hence the Governor of the Central Bank had to be present in any meeting that accepted or rejected the numbers as a whole. Up until that time he had little to do with the mission, all of the analytical work undertaken at that bank involving more junior officials and his deputies. But for that work to count, this individual had to sign off the product of that work. The reverse holds true as well. Just as the various junior members of the mission were able to present what in effect were the mission figures to the officials they met in the Ministries of Finance and Planning, their views were ultimately subordinate to the mission chief's. To be transformed into the official team's view, the chief had to present them as his own. This he did in his oration to the authorities. It was in this sense that power showed itself in the meetings. One should not be surprised by the fact that the chief had to sanction his team's views or that Arcadians had to do the same. There is no news in pointing towards the fact that institutions are hierarchical. But there is much to be learned from drawing attention to what one might call the moral transformation in question. It is to expand on what is meant by this that I now turn.

The raw and the cooked

The process of converting 'raw numbers' into meaningful and 'useable' information constitutes, in part, a *moral transformation* and not just an arithmetical or econometric one. I want to suggest that this does not just hold for the events within the policy meetings, although they highlight the issues most clearly. Mission work as a whole consists of a process of gathering data, subjecting these data to various assessments and sanctionings and, if the data pass these tests, using them in analytical tasks. This is in part a moral process because the data in question will often remain the same (i.e. the actual numbers at issue) irrespective of whether they are signed off, as in earlier stages of a mission, or ritually accepted, as in the policy meetings at the end. 'Passing the test', being signed off, being accepted, may make no difference to the number as a number (though sometimes it does). The difference made is to its moral status. Once data have been transformed (signed off), they come to exist in a moral field. By this I mean that when a number is signed off, it can jostle other numbers, sometimes resulting in those other numbers being ejected or returned to a non signed-off status (that is, thrown out of the figures). In this regard, one might say that missions are to some extent in the business of creating a moral order, an order upon which the Fund's analytical apparatus can operate.

It is worth noting that this process did not appear to involve a preference to seek agreement in the sense that both sides always try to agree with each other, as is the case with ordinary conversation. In this mission, there were distinct occasions when difficulties reaching agreement were confronted. These difficulties were solved through small, 'intimate' meetings between the chief and his equals in the authorities, including the Governor of the Central Bank. The chief and the mission team believed that these meetings would be difficult, and so asked for them to be held *in camera*. The Arcadians too asked for certain meetings to held in the same private manner.[5]

Be that as it may, all this discussion of the moral transformation of economic facts could lead one to think that economic reality is 'merely' a social construct, in this case, a construction based on audited numbers. If so, then it might lead one to believe that the concern of a mission and their counterparts in the authorities is not the real, hard, economic facts, but to ensure that the process of building a picture results in agreement, the difficulties in achieving this notwithstanding. This would give the impression that the exact nature of the picture does not matter, the main concern being simply that two sides, mission and authorities, agree to it.

In these respects, the process of social agreement confirms part of the thesis put forward by Porter (1995). According to Porter, the use of numbers and their collaborative investigation, their construction by various parties in government and other powerful institutions, is a means whereby the individuals involved come to display the objectivity of their work. The evidence I have presented confirms this view. But Porter goes further and argues that the need for this display is related to the fact that the individuals (and the institutions they work for) have no other way of justifying their social authority. According to him, numbers are a method to manifest and justify positions of power. From this view, the purpose of sanctioning numbers is to provide a device that justifies not only the numbers themselves, but also the status of those involved. However, evidence from mission work suggests that this is not the reason why numbers are agreed to. It suggests that given the nature of the material used on Fund missions, its mix of high-level numbers, estimates, projections and so on, it is necessary for all those using those numbers to agree what they might be. Agreement between the Arcadian authorities and the mission, as in this case, was the *basis* of the policy analysis, not a means whereby the power of those involved was justified to the outside world.

This does not mean to say that power is not involved. But it is involved in a different sense from how Porter construes it. Power is at issue insofar as the participants to these meetings – members of the Fund, senior officials in the Arcadian authorities – are socially sanctioned by their status to discuss these matters. Their positions in power enable them to do so. From this view, it is the assumption of and the fact of power that allows the work to be done, rather than the work justifying that power.

This leads me back again to the second stage of the meetings. I noted in the vignette that the Arcadians wanted to add up the numbers for themselves. I mentioned this not to point towards the possibility that they did not trust the mission numbers. Rather, it drew attention to how the Arcadians were cognizant of the practical fact that people understand numbers better if they handle those numbers themselves. But behind this was something much more significant, which relates to the economic reality of concern to all parties in the meetings and the relationship of that reality to the process of determining it. For this apparently inconsequential running through of the numbers points towards the fact that, for participants in these meetings, objective reality could only be brought into view through extensive investigations of the numbers.

This process was both a hands-on econometric undertaking and a social one, wherein the various participants tested and corroborated their investigations with their colleagues. These testings and corroborations were crucial since the meetings were populated by those people whose status and business was to determine what was the right way and the wrong way of doing these things. These were the experts doing their work. It is in this sense that there was a moral basis to the policy meetings: the activities in these meetings were being undertaken by the experts this field. It was their determinations that counted, their assessments of what was the right way of doing things that mattered. There is more here than the fact that their views came to hold sway: their views were the product of analytical work. This involved unpacking and investigating how the figures fitted together. That in turn meant working through the figures, presenting views on the figures, and investigating the numbers and their implications with calculators in hand, there and then. This was the way in which the economic reality came into sight. The economic facts were constituted in the methodical ways the mission team and the authorities jointly worked out an intelligent basis for their analysis. Yet at the same time the adequacy of the methods used were attested to by the willing participation of members of those meetings in those investigations.

By willing I do not mean that they were uniformly compliant to what was done – far from it. For they discussed and reasoned through together what were the appropriate ways of proceeding. The point is that these meetings were so designed as to provide the opportunity for *these* people to demonstrate, use and participate in the determination of facts in policy work. This was a group of experts doing their work, together. These were meetings that 'counted' by dint of those who did the counting.[6]

Conclusion

Each and every Fund mission is unique; furthermore, the pattern of relations between the Fund and particular members is also always unique, reflecting the kinds of problems a member has, its expertise, its institutional structures and so on. In this case, the member authorities were somewhat reliant on the Fund mission to guide and instruct them on policy work. As one of the Arcadians quipped toward the end of the mission: 'We've been waiting for you [*the mission*] to come back again to help us solve these policy dilemmas. You should come back more often!' The specifics of the Arcadian institutions also showed themselves in the mission process and in the character of the policy meetings. The desk officer explained to me (during the event) that one of the reasons why the Central Bank staff took so long deliberating on the figures the chief presented was that they were trying to determine which of those figures were their responsibility and which were other departments' within the government. They were concerned to make sure that the numbers they had produced did not indicate that they had done a bad job.

These particularities aside, I have been wanting to highlight a number of general, key features of mission work whether it be to Arcadia or anywhere else. I have shown that getting to the right information involves both an analytic and social process. It is analytical in the sense that it requires the understanding of the representational apparatus that will be given to a mission (the numbers, the tables, the National Accounts). It is social in the sense that it means talking to those who devise this apparatus, which enables a mission to understand the motives and purposes behind these tools. It is also social in the sense that when a mission begins to develop an apparatus of its own (their own set of numbers, tables, and so forth), they have to have it signed off by the authorities.

I reiterate, however, that mission work itself is fraught with the possibility of not coming to understand what the policy situation is, not in the sense that the two sides (mission and authorities) might not agree, but because determination of the facts of the case may be difficult to achieve. The Arcadian team became more and more tired towards the end of the mission not simply because they were trying to get all the work done in time but because the work was turning out to be very difficult. Of course they wanted to get the work done in time, but first and foremost they had to get the numbers right. This holds true for all missions. Mission work is, in other words, a hands-on empirical science, albeit bound up with and immersed in social practice.

Finally, I have wanted to note that missions come to an agreement as to the numbers representing the economic situation not in a fashion that is 'merely ritualistic' (that is, an agreement that is inevitable). The numbers a mission team generates achieve transformation in the very useability of numbers only because the analytical work for the construction of those numbers is done successfully. This may take more time, or it may take less. Such transformations are likely to be salient in all organizations and institutional contexts subject to audit. Here the numbers represent the enormously complex and indeed vast scale of national economies; in other situations they may represent much finer grained phenomena. As I mentioned at the outset, the ubiquity of auditing is affecting all aspects of our lives. It goes without saying that such auditing is being undertaken with a view to assess quality, productivity, and so on. Often doing so is treated as essential to a rational society. But if it is the case that the transformations I have described are common to all audit processes, then the society we are moving toward – Power's Audit Society – is perhaps much less rational in the Weberian sense than we may think. It may well be that though the raw material of those processes may be wholly mundane, agreeing to count them may make them seem sacred. The empirical materials I have presented from the IMF lead me to make this suggestion; it is for others to investigate whether this is so.

Notes

1 This is normal practice for all desk officers.
2 Sometimes local authorities 'reject' the figures and analysis of Fund missions, and insist that a mission goes through its numbers again.

3 It should be added that costs for stocks were carried by the government since it had a policy of purchasing unsold stocks off the suppliers.
4 Just as the meeting I have described focused on one area of concern, other meetings dealt with the remaining areas. By the time the team had completed the meeting cycle, all sectors of the economy had been covered.
5 I was not able to understand what the difficulties in question were. One reason was that I could not participate in the prior meetings that had led to the discovery of difficulties. These meetings, which had apparently also broached the various ways they could be solved, were held between the deputy chief and the official in the Ministry of Planning, one of the earliest of which I have described. As I explained at that point, this individual was a key informant for the mission. Apparently the team knew that, at a certain time in the mission, difficult topics would have to be discussed with this individual. Therefore they were happy to let me observe some of the early meetings, less so later ones. The team felt that my presence might make these discussions more difficult. Thus, it is hard for me to assess what impact my own presence (or in this case absence) throughout the mission had. As it happened, the chief remarked that my cheerful countenance kept his team's spirits up. The Arcadian themselves thought it amusing that the Fund would allow an outsider to watch them at work. Beyond this I cannot determine what my influence may have been. The meetings held in camera may be indicative of how certain tasks were undertaken in a way that made them invisible. But one might reasonably take the view that this was a reflection of the fact that the mission team had hard work to do, and they simply did not want a stranger breathing down their neck.
6 This is a point often lost in sociological descriptions of experts at work. For a good exposition see Button and Sharrock (1993).

References

Anderson, R., Hughes, J. and Sharrock, W. (1989) *Working for Profit: The Social Organisation of Calculation in an Entrepreneurial Firm*, Aldershot: Avebury.
Button, G. and Sharrock, W. (1993) 'A Disagreement over Agreement and Consensus in Constructionist Sociology', *Journal for the Theory of Social Behaviour* 23(1): 1–25.
Gardner, L. and Lewis, D. (1996) *Anthropology, Development and the Postmodern Challenge*, London: Pluto Press.
Harper, R.H.R. (1987) 'The Fate of Idealism in Acccountancy', *Proceedings of the Third Multi-disciplinary Approaches to Accountancy*, Manchester University, Summer.
—— (1988) 'Not Any Old Numbers: an Examination of Practical Reasoning on an Accoutancy Environment', *The Journal of Interdisciplinary Economics*, 2: 297–306.

—— (1989) 'An Ethnographic Examination of Accountancy', unpublished PhD Thesis, University of Manchester.

—— (1998) *Inside the IMF: An Ethnography of Documents, Technology and Organisational Action,* London and San Diego: Academic Press.

Harper, R.H.R., Randall, D. and Rouncefield, M. (2000) *Organizational Change and Retail Finance: an Ethnographic Perspective,* London and New York: Routledge.

Lynch, M. (1985) *Art and Artifact In Laboratory Science,* London: Routledge and Kegan Paul.

Lynch, M., Livingston, E. and Garfinkel, H. (1983) 'Temporal Order in the Laboratory' in K.D. Knorr-Cetina and M. Mulkay (eds) *Science Observed,* London: Sage.

Porter, T. M. (1995) *Trust in Numbers: The Pursuit of Objectivity in Science and Public Life,* Princeton, New Jersey: Princeton University Press.

Power, M. (1997) *The Audit Society: Rituals of Verification,* Oxford: Oxford University Press.

Part II

Chapter 2

Coercive accountability

The rise of audit culture in higher education

Cris Shore and Susan Wright

One of the questions raised in the introduction to this volume is how one recognizes epochal change, particularly when one is in the midst of it. The rise of what some authors have termed 'audit culture', and the rapid and relentless spread of coercive technologies of accountability into higher education is a case in point. Few processes have had such a profound impact in re-shaping academics' conditions of work and conditions of thought since the post-war expansion of the university sector in Britain, yet this major transformation remains curiously under-researched and un-theorized. If, as anthropologists argue, culture is constantly being invented and re-invented, nowhere is this becoming more evident than in the milieu in which most anthropologists themselves operate: the university sector.

This chapter focuses on the rise of technologies of audit and accountability and their transfer from the financial domain to the public sector, particularly higher education. But why does something as seemingly mundane as a 'technology transfer' merit the grand term 'epochal cultural change'? The French philosopher Foucault provides ample evidence of ways in which seemingly dull, routine and bureaucratic practices often have profound effects on social life. Our analysis underlines the fact that audit technologies being introduced into higher education and elsewhere are not simply innocuously neutral, legal-rational practices: rather, they are instruments for new forms of governance and power. They embody a new rationality and morality and are designed to engender amongst academic staff new norms of conduct and professional behaviour. In short, they are agents for the creation of new kinds of subjectivity: self-managing individuals who render themselves auditable.

In tracking these changes in higher education and other sectors in Britain, we show how audit culture is intimately connected to what is often referred to as 'new managerialism'. In turn, new managerialism is but one expression of a more global process of neo-liberal economic and political transformation manifest in the structural adjustment policies of the IMF (Gray 1998), the recruitment and management strategies of American corporations (Martin 1997) and tenant self-management in British council housing estates (Hyatt 1997). Ideas and practices associated with auditing have not only migrated across sectors but, through various 'transnational connections' (Hannerz 1996), they have travelled across different parts of the world. Although their name and form seem to be everywhere the same, each time these technologies enter a new context, their impact varies, often in unpredictable ways. Building on this, we show how the introduction of new methods of audit and accountability that originated in financial management take on very different meanings – and often coercive functions – when introduced into the pubic sector.

We suggest three ways of identifying and analysing the character and direction of the new cultural epoch of managerialism and its impact on higher education. The first is through tracking key changes in language, including the emergence of new discourses and the 'semantic clusters' from which they are constituted. The second is by identifying the new kinds of practices associated with these discourses, and the new institutions, norms, and areas of expertise that they hail into existence, and through which they are implemented. The third is the effect of these norms and practices – embedded in mundane routines and duties – on conditions of work and thought and, more importantly, on the way in which individuals construct themselves as professional subjects. The question is: how do individuals confront the new cultural logic, with its implicit morality and its reworked notions of professionalism, when they are 'inside' – and therefore subject to the disciplines of – the new regime itself?

The meaning of audit

The past two decades have witnessed a striking proliferation in the use of the term audit and its extension into contexts where it was seldom previously used. It has become a key term in the lexicon of contemporary management, and a major interest of policy-makers and governments throughout the Western world. As the Oxford English Dictionary shows, its roots lie firmly in financial management. The dictionary gives five main definitions for the noun 'audit': (1) statement of account, balance sheet; (2) (from Late Medieval English) periodical settlement of accounts between landlord and tenants; (3) official examination or verification; (4) hearing, enquiry, judicial examination; (5) (figurative) reckoning, settlement, especially Day of Judgement.

These definitions all stem from the Latin *audire*, 'to hear' or 'hearing'. Each evokes the principles of scrutiny, examination and the passing of judgement. In every case the hearing (or monitoring) is a public inspection – what Power (1997: 123) calls a 'ritual of verification'. Moreover, the second definition tells us that the nature of the relationship created or implied by audit is hierarchical and paternalistic. Audit is essentially a relationship of power between scrutinizer and observed: the latter are rendered objects of information, never subjects in communication (Foucault 1977: 200).

During the 1980s and 1990s, audit migrated from its original association with financial accounting into new domains of professional life, and in the process came to acquire a new set of meanings and functions. We call this an example of *conceptual inflation*. As Martin (1994) demonstrated for the word 'flexibility', audit has been released from its traditional moorings, inflated in importance, and now, like a free-floating signifier, hovers over virtually every field of modern working life. There are now 'academic audits', 'government audits', 'health and safety audits', 'company audits', 'value for money audits', 'computer audits', 'data audits', 'forensic audits', 'environmental audits', even 'stress audits' and 'democratic audits'. The term was never previously associated with any of these fields. Following Williams (1976), we call nouns that migrate in this way *keywords*. As Williams argued, over time, keywords acquire a range of contingent meanings, and as words are used in new contexts, either old meanings gain new prominence or existing meanings are stretched in novel and unpredictable directions. In the case of audit, as the word spread from its initial association with financial accounting and entered new areas of professional life, the meanings from among its original repertoire that have risen to prominence are 'public inspection', 'submission to scrutiny', 'rendering visible' and 'measures of performance'.

As concepts migrate, their relationship to other key terms change and new semantic clusters form. These provide the threads from which discourses and ideologies are woven and, when successful, form the conceptual bedrock upon which new institutions acquire cultural legitimacy. This process, by which a migrating keyword becomes the centre of a new semantic cluster, exemplifies what Strathern (1992) labels the 'domaining effect', whereby the conceptual logic of an idea associated with one domain is transposed into another, often with unanticipated outcomes. A good example is the transformation of the notion of 'the people' during the rise of nationalism and the establishment of the institutions of the nation-state in Europe after 1789. Hitherto, 'the people' had referred to subjects of a ruler or followers of a religion, but after the French Revolution the concept of 'the people' became increasingly associated with that of 'the nation', and formed a semantic cluster with 'language', 'territory', 'citizenship' and 'statehood' (Hobsbawm 1990). This constellation of concepts, and the equation of people with nation and with state, migrated quickly from Revolutionary France to the rest of Europe and beyond, giving rise to the political institutions of modernity, yet in entering each new context, acquiring different forms and outcomes.

In the case of new managerialism and British higher education in the 1980s, audit was divorced from its strictly financial meaning and became associated with a cluster of terms: 'performance', 'quality assurance', 'quality control', 'discipline', 'accreditation', 'accountability', 'transparency', 'efficiency', 'effectiveness', 'value for money', 'responsibility', 'benchmarking', 'good practice', 'peer-review', 'external verification', 'stakeholder' and 'empowerment' (Audit Commission 1984: 3). Writing on this audit explosion in general, Power (1994: 43) observes how Value For Money Auditing was translated from private sector administration into the management of the public sector. This appears to be particularly evident in those countries which have experimented with neo-liberal reforms. It is difficult to trace the precise path along which audit rationality has moved; however, since the early 1980s a wave of change has swept over the public sectors of most OECD countries and various market mechanisms have been introduced in an effort to increase efficiency, accountability and consumers' power over the public sector. Higher education has been particularly affected by these policies, and the first comparative studies have begun to emerge (Niklasson 1996).

Audit as instrument of government

The consequence of introducing the new vocabulary of audit into higher education has not simply been to re-invent academic institutions as financial bodies (Strathern 1997: 309). More importantly, the introduction of the language and norms of audit has given rise to a host of new institutions and agencies. It has also facilitated the emergence of a new ethics and politics of governance in which 'a particular style of formalised accountability' has now become the 'ruling principle' (Power 1997: 4). These changes are symptomatic of a new rationality of government, or what, following Foucault (1991), we might call 'neo-liberal governmentality'. By this, we refer to a wholesale shift in the role of government premised on using the norms of the free market as the organizing principles not only of economic life, but of the activities of the state itself and, even more profoundly, of the conduct of individuals. The key to this system of governmentality lies in inculcating new norms and values by which external regulatory mechanisms transform the conduct of organizations and individuals in their capacity as 'self-actualizing' agents, so as to achieve political objectives through 'action at a distance' (Miller and Rose 1990: 1). These regulatory mechanisms act as 'political technologies' which seek to bring persons, organizations and objectives into alignment.

Disguising how power works is, as Foucault (1977) observes, central to political technology. As Dreyfus and Rabinow (1982: 196) note, 'political technologies advance by taking what is essentially a political problem, removing it from the realm of political discourse, and recasting it in the neutral language of science'. Thus, audit procedures present themselves as rational, objective and neutral, based on sound principles of efficient management - as 'unopposable as virtue itself' (Pollitt 1993: 49). However, these procedures revolve around normative statements and measurements which are used to construct evaluative grids – such as competitive league tables and performance charts – that simultaneously rank institutions and individuals against each other. Audit is thus a 'dividing practice' which is, to use Foucault's phrase, both 'individualizing and totalizing'. The supposed 'self-empowerment' of this system rests upon a simultaneous imposition of external control from above and internalization of new norms so that individuals can continuously improve themselves. In short, external subjection and internal subjectification are combined so that individuals conduct themselves in terms of the norms through which they are governed. Audit thus becomes a political technology of the self: a means through which individuals actively and freely regulate their own conduct and thereby contribute to the government's model of social order.

A key aspect of this process has been its effect in changing the identity of professionals and the way they conceptualize themselves. The audited subject is recast as a depersonalized unit of economic resource whose productivity and performance must constantly be measured and enhanced. To be effective, audit technologies must somehow re-fashion the way people perceive themselves in relation to their work, to one another and to themselves. In short, they are used to transform professional, collegial and personal identities. This process often goes under the name of 'empowerment'. It contends that audit 'enables' individuals and institutions to ensure quality and improve performance not by imposing external standards of conduct, but by allowing people to be judged by the targets that they set for themselves. According to this perspective, audit is an open, participatory and democratic process whose benign objectives are surely beyond criticism. However, what the language of 'efficiency', 'effectiveness', 'best practice', 'self-management', 'self-enhancement' and 'value for money'[1] disguises is that audit culture relies upon hierarchical relationships and coercive practices. The self-directed, self-managed individual is encouraged to identify with the university and the goals of higher education policy: challenging the terms of reference is not an option.

Central to the development of new political technologies in higher education has been the creation of new categories of experts including 'educational development consultants', 'quality assurance officers', 'staff development trainers' and 'teaching quality assessors'. These specialists fulfil four main roles. First, they develop a new expert knowledge and a discourse which create the classifications for a new framework or template of norms, a normative grid for the measurement and regulation of individual and organizational performance. Second, their grid and expertise are used for the design of institutional procedures for setting targets and assessing achievements. Third, certain of these experts staff and manage the new regulatory mechanisms and systems, and judge levels of compliance or deviance. Fourth, they have a therapeutic and redeeming role: they tutor individuals in the art of self-improvement and steer them towards desired norms.

The point to note here is that the combination of new expert knowledges, regulatory mechanisms and categories of specialists has had a different impact in different parts of the public sector and the response of professionals has also varied. This is well exemplified by the growing body of literature (Ball 1990; Hyatt 1997; du Gay 1996; Exworthy and Halford 1999). Particularly interesting has been the response of doctors in the British National Health Service (NHS). According to Walby and Greenwell (1994), hospital doctors in the UK have successfully embraced the threat to their professionalism from the onslaught of new managerialism by developing managerial competencies themselves. They have initiated their own practices of medical audit and implemented the language of accountancy to transform the NHS in such a way as to enhance their professional status and clinical autonomy. However, as a result, new categories of 'managerial professionals' have emerged, resulting in a loss of collegiality and new power hierarchies among doctors (Exworthy and Halford 1999: 125). By contrast, some professions such as social workers have done little to contest new managerial technologies and as a result have experienced a clear erosion of their professional values and status (Jones 1999: 48). Others, such as school teachers and head teachers have responded ambiguously, some enthusiastically accepting the new norms, others feeling professionally compromised and doing what they can to resist them (Menther and Muschamp 1999). As Exworthy and Halford (1999) point out, however, in all these professions collective values and lateral solidarities have been disrupted. The question that forms the focus of our enquiry is: how are lecturers in higher education responding to the orthodoxies of new managerialism, both individually and collectively?

New managerialism and the rise of audit

The emergence of new managerialism in Britain is associated with the strategies of the 1979 Thatcher government to reduce public expenditure, 'roll back the state' and increase the efficiency of public servants by subjecting them to simulated disciplines of the free market. Throughout the 1980s, government assumed, despite ample evidence to the contrary, that the private sector was regulated effectively by market mechanisms, and that this sector provided an ideal model also for the public sector (Shore and

Wright 1999). Increasing efficiency invariably meant cost-cutting and reforms designed to transform public institutions into pseudo-businesses. In central government departments, civil servants were cut by 14 per cent over five years, cash limits were imposed on most public service activities, and each department was set up as a 'cost centre', with performance indicators for its work and annual personal objectives for each individual. Those individuals who achieved their targets received 'merit awards' and promotion.

Following Pollitt (1993), one may characterize this new managerialism as neo-Taylorian. Other neo-Taylorian features included the following. First, of the three virtuous E's, the emphasis was clearly on Economy and Efficiency rather than Effectiveness. This had the effect that civil servants' energy was concentrated on money, time and staff-saving revisions to internal procedures rather than on larger questions concerning the ultimate effectiveness of programmes, their impact on the public and on issues of social justice, and whether their outcomes were consistent with expressed policy aims. Second, there was an emphasis on the rhetoric of decentralization, which disguised the true extent of centralization but had the advantage of putting responsibility for imposing unpopular cuts on local management. Third, the old, discredited terminological division between politics and administration was reproduced in the guise of 'strategic objective setting' on the one hand and 'management' on the other. Better management was presented as a politically neutral good and fundamentally a matter of efficient implementation. Fourth, staff were treated as 'work units to be incentivised and measured' rather than 'people to be encouraged and developed' (Pollitt 1993: 60). The overall emphasis was on controlling employees rather than staff development, on 'measurement rather than encouragement', and 'on money rather than leadership or morale' (Pollitt 1993: 59). The benefits of this approach were summed up by one of its most influential advocates, the Conservative minister Heseltine. In a statement which captures the spirit of neo-Taylorian managerialism and its accounting mentality, he opined:

> When the literacies of the Civil Service and the generalities of their intentions are turned into targets which can be monitored and costed, when information is conveyed in columns instead of screeds, then objectives become clear and progress towards them becomes measurable and far more likely.[2]

Following the third electoral victory of the Conservative Party under Mrs Thatcher in 1987, a second wave of reforms known as the New Public Management (NPM) was embarked upon with renewed vigour and confidence. There were continuities with the forms of neo-Taylorian managerialism introduced earlier as well as two major innovations. Among the former were first, a much bolder and larger scale use of quasi-market mechanisms for those parts of the public sector that could not be privatized. However, these 'markets' were highly managed. For example, the then Universities Funding Council (UGC) determined how each university was rewarded or penalized for its performance in the race to recruit more students. Second, an emphasis on greater arms-length control via government intermediary bodies (such as the Higher Education Funding Council for England) and sub-contracting of services. What was new in the second wave of reforms was a rhetorical emphasis on 'quality' and on the need to meet and improve upon 'customer's requirements' (Pollitt 1993: 184–5). However, in many instances it was economic issues and central political control which predominated: customers were typically other public sector agencies and often it was ministers, not the public, who prescribed what the 'right services for customers' ought to be.

Commentators have not always made the link between the new managerialist agenda and the explosion of audit systems.[3] Accompanying the introduction of new managerialism into central government departments, a long-established Exchequer and Audit Department was transformed in 1983 into the new National Audit Office. Audit became an even more visible instrument of political rule in the context of the Thatcher government's equally important rolling back of the local state. The Local Government Finance Act of 1982 was designed first to control and cut local authority spending (a major area of public expenditure) and second to ensure that local authorities used their resources with 'economy, efficiency and effectiveness' (Audit Commission 1984: i). Local government's adherence to the three virtuous E's was to be scrutinized by a new agency, the Audit Commission, also created in 1983. The Audit Commission was to be 'a driving force in the improvement of public services' and its main functions were threefold: to establish a national Code of Audit Practice; 'to carry out national studies designed to promote economy, efficiency and effectiveness in the provision of local authority and NHS services' and 'to apply

national findings to the audited body to help assess local performance' (Audit Commission 1996: 4). The birth of this agency
marked the moment when the language associated with financial
accounting shifted to embrace 'monitoring performance', identifying 'best practice', improving Value For Money (VFM) and
'ensuring effectiveness of management systems' (Audit Commission
1984: 3). Audit came to mean not just checking the books but the
scrutiny of good government, and in the process, became instrumental in the formation of policy itself.

The new Audit Commission was launched with a complement of
no fewer than five hundred staff, of whom three-quarters were
seconded from the Department of the Environment, and a quarter
were drawn from private financial accountancy firms. These firms
(such as Price Waterhouse, Touche Ross, Coopers and Lybrand and
Peat, Marwick, Mitchell) were undergoing the same enlargement
of their remit as the Audit Commission itself. They grew expo-
nentially during the 1980s and expanded from purely financial
accounting to become leading consultants in the new and global
business of audit and management.[4]

The Audit Commission epitomized the arms-length agencies
established by central government during this period. The
Commission emphasized that its staff operated independently of
central and local government and were not even Crown Servants
(Audit Commission 1984: i). Its claim to independence is based on
the fact that it receives no grant or subsidy from government.
However, this claim is somewhat disingenuous as, in the words of
its Annual Report, 'its income derives entirely from fees charged to
local authority and NHS bodies for audit work' (1996: 4). That is,
these bodies are compelled to pay the Audit Commission for
regular inspections and to participate in targeted reviews of
particular services. Professing 'independence' from government is a
good example of how power disguises the mechanism of its own
operations.

As will be shown, similar arms-length bodies have been established to audit performance in higher education. The political
technologies which these agencies have developed to transform this
sector combine the neo-Taylorist features of managerialism as
applied to central government departments with the kind of
instruments and procedures initially used by the Audit Commission
to review local authority purchasing and refuse collection. By the
1990s, and even after a change of government, audit had become

the mechanism for reviewing public sector performance and validating claims to good governance.

Auditing universities

Many features of new managerialism and audit culture have been introduced into higher education in the UK. However, this process has been protracted and not without occasional hiccups and resistance. Throughout the 1980s, the education system – and particularly higher education – was accused of having 'failed the economy'. This criticism was justification for introducing new managerialist methods to increase efficiency and productivity. Furthermore, British universities were considered to be elitist in catering for only some 5 per cent of the population, a much smaller percentage than their counterparts in Europe and North America. Government policy aimed to create a system of mass higher education without a loss of 'equality', at the same time as driving down the unit of resource. Consequently, attempts were made to instil a pseudo-market, and for a sequence of years the University Funding Council asked universities to compete for expanding student numbers. Suddenly, in the late 1980s, when the implications of increasing numbers of student grants for local authority budgets were realized, the funding body reversed the policy, reduced intake targets and penalized universities that over-recruited. The result was a muddled market that was anything but 'free'.

The 1985 Jarratt Report on 'efficiency studies in universities' that was set up by the Committee of Vice Chancellors and Principals (CVCP) and the government's University Grants Council (precursor to HEFCE, see below) recommended that universities introduce the language of new managerialism to the university sector. Its view was that 'universities are first and foremost corporate enterprises' and that '[the] crucial issue is how a university achieves maximum value for money'. To this end Jarratt recommended that the Vice Chancellor should be considered not only as an academic leader, but also as a 'chief executive' whose role entails 'ensuring that "strategic plans" link "academic, financial and physical aspects" into "one corporate process"'.[5] Furthermore, he recommended that, as part of the process of re-inventing themselves as enterprises, university faculties be broken up into private sector-style 'cost-centres' and that they be managed through 'the centralisation of executive control, the linkage between budgetary and academic considerations and the decentralisation of account-able budgets to the lowest level'.[6] However, as critics have noted, British universities have followed a narrow and financially-deter-mined agenda of efficiency and economy in which once again the third virtue – effectiveness – has hardly been considered at all. The overall picture of educational achievement and the role of uni-versities in British society has largely been ignored.

The logical corollary of creating cost centres and performance indicators is the setting of annual personal objectives for individual staff – with rewards for those who achieved their targets. In 1988, there was a major conflict between the Vice Chancellors and the Association of University Teachers (AUT) who reported that:

> [The Vice Chancellors] saw appraisal as an additional tool for managing the institution and wanted to associate it with a system of rewards and punishments. We wanted a scheme which focused on supporting the professional development of individual members of staff.[7]

The outcome was an agreement to establish a system in which there was to be no linkage between appraisal, any process of target-setting, differential pay or promotion. However much this agree-ment may have been compromised in practice, Pollitt cites this case as an example where 'a profession was able to resist' the more strident aspects of new managerialism by articulating 'alternative schemes of a less hierarchical or authoritarian character' (Pollitt 1993: 80).

If this was one instance where the thrust of new managerialism towards diminishing the status and solidarity of a group of profes-sionals was contested, another instance came with the 1988 Education Reform Act. One clause of that Act severely weakened academic tenure which had been lecturers' guarantee of freedom of speech as well as job security. Although university lobbying resulted in the insertion of a formal statement of academic freedom in the 1988 Education Reform Act, security of tenure was lost.

State funding of university education had not, hitherto, been used to interfere with the manner in which universities conducted themselves. Under royal charters, universities set their own standards and were the sole arbiters of their own quality. Audit heralded a significant break with the principle of academic autonomy. Rather than attacking university autonomy head on, the government concealed the extent of its intervention by recruiting a host of intermediary agencies and by mobilizing academics themselves as managerial professionals and active accomplices in this process. Although the introduction of audit culture into higher education in the early 1980s made some progress, it was not until the post-1987 wave of New Public Management reforms that, under the guise of 'enhancing quality' and 'achieving cultural change', the effect on the structure of universities and the professionalism of individuals really began to bite.

These themes were epitomized in the 1993 White Paper on science and technology, entitled *Realising Our Potential*. This argued not only for tighter financial control, but called for 'a key cultural change' in education, science and research that would 'enforce accountability' to the taxpayer (HMG 1993: 5). The White Paper again stressed the government's priorities of competitive wealth creation, closer links between businessmen and scientists, and greater responsiveness to 'user groups' (including industry, commerce and government departments). Its language exemplified the key themes and metaphors associated with markets and 'Enterprise Culture': 'cost-effectiveness', 'improving efficiency'; 'enhancing productivity', 'driving down unit of resource' and 'providing value for money" (Selwyn and Shore 1998). The new managerial strategies required to improve the quality and efficiency of teaching and research were set out clearly. These included strong 'line management', the 'rationalization' of teaching resources, a more comprehensive definition of lecturers' duties, and a whole new gamut of business practices from 'mission statements', 'strategic plans' and 'performance indicators', to competitive league tables.

In the view of the government, 'efficiency savings' (alias 'budget cuts') would not diminish standards of academic research or teaching thanks to new procedures of 'quality assurance' based on a rough translation of Total Quality Management (TQM) from the private sector. The core features of TQM in British education were summed up by one college principal thus:[8] organizations must put their customers at the centre of all they do and strive for continuous quality improvement; everyone in the organization should be 'empowered' by being the manager of their own areas of responsibility; finally, quality assurance must be management-led and driven, but 'quality is in fact everyone's responsibility'. Thus a key aim of TQM is the (*sic*) 'responsibilization' of the workforce.

For most lecturers and middle managers, however, the result has not been empowering but increased pressure to conform, reduced autonomy and responsibility without power.

An audit process to ensure 'quality' was set out in the government's 1991 White Paper, *Higher Education: A New Framework* and a new government agency, the Higher Education Funding Council for England (HEFCE), was charged with ensuring the quality of teaching and learning in institutions. The auditing procedures adopted by the Council followed the principle that individuals and departments were responsible for managing their own performance and ensuring the quality of their provision (HEFCE 1992; 1993). However, HEFCE required departments to submit 'bids' claiming their provision to be 'excellent', 'satisfactory' or 'unsatisfactory'. These had to be supported by documented evidence based on 'performance indicators' (PI's) demonstrating 'output' and 'fitness for purpose'. HEFCE then sent teams of inspectors composed of senior academics from the relevant discipline and their own officials to visit, observe and grade the department. Any department deemed unsatisfactory had to rectify the situation within twelve months, or else 'core funding and student places for that subject will be withdrawn' (HEFCE 1995: 14).

By the early 1990s, universities experienced a veritable panopticon of inspection, with Academic Audits (AA) one year, a competitive Research Assessment Exercise (RAE) another, and a Teaching Quality Assessment (TQA) the next. Leaving aside the high cost of these audits to the HEFCE, they also placed enormous financial burdens on the universities, generating additional workloads for university staff. By turning some academics into managerial professionals, and by ranking departments competitively against each other through RAE and TQA league tables, these audits have often had a damaging effect on collegiality. Reports from erstwhile peers became the basis on which HEFCE determined departmental funding. The system was also punitive in that, as the AUT (1993: 1) pointed out, those departments with problems experienced a withdrawal of their funding, rather than encouragement or support. Thus, academic peers found themselves in a policing role in a punitive and divisive system.

In 1996 the government established a bipartisan committee under the chairmanship of Dearing in order to make 'recommendations on how the purposes, shape, structure, size and funding of higher education, including support for students, should develop to meet the needs of the United Kingdom over the next 20 years' (Dearing 1997: 1). The Dearing Report recommended that two new agencies be created to implement its reforms. The accreditation of academics as teachers fell to the first of these, the Institute for Learning and Teaching (ILT). The second, the Quality Assurance Agency (QAA) – a registered charity and a 'company limited by guarantee' technically owned by universities – has set out a 'quality assurance framework', with the following elements: (1) a Qualifications Framework to ensure that degrees with the same title (BA, MA, PhD) are of a common level and nature; (2) Subject Benchmarks of agreed national standards in each subject; (3) a Programme Specification setting out the intended outcomes for each programme in each institution; (4) Academic Reviewers, a panel of senior academics and practising professionals for each discipline; (5) a six-yearly cycle of Reviews to scrutinize quality assurance mechanisms in each institution, and 'secure national consistency and comparability of judgements' on the same subject (QAA 1998: 4).

All the elements of new managerialism are evident in these new bodies. First, they set up pseudo-markets and reorganize institutions into quasi-businesses. Second, they police organizations' own systems of control, through intermediary bodies and 'action at a distance'. Third, they create new, ostensibly independent experts whose knowledge is used as the basis for systems of audit and is also accessible to individuals wishing to improve themselves. Fourth, they rely on techniques of the self which render political subjects governable by requiring that individuals behave as responsible, self-activating, free agents who have internalized the new normative framework. Fifth, through requiring disciplines to formulate Subject Benchmarks they encourage disciplines to reorganize themselves and, paradoxically, to act more collectively. Sixth, where successful, 'they bring persons, organizations and [political] objectives into alignment' (Miller and Rose 1990: 1), thus, squaring the circle of efficiency, economy and arms-length control.

How audit transforms organizations

We have described how new managerialist audit practices have been diffused throughout the tertiary education sector and the new norms and values they have promulgated. The question raised in this section is what effect have these had in changing university culture and the organization of the discipline.

Power argues that to be audited, an organization must actively transform itself into an auditable commodity: one 'structured to conform to the need to be monitored ex-post' (Power 1994: 8). Thus, a major feature of audit is the extent to which it reshapes in its own image those organizations that are monitored. What is required is auditee compliance with the norms and procedures demanded by inspectors. While it is claimed that the standards against which university departments and individuals are assessed are those which they set for themselves, as Power points out, audits 'do as much to construct definitions of quality and performance as to monitor them' (Power 1994: 33).

Universities have prepared for audit by appointing new 'quality assurance officers' and creating special 'monitoring committees' to bring their procedures into line with the anticipated standards demanded by external assessors. The result has been the invention of a host of 'auditable structures' and paper trails to demonstrate 'evidence of system' to visiting inspectors. To make such structures visible has become a major new aspect of university work, not only for these new specialists, but also for lecturing staff who are now required to devote their time to producing auditable records – time that would otherwise be spent on teaching and research. For many university lecturers, all this activity appears superfluous to their real work and indeed the whole audit procedure takes on the feel of an artificial and staged performance. Some universities, for example, now run dress rehearsals in preparation for the TQA visits. Most staff and students are tutored on what to say and what not to say about the quality of provision in their institution. 'Careless talk costs money' is an apt motto for the new ethos of caution and careful preparation. Audit visits produce a climate of unease and hyperactivity. Like the periodic school inspections, teaching and research audits in universities have become the key events in the academic calendar for teachers and in the Business Plans of the new university Management Teams. These staged events have acquired all the characteristics of what Abélès (1988) calls 'modern political ritual': formalized, choreographed, theatrical and ideologically loaded. The enhanced performance induced by audit, with its pressure to play to the gallery, is thus of a very different kind to that intended by the government and the HEFCE.

The meaning of 'teaching quality' has similarly been transformed by the audit process. It is now defined largely in Mission Statements by management teams, from within the university but often remote from classroom practice. To be audited, the learning experience must now be quantified and standardized so that it can be measured. The curriculum's merits are today measured in terms of finite, tangible, transferable and, above all, marketable skills. 'It no longer really matters how well an academic teaches and whether or not he or she sometimes inspires their pupils,' writes Johnson (1994: 379); 'it is far more important that they have produced plans for their courses, bibliographies, outlines of this, that and the other, in short all the paraphernalia of futile bureaucratization required for assessors who come from on high like emissaries from Kafka's castle.'

The emphasis on creating auditable paper trails and visible systems illustrates a key point made by Power (1994: 19):

> what is being assured is the quality of control systems rather than the quality of first order operations. In such a context accountability is discharged by demonstrating the existence of such systems of control, not by demonstrating good teaching, caring, manufacturing or banking.

The economy and efficiency of the audit process itself requires that the emphasis is on the 'control of control'.

Some critics argue that the imperatives for control that follow audit could 'undermine staff and institutional autonomy . . . and would have a debilitating effect on teaching and academic freedom'.[9] Others argue that audit has created a 'culture of compliance' and an 'invitation to outward conformity' (AUT 1993). It has also generated a climate of fear that non-compliance with the managerial drive for normalization and standardization will be punished (Alderman 1994; Shore and Roberts 1995). The need for universities to protect and improve their position in the competitive league tables is increasingly placing obligations on staff to conform to a university line. For example, one professor wrote to a national newspaper correcting his university's claim that larger class sizes and reduced resources had in no way lowered educational standards. As a result, the professor was given an official warning that staff should not bring their institution into disrepute as this was a sackable offence.[10] In short, those who express public concern

about the 'effectiveness' of higher education (for example, standards of teaching and learning and issues of social justice), rather
than 'economy and efficiency' are labelled 'whistleblowers' and a
threat to corporate reputation.

The impact of audit procedures on university culture is therefore
to engender a coercive type of accountability. To admit that standards
have declined is tantamount to an admission of failure, and in a
regime of competitive allocation of declining funds, 'failure' must
be punished if 'excellence' is to be rewarded.

Audit's mobilization of disciplines

Audit procedures are not only transforming universities, but also
propelling academic disciplines into new roles which demand that
they modify their organization. Until recently in the UK, the discipline of anthropology constituted a loose network of colleagues
who shared certain discourses and ways of conceptualizing issues.
The Association of Social Anthropologists holds an annual
conference, but the Annual Business Meeting is not an occasion for
discussing how the discipline is faring. Heads of anthropology
departments have met annually since the mid-1980s to report on
developments in their institutions. This meeting was a remnant
from the last time the discipline had to become politicized, when
the Rothschild review threatened the future of research funding,
but by the 1990s it rarely resulted in collective action. Audit
procedures however, recognize that academics identify above all
with their discipline, and call on 'the discipline' to be a more
effective and 'disciplinary' organization, capable of assembling
panels of peer reviewers for both RAE and TQA. Moreover, the
post-Dearing audit procedures proposed by the QAA assume that
'a discipline' is a corporate entity with an organization capable of
speaking or acting on behalf of its members.

This assumption has already had considerable effects. The need
for heads of departments to respond to the decisions and
consultations of HEFCE, QAA and ESRC, which have implications
for their funding, resulted in the establishment of a Standing
Conference of Heads of Anthropology Departments (SCHAD).
Heads of departments now communicate several times a week by
email, effectively reach consensus decisions and write collective
letters. The QAA's consultation document gave 'disciplines' an
important role in the new teaching quality assessment procedures,

and this prompted SCHAD, the ASA and the four other national anthropology organizations to form a Coordinating Committee for Anthropology so that 'the discipline' could speak to government agencies with one voice. In creating an organizational presence in response to the expectations of QAA, several anthropologists voiced concern that the discipline could itself become a bureaucratic instrument in the machinery of audit (Mascarenhas-Keyes 1998). To try to avert this possibility, they rejected the QAA's assumption that disciplines would be centralized and hierarchical and decided to develop a horizontal web of networks instead.

Whilst government agencies expect disciplines to have a corporate presence and decision-making capacity, Exworthy and Halford (1999) point out that new managerialist procedures promote divisiveness, even internal combustion, within professions. Divisions form as some academics develop the skills of managerial professionals, which others eschew for traditional knowledge-based status, and collegiality is further endangered as peer reviewers take on the role of policing. Yet according to Exworthy and Halford it is those professions that are able to maintain 'lateral solidarities' that sustain their values and status in the face of new managerialism's attack on 'vested interests'.

Anthropology's attempts to act with disciplinary solidarity have so far misfired. A significant moment was when all departments submitted bids claiming 'excellence' in the TQA. The process thereafter followed the usual pattern of critical peer assessment. The results were that 18 out of 20 departments gained 'excellent' status. These good results were perhaps unsurprising as the discipline is almost entirely based in the so-called old universities. Moreover, the discipline is characterized by the speed with which lecturers feed the latest research into teaching, and by the predominant practice of staff at all levels of seniority not only to be research-active but also to do their own teaching with very little use of teaching assistants (Mascarenhas-Keyes with Wright 1995). When other colleagues heard about the outcome of 'excellence', a rumour started that anthropologists' solidarity extended to giving one another good results. When the RAE and the ESRC's reviews of master's courses and of doctoral research training also produced good results for the discipline, rumours multiplied that anthropologists do not criticize one another.[11] The discipline has been unsuccessful at quashing these rumours. The issue came to a head when the QAA refused to recognize 'anthropology' as a discipline and subsumed it under 'sociology' in the new Quality Assurance Framework. The reason given by a senior official was that the discipline's outstanding TQA scores 'stood out like a sore thumb' when they were presented to the Department of Education. Anthropologists, according to the official, had 'shot themselves in the foot' by being too 'generous' to one another. The discipline had been put in with sociology because it was considered 'cosy' and in need of being broken up. The response that both peer reviewers and auditees had taken these exercises extremely seriously and that anthropology should not be punished for working hard to achieve good results cut no ice. Nor did a promised meeting materialize. The new Coordinating Committee for Anthropology then enabled the discipline to make a corporate response: all departments have refused to co-operate with the QAA's benchmarking process until the agency gives anthropology separate disciplinary status.

This episode exemplifies how the model of audit applied to higher education is muddled and has contradictory effects. Some aspects of the process compel disciplines to act as corporate bodies, other aspects cause competition and fragmentation. Where anthropology has mobilized itself to act corporately, it is charged with cosiness and being insufficiently competitive. This is a good example of what Power (1997) identified as the contradiction inherent in audit: authorities distrust socially embedded and motivational guarantees of professionalism and attempt to replace them with coercion and control, yet they need to trust the peer reviewers who implement the process.

Audit and the construction of the professional self

However much academics might try to remain immune from the rationality of audit, it has become a powerful and pervasive technology, and non-compliance is not an option.[12] One may disapprove of competitive league tables comparing the relative performance of departments as crude and reductionist, but their publication directly impinges on an institution's reputation, its funding and student applications. A pecking order is created not only between differentially ranked universities and departments, but increasingly between individuals – who are now being informally referred to, in reference to research assessment grades, as a '3b', a '4' or a '5' rated academic performer. The rationality of audit thus appears similar to that of the panopticon: it orders the whole system while ranking everyone within it. Every individual is made acutely aware that their conduct and performance is under constant scrutiny. As Foucault (1977) noted, the effect of constant surveillance in prison is to instil anxiety such that inmates come to scrutinize their own behaviour and eventually adopt the norms of conduct desired by the disciplinary institution – whether or not the guards are in the watchtower. In British higher education we are witnessing a similar process in the way research assessment exercises have engendered constant institutional and individual anxiety about each lecturer's performance. The audit procedure is intended to be stressful: HEFCE policy has been to keep moving the assessment goalposts. As one HEFCE inspector admitted, performance indicators only have a shelf-life of about two years because 'after that time people get wise to them'. The intention, it seems, is to keep people on their toes by making them feel insecure.

Engendering insecurity in the workplace appears to be consistent with new managerialism throughout the public and private sectors. A recent survey of 6,000 British managers found that, if they were to meet their own targets and those of their department, they had to push both themselves and their staff too hard (Olver 1998). Academics, similarly, are overworking. According to a recent survey, the average length of the university lecturer's working week is 53.5 hours, and one quarter had, in the last twelve months, taken sick leave due to stress (AUT 1998: 1, Court 1994). Academics, like managers, are thus caught in a disciplinary system whose negative characteristics they are actively reproducing, yet over which they feel increasingly powerless.

Linked to this panopticon model of accountability is its damaging effects on trust. Audit encourages the displacement of a system based on autonomy and trust by one based on visibility and coercive accountability. As Power (1994: 13) argues, audit is introduced largely when trust has broken down, and yet the 'spread of audit actually creates the very distrust it is meant to address', culminating in 'a "regress of mistrust" in which the performances of auditors and inspectors are themselves subjected to audit'. In one London college, for example, a self-critical review from the first round of CVCP-led Quality Audit had been used to make constructive departmental changes and was no longer relevant by the time that it came to the notice of HEFCE inspectors. Nonetheless, they used it to make damning criticisms of that department.

The substitution of trust by measurement, the replacement of academic autonomy by management control, the deliberate attempt to engineer competition and a climate of insecurity are all features of new managerialism's disciplinary grid of audit. Its aim is to inculcate new norms that supposedly 'empower' audited individuals to observe and improve themselves according to new neo-liberal notions of the performing professional. The logic of the modern audit system is to produce not 'docile bodies' but 'self-actualized' auditable individuals.

Herein lies another contradiction of the audit process: it encourages a form of 'reflexivity', but the reflexive subject is caught within tightly fixed parameters that appear to render opposition futile. But how inescapable and panopticon-like is this system? What options for manoeuvre exist and how should anthropology respond to this advancing audit culture and the new managerialist norms that are propelling it forward? How can anthropology as a discipline resist the pervasive and seemingly unstoppable advance of audit culture beyond its original terms of reference?

Conclusion: anthropology and the critique of new managerialism

The question asked at the outset was how one recognizes epochal change when one is in the midst of it. It is first important to stress that we are not arguing against the principle of accountability, nor are we opposed to audit *per se*, to new styles of management or to the idea of enhancing the quality of provision in the public services. Our argument is that British higher education has witnessed the introduction of one particular version of new managerialism that is anything but progressive or effective in the university context. The restructuring of universities according to the dictates of financial audit and the attempt to create a 'culture of accountancy' is not, in our view, likely to enhance the quality of teaching and research. On the contrary, the impoverished version of new managerialism that has risen to prominence in the university sector seems to ignore much of what is sensible in the literature on new management. As Wright (1994) observed in the early 1990s, the post-Fordist trend in organizational studies and management was moving in two very different directions. On the one hand, there was a move towards new forms of command and control from above in the style of neo-Taylorism, but, on the other, there was an emphasis on the need for greater worker flexibility and empowerment. It is the first, neo-Taylorian strand of managerialism that has predominated in higher education, whereas some version of the second, 'flexible worker', approach would seem more suitable. University lecturers have always been flexible workers: adaptable, multi-skilled, self-managed and largely self-driven professionals who are willing to work far longer hours than they are contractually obliged to do. What is perverse and counter-productive about the new audit culture is that it militates precisely against that kind of professionalism. Anxiety and insecurity among professionals, as Power (1994: 42) notes, often destroy the commitment and loyalty of individuals to their organizations 'to such an extent that this may undermine performance'. This is just one of the dysfunctional consequences of academic audits frequently overlooked or ignored.

We conclude by suggesting four ways in which anthropology might usefully analyse and respond to the current systems of audit that are being introduced into the public sector. The first is simply to raise critical awareness of the nature of the audit explosion, the conditions that have fuelled its rise, and the interests that it serves. As often noted, power works most effectively when it is disguised: when the discourses of governing elites have become so naturalized that they go unchallenged and cease to be recognized as political or ideological. This appears to be the case with audit. As Power (1994: 41) rightly observes:

> We seem to have lost an ability to be publicly sceptical about the fashion for audit and quality assurance; they appear as 'natural' solutions to the problems we face. And yet, just as other fashions have come and gone as the basis for management thinking, the audit explosion is also likely to be a passing phase.

However, the continuation and, indeed, the extension of indirect control in the UK through audit technologies since New Labour came to power in 1997 suggests that Power's optimism may be unfounded. If our analysis is correct, the audit explosion is not so much a passing fashion as the expression of a much more permanent and profound system of governmentality that is radically transforming all areas of working life. Where we would agree with Power, however, is in his observation about the paucity of intellectual opposition to the values and assumptions that legitimize audit practices. Despite increasingly vocal dissatisfaction with what we might call the new audit industry, its draconian regulations and prescriptions, and the plethora of new parasitical professions it has created, there is still no effective (in the sense of publicly articulated) critique of audit rationality.

This leads us to a second way to contest audit: through language. Power (1994: 42), who makes a similar point, puts it in terms of the need to create 'an institutionally acceptable language' to express shared grievances about the preoccupation with measuring performance and quality and to rehabilitate concepts of trust and autonomy in managerial discourses. We would put this in a slightly different way: what is required is the reappropriation of key concepts such as 'quality', 'accountability' and 'professionalism' so that they come to reflect our meanings rather than those of account- ants and managers. Before the neo-liberal 1980s, universities had a shared and institutionally acceptable language for articulating the values and charters upon which they had been founded that was very different from the accountancy-led mission statements of today. While many of the key concepts remain, there can be little doubt that their meanings have been distorted out of all recog- nition by the Orwellian Newspeak of New Managerialism. What values would lecturers now wish to emphasize in these terms? If the first task is to contest and unmask the way key organizing concepts are being used (i.e. to encourage a posture of critical scepticism), the second task is to reclaim those concepts by pointing out what they should stand for.

The third way for anthropologists and other intellectuals to challenge New Managerialist policies and practices lies in the scrutiny of their effectiveness. We have stressed that the neo-Taylorian approach leads to a narrow emphasis on economy and efficiency to the neglect of effectiveness. There is much talk of the need for an audit culture to create a non-elitist and all inclusive higher education sector, but audit 'talks up' expectations about itself; it manufactures 'images of control' and produces a form of 'social control talk' that reinforces the powerful about their inten- tions (Power 1997: 140–3; see also Jary 1999). Who is assessing whether audit procedures are actually helping the sector to achieve the aim of high quality mass higher education? Power also points out that 'effectiveness' itself has been redefined in the discourses of audit: it now focuses on whether systems of command and control work, rather than on the impact of higher education on society.

However, the effectiveness of audit, even in its own terms, has to be questioned. As critics point out, audit systems are themselves immune from public accountability and are rarely subject to the pseudo-market forces which their advocates claim are so essential in the sectors to be audited. It is not simply the increasing examples of audit incompetence and regulatory failure (such as the Maxwell financial empire and pension fund scandal, the collapse of the Bank of Credit and Commerce International, or fraud in the European Commission): there is now growing evidence that audits are failing to deliver their claimed benefits of enhanced quality and effectiveness across the public sector.

For example, the auditing of schools in England and Wales, by a schools' inspectorate created by the Conservative government in 1992, has come under mounting criticism for failing to deliver its most basic of desired outcomes. A team from Huddersfield University recently carried out detailed research comparing examinations scores (the GCSE 16+ national examination) in schools that had been inspected with those that had not been visited. What it found was that average examination scores actually went down in those schools that had been inspected.[13] Not only are such inspections costly and highly stressful for schools and their staff, they also have a negative effect on performance and results. This confirms Power's point about the way audit transforms the environments in which it operates: not only does it render people and institutions 'auditable', it actively encourages the ritualization of performance and tokenistic gestures of accountability – such as rigid paper systems and demonstrable audit trails – to the detriment of real effectiveness.

Recent criticisms of the Quality Assurance Agency for failing to operate effectively in its own terms, go even further. Its institutional audit reports are excessively long, unclear, of little use within the institution or more widely, and capable of diametrically opposed interpretations (Baty 1999: 4). The QAA was set up with the purpose of integrating the various university audits to reduce the burden on staff and the costs to universities whilst promoting public confidence that standards are being safeguarded. Yet it is unclear whether the financial burden of audit was a priority in constructing the new Quality Assurance Framework. James, who has studied the growth of regulatory bodies, questions whether the QAA has done any work on the costs to universities of compliance with their new Quality Assurance Framework, whereas in the private sector, the costs of compliance are always calculated (quoted in Baty 1999: 5). Nor does the QAA make available to the universities or the public at large any information on the way it assesses the value for money of its own operations: salaries and administration constituted 24 per cent of its expenditure in 1997/8. The QAA's lack of cost effectiveness is attributed by critics to the fact that the agency is itself not publicly audited and it is unclear to whom QAA is accountable. Half of the agency's £8 million income in 1997/8 came from contracts to implement quality assessments for the English, Scottish and Welsh funding councils (Baty 1999: 5). In keeping with these contracts, the QAA was audited by the English funding council (HEFCE) in 1999, yet neither the QAA nor HEFCE will publish the report. It is only known that the report contained twenty-two recommendations for improved management and governance. Thirty-eight per cent of the QAA's income is from compulsory subscriptions of individual universities, for whom the Committee of Vice Chancellors and Principals (CVCP) and equivalent bodies in Scotland and Wales set up the agency as a form of self-regulation within the higher education sector. Yet recent behaviour by the QAA suggests that it thinks of itself as an agent of government rather than of higher education self-regulation.[14] Critics argue that the QAA will only become accountable if it is subject to the same quasi-market and audit disciplines as the rest of the quality assurance industry. One suggestion is to subject the QAA to third-party scrutiny, for example by the UK Accredition Service which audits most of the other quality assurance agencies (Baty 1999: 4). Alternatively, instead of guarding the guards, if the QAA lost its monopoly position and if universities could choose among the accreditation systems of competing regulators, in James' view the regulators would become more responsive to the sector and accountable to the public (quoted in Baty 1999: 5).

One further aspect of the lack of emphasis on effectiveness in the neo-Taylorian approach is its notorious disregard of 'human resources' issues. Increased stress among employees is an inevitable and, to a large degree, intentional consequence of the emphasis audit places on enhancing performance and efficiency. However, the pressure many organizations now place on their staff has reached such unprecedented levels that it is clearly damaging the physical and mental health of their workforce. A recent report for the Joseph Rowntree Foundation by Cambridge University's Centre for Business Research concluded that the drive for ever-greater efficiency and profits is putting an unsustainable burden on workers, which is reflected in increasing job insecurity, ill-health and unhappiness. It notes that by far the biggest increase in employment insecurity has occurred among professionals, 'who went from being the most secure group of workers in 1986 to the most insecure in 1997' (Burchell *et al.* 1999: 2). Significantly, only 26 per cent of those workers surveyed said they believed that management and employers were 'on the same side', and when asked whether management could be expected to look after their best interests, 44 per cent responded 'only a little' or 'not at all'. Lack of trust and dysfunctional levels of stress appear to have become endemic in the workplace in Britain at the turn of the twentieth century, much as they were at the close of the nineteenth century. A parallel can be drawn here with the agricultural industry's approach to its resources. As Elliott (1999: 29) observes, few people would now dispute that environmental sustainability matters, and most farming companies accept, however reluctantly, that there is a price to pay for 'sweating assets too hard'. But while farm managers acknowledge that intensive use of fertilizers and genetic engineering to boost short-term yields could have detrimental long-term environmental costs, many human resource managers appear relatively indifferent to the long-term health and social costs of their relentless quest for efficiency gains and productivity. The Labour government repeatedly emphasizes the need to temper competitiveness with social justice, but despite its rhetoric about 'the Third Way' the reality has been intensification of new managerialist methods and little in the way of enhancing labour-market protection. On a number of counts, therefore, the 'effectiveness' of audit systems has to be questioned.

This brings us to the fourth and final point: understanding the cultural logic of audit. In *The Audit Explosion,* Power (1994: 41) suggests that the rise of audit should be interpreted not as a 'conspiracy of the vested interests of accounting practitioners', but rather as a phenomenon driven by 'a pervasive belief . . . in the need for the discipline which it provides' (1994: 45). In *The Audit Society* (1997) he argues that the rise of audit can be explained as a response to the uncertainties of 'risk society'. Taking up ideas of social theorists such as Beck and Giddens, Power proposes that the audit explosion represents 'a distinctive response to the need to process risk': a process designed to provide 'visions of control and transparency which satisfy the self-image of managers, regulators and politicians' (1997: 143). In short, audit is an expression of the attempt by managers 'to confront the uncomfortable policy reality of loss of control' (1997: 140). Rituals of verification such as quality audits and research assessment exercises thus reflect management's need for security in an age where professional autonomy and trust have been lost. What is needed, Power says, is a dialogue between all interested parties to develop a more democratic form of accountability: a type of 'reflexivity' that would open up the possibility of imagining alternative futures (Jary 1999). For Power this involves the substitution of 'at-a-distance control with more face-to-face forms of peer group accountability' because 'corporate community is a necessary precondition for corporate governance' (1994: 43).

In our view, this analysis echoes many of the weaknesses of traditional functionalist approaches to ritual. To interpret the character of New Managerialism in terms of psychological and organizational 'needs' for comfort and security is to miss the key point that what is driving current concerns with audit is the economic and political imperatives of neo-liberalism. For Power, audit is an essentially benign tool that has errors, but these can be rectified by the introduction of more personal forms of accountability and the restoration of a sense of 'corporate community'. His argument is premised on the questionable belief that 'corporate governance' is a self-evidently desirable way to manage public bodies. Despite his evident debt to Foucault and to critical social theory, Power draws back from the radical conclusions to which such approaches can lead. The problem with audit, he says – and this is his main message – is that it has put itself beyond empirical knowledge about its own effects so that it is 'impossible to know when it is justified and effective' (Power 1997: 142). The question is: effective for whom?

Power's idea of reflexivity is also inadequate and a far cry from the anthropologically informed 'political reflexivity' for which we have argued (Shore and Wright 1999). It is all very well to imagine alternative futures but what is required is a reflexivity that offers a critique of the present so as to unmask the ways that technologies of audit work and that helps us to understand how, as social persons, we are positioned within systems of govenance. Our argument is that audit must be understood not simply in terms of whether it meets its professed aims and objectives, but in terms of its political functions as a technology of neo-liberal governance.

The current management-led obsession with audit and efficiency arises not from 'psychological insecurities' of managers (although these may contribute), so much as from the pressure on firms to obtain ever-greater profits and productivity from the workforce. The weakened position of trade unions has made it easier for managers to return to a more aggressive form of business in which the pursuit of profit is unencumbered by concerns about job security. Set against this background, pleas for 'corporate community' and more 'face-to-face control' hardly offer a solution to the problems caused by a system of governmentality that is itself deeply exploitative and anti-communitarian.

In short, the market model of audit and accountability, which treats people as commodities, has inevitably damaging consequences when applied to the public sector. The current social environment and conditions of work have not arisen by accident. Making a flawed, ideological and market-driven system of accountability work better is not the solution. The time has come to hold audit itself to account so that we may realize the true extent of the disastrous social costs of this coercive new form of governance.

Notes

1 For examples of this kind of discourse, see the Audit Commission (1984).
2 Michael Heseltine (1987: 21), cited in Pollitt 1993: 58.
3 The word 'audit' scarcely appears in the indexes of Metcalfe and Richards (1993) or Kirkpatrick and Lucio (1995), and not at all in that of Zifcak (1994).
4 According to a recent newspaper report, the industry of management consultancy is now growing at 16 per cent per year and employs around one quarter of a million staff. In 1998/9, 90 per cent of Britain's top 300 companies employed management consultants. Increasingly a consultancy firm is becoming a permanent adjunct to the management of large organizations. For example, McKinsey and Co. now has a permanent presence in the BBC which spent £22m on consultancies in 1998/9 (Younge 1999).
5 Jarratt Report 1985: 36, cited in Clarke, Barry and Chandler 1998: 210.
6 Ibid.
7 Cottrell (1998: 6), cited in Pollitt 1993: 78.
8 Tower Hamlets College, 1992, *Newsletter*, 30 November: 8–10.
9 AUT, Update Issue No. 51, 2 June 1998: 4.
10 This pattern is also increasingly evident in the health service where new 'gagging clauses' are being incorporated into staff contracts (Mihill 1994; Waterhouse 1994). The editor of the *British Medical Journal*

observed in an article entitled 'the rise of Stalinism in the NHS', senior
staff 'were convinced that the NHS was becoming in organization in
which people were terrified to speak the truth' (Smith 1994: 1640).
11 Contrary to this view, the outside 'User' brought on to the ESRC
Recognition Panel for master's courses in anthropology reported that
the procedure was more rigorous than any she had experienced in the
private sector.
12 League tables are another example of the domaining effect. There are
now league tables comparing hospital deaths, police responses,
academic output, treatment of cervical cancers, benefit fraud, court
occupancy, beach cleansing, rent collecting and local council efficiency.
The league table idea was seized upon by Patten as Tory Education
Secretary in the 1980s and extended to state schools. Exam results
have been made the index by which to judge a school and their annual
publication has been turned into 'a nation-wide carnival of institutional
success or failure' (Jenkins 1996).
13 Cullingford, Cedric *et al.* (1997), 'The Effects of Ofsted inspection on
school performance', School of Education and Professional Development, University of Huddersfield, cited in the *Guardian*, 28 October
1998: 21.
14 For example, in 1999, without consulting the CVCP, the QAA proposed to government a change in the law to allow the removal of a
university's degree-awarding powers. The CVCP said the plans showed
the QAA's 'profound distrust of the whole university sector' (quoted
in Baty 1999: 4). This example suggests that the QAA sees itself
accountable to government rather than to its funders.

References

Abélès, M. (1988) 'Modern Political Ritual: Ethnography of an Inaugur-
ation and a Pilgrimage by President Mitterand', *Current Anthropology*
29, 3: 391–404.
Alderman, G. (1994) 'Who Scores the College Dons?', *Guardian* (Edu-
cation Supplement), 25 January p. 3.
Audit Commission (1984) Audit Commission for England and Wales.
Report of Accounts for Year Ended 31 March 1984, London: HMSO.
—— (1996) Annual Report and Accounts for Year Ended 31 March 1996,
London: HMSO.
AUT (Association of University Teachers) (1993) 'Letter to Council
Members Concerning Quality Assurance', LA/5061 (November).
—— (1998) UpDate, No. 50 (30 April).
Ball, S. (1990) 'Management as Moral Technology. A Luddite Analysis', in
S. Ball (ed.) *Foucault and Education: Disciplines and Knowledge*,
London: Routledge.
Baty, P. (1999) 'A Piper who Does Not Play the Payer's Tune' *Times
Higher Education Supplement*, 20 August: 4–5.
Burchell, B., Day, D., Hudson, M., Ladipo, D., Mankelow, R., Nolan, J.,

Reed H., Witchert, I. and Wilkinson, F. (1999) *Findings: Job Insecurity and Work Intensification*, Ref. 849, York: Joseph Rowntree Foundation.

Clarke, H., Barry, J. and Chandler, J. (1998) 'On Whether it is Better to be Loved than Feared: Managerialism and Women in Universities' in D. Jary and M. Parker (eds), *The New Higher Education: Issues and Directions for the Post-Dearing University*, Stoke on Trent: Staffordshire University Press.

Cottrell, P. (1998) 'Agreement on Promotion and Appraisal Guidelines' AUT Bulletin, 151 (January): 6–7.

Court, S. (1994) 'Long Hours, Little Thanks'. A Survey of the Use of Time by Full-time Academic and Related Staff in the Traditional UK Universities, London: AUT.

Dearing, R. (1997) *Higher Education in the Learning Society*. The National Committee of Inquiry into Higher Education, London: HMSO.

DES (Department of Education and Science) (1987) *Higher Education: Meeting the Challenge*, Cmnd 114, London: HMSO.

—— (1991) *Higher Education: A New Framework*, London: HMSO.

Dreyfus, H. and Rabinow, P. (1982) *Michel Foucault: Beyond Structuralism and Hermeneutics*, Brighton: Harvester Press.

du Gay, P. (1996) *Consumption and Identity at Work*, London: Sage.

Elliott, L. (1999) 'Ease Up, Before the Workforce Cracks Up', *Guardian*, 23 August: 29.

Exworthy and Halford (eds) (1999) *Professionals and the New Managerialism in the Public Sector*, Buckingham: Open University Press.

Foucault, M. (1977) *Discipline and Punish*, Harmondsworth: Penguin.

—— (1991) 'Governmentality' in G. Burchell *et al.* (eds), *The Foucault Effect: Studies in Governmentality*, London: Harvester Wheatsheaf.

Gray, J. (1998) *False Dawn. The Delusions of Global Capitalism*, London: Granta.

Guardian (1998) 'Analysis: School Inspectors' 28 October: 21.

Hannerz, U. (1996) *Transnational Connections*, London: Routledge.

HMG (Her Majesty's Government) (1993) *Realising Our Potential . A Strategy for Science, Engineering and Technology*, London: HMSO, Cm 2250.

Heseltine, M. (1987) *Where There's a Will*, London: Hutchinson.

HEFCE (1992) 'Quality Assessment' (HEFCE circular, 10/92).

—— (1993) 'Assessment of the Quality of Education' (HEFCE circular 3/93).

—— (1995) 'A Guide to Funding Higher Education in England', Bristol: HEFCE.

Hobsbawm, E. (1990) *Nations and Nationalism Since 1780*, Cambridge: Cambridge University Press.

Hyatt, S. (1997) 'Poverty in a "post-welfare" landscape: Tenant management policies, self-governance and the democratization of knowledge in

Great Britain', in C. Shore and S. Wright (eds) *Anthropology of Policy: Critical Perspectives on Governance and Power*, London: Routledge.

Jary, D. (1999) 'The Implications of the Audit Society? The Case of Higher Education' in M. Dent, M. O'Neill and C. Bagley (eds) *Professions, New Public Management and the European Welfare State*, Stoke on Trent: Staffordshire University Press.

Jenkins, S. (1996) 'In League with Ignorance', *The Times*, 20 November: 20.

Johnson, N. (1994) 'Dons in Decline', *Twentieth Century British History*, 5(3): 370–85.

Jones, C. (1999) 'Social Work: Regulation and Managerialism' in M. Exworthy and S. Halford (eds) *Professionals and the New Managerialism in the Public Sector*, Buckingham, Open University Press.

Kirkpatrick, I. and Lucio, M. M. (eds) (1995) *The Politics of Quality in the Public Sector*, London: Routledge.

Martin, E. (1994) *Flexible Bodies. Tracking Immunity in American Culture from the Days of Polio to the Age of AIDS*, Boston: Beacon Press.

—— (1997) 'Managing Americans: Policy and Changes in the Meanings of Work and Self' in C. Shore and S. Wright (eds) *Anthropology of Policy. Critical Perspectives on Governance and Power*, London: Routledge.

Mascarenhas-Keyes, S. with Wright, S. (1995) 'Report on Teaching and Learning Anthropology in the UK', Sussex University: National Network for Teaching and Learning Anthropology.

Mascarenhas-Keyes, S. (1998) 'Higher Education Policy and the Implications for Pedagogic Practice in Anthropology', report of workshop held at Manchester University, 24–25 April 1998, Birmingham University: National Network for Teaching and Learning Anthropology.

Menther, I. and Muschamp, Y. (1999) 'Markets and Management: The Case of Primary Schools' in M. Exworthy and S. Halford (eds) *Professionals and the New Managerialism in the Public Sector*, Buckingham, Open University Press.

Metcalfe, L. and Richards, S. (1993) *Improving Publc Management*, London: Sage.

Mihill, C. (1994) 'Health Service "Gagging Doctors"', *Guardian*, 16 December: 6

Miller, P. and Rose, N. (1990) 'Governing Economic Life', *Economy and Society*, 19 (1): 1 –31.

Niklasson, L. (1996) 'Quasi-Markets in Higher Education – A Comparative Analysis' *Journal of Higher Education Policy and Management*, 18 (1): 7–22.

Olver, J. (1998) 'Losing Control', *Management Today*, 2 June (Online search of FT Profile database).

Pollitt, C. (1993) *Managerialism and the Public Services. Cuts or Cultural Change in the 1990s?* (2nd Edition), Oxford: Blackwell.

Power, M. (1994) *The Audit Explosion*, London: Demos.
—— (1997) *The Audit Society: Rituals of Verification*, Oxford: Oxford University Press.
QAA (Quality Assurance Agency) (1998) 'The Way Ahead', *Higher Quality* no. 4, October.
Selwyn, T. and Shore, C. (1998) 'The Marketisation of Higher Education: Management Discourse and the Politics of Performance' in D. Jary and M. Parker (eds) *The New Higher Education: Issues and Directions for the Post-Dearing University*, Stoke on Trent: Staffordshire University Press.
Shore, C. and Roberts, S. (1995) 'Higher Education and the Panopticon Paradigm: Quality Assurance as "Disciplinary Technology"', *Higher Education Quarterly*, 27 (3): 8–17.
Shore, C. and Wright, S. (1997), 'Policy: a New Field of Anthropology', in C. Shore and S. Wright (eds) *Anthropology of Policy: Critical Perspectives on Governance and Power*, London: Routledge.
—— (1999) 'Audit Culture and Anthropology: Neo-Liberalism in British Higher Education', *Journal of the Royal Anthropological Institute* 5(4): 557–75.
Smith, R. (1994), 'The Rise of Stalinism in the NHS', *British Medical Journal*, 309 (17 December): 1640.
Strathern, M. (1992) *After Nature. English Kinship in the Late Twentieth Century*, Cambridge: Cambridge University Press.
—— (1997) '"Improving Ratings": Audit in the British University system', *European Review* 5 (3): 305–21.
Walby S. and Greenwell, J. (1994), 'Managing the National Health Service', in J. Clarke, A. Cochran and E. Mclaughlin (eds) *Managing Social Policy*, London: Sage.
Waterhouse, R. (1994) 'NHS Staff Subject to "Reign of Terror"', *The Independent*, 16 December: 5.
Williams, R. (1976) *Keywords*, London: Fontana.
Wright, S. (ed.) (1994) *Anthropology of Organizations*, London: Routledge.
Younge, G. (1999) 'Called to account', *Guardian*, 30 August, G2: 2–3.
Zifcak, S. (1994) *New Managerialism. Administrative Reform in Whitehall and Canberra*, Buckingham: Open University Press.

Chapter 3

Generic genius – how does it all add up?

Eleanor Rimoldi

In an essay titled 'Only quality can save universities' in *The Times*, December 6, 1993, the then U K Education Secretary Patten set out his 'vision for the future of higher education' in England. The essay opens with a reference to a New Zealand university that is meant as a kind of cautionary tale:

> Some 11,000 miles away at New Zealand's University of Otago, courses are being offered to the 'intellectually challenged'. Opening the doors of universities to all and sundry is one way of growing a higher education sector. It is, however, not a good one if universities are to remain the pinnacles of excellence, the ivory silos fit for the toil of scholarly elites that we expect them to be. The day we sacrifice these essential principles on the ever-growing altar of political correctness will mark the beginning of the self-destruction of one of the nation's greatest assets.[1]

As part of the international family of tertiary scholars, New Zealand academics also struggle to maintain 'excellence' and it would be a mistake to assume that our universities are unthinkingly driven by what Patten called 'political correctness'. A far greater challenge is posed by government initiatives such as those that seek to codify 'excellence' or to itemize the 'skills' inherent in a discipline so that they can be branded, marketed and purchased from any number of 'providers'. This chapter will explore the New Zealand manifestation of the global phenomenon of 'audit culture' (Strathern 1997), including the influence of the New Zealand Qualifications Authority and the Government 'Green Paper' ('A Future Tertiary Education Policy for New Zealand: Tertiary Education Review',

1997). Such initiatives have real implications for social anthropologists in how their discipline is defined and taught. At the same time, ethnographic method could prove a powerful basis for the critique of these very systems which, I suggest, not only blur disciplinary distinctions but also potentially redefine aspects of private or everyday life as education commodities or skills that can be accredited to formal schooling or tertiary qualifications.

Quality control

The rather acid remarks made by Patten about Otago did not go unnoticed at that university. The reply of the University's Registrar in *The Times* of 22 December 1993 not only made mileage out of Patten's error in situating Otago 11,000 miles away (it is 13,000 miles from the British Isles) but pointed out, 'The University of Otago adheres rigidly to the entrance standards set and controlled by the New Zealand Qualifications Authority', and there 'has never been the slightest suggestion that courses at the University of Otago are "open to all and sundry"'. The Registrar further commented: 'Our degrees and the quality of our research are well known in the academic world, as those several hundred of our graduates living and working in the United Kingdom will affirm' (Girvan 1993). This bit of sniping across academic borders exposes the rawness of academic nerves in the age of audit culture. In the rush to prove excellence, or more excellent than thou, a multitude of measures, reviews and strategies have emerged. The 'expert consultant' produces weighty unreadable tomes that claim to *really* reveal quality processes, and words such as stakeholders, benchmarking, efficiency, and change processes stand like sentries beside the bullet points of our mission statements. The uneasy sociologist, Meade (1997), who produced one such report for that excellent university, Otago, suffered some embarrassment when his colleagues referred to him as belonging to 'the new right' and clearly did not want such a label – he only wanted members of the university to join him on a 'journey' towards 'quality' as he set out to 'codify quality processes'.

As a social anthropologist, I am curious as to how these ideas have become so quickly internationalized. Is this some twenty-first century version of nineteenth-century diffusion creeping up on us as the millennium approaches? Perhaps part of the answer lies in the way that university administrators are drawn together as a global power elite. In his introduction to Meade's report, Fox, the then Head of English at Otago, recounts his journey with Meade on the road to quality:

in late 1995 . . . the University of Otago faced its first quality audit by the newly established Academic Audit Unit of the New Zealand Vice-Chancellors' Committee. In anticipation of this event, the University had appointed an expert in quality assurance systems, Dr Phil Meade, in the newly established position of Deputy Vice-Chancellor (Academic). 'Through a stroke of good fortune, I was asked to assist in the writing of the first draft of the Quality Portfolio that was to be prepared for the team conducting this audit. . . . The next crucial stage in my personal journey was to attend a course for senior university administrators (SUAC) run by the Centre for Higher Education Research and Development at the University of Manitoba, Canada. It quickly became apparent at this course that the circumstances we were confronting at Otago merely mirrored those that university leaders from around the world were needing to tackle'.[2]

As a senior lecturer responsible for developing a social anthropology programme at Massey University's new campus at Albany in Auckland, and expected to lecture and research and publish as usual, I feel that I and my colleagues are at the end of the food chain in this auditing feeding frenzy. The outcomes always seem to be in the area of 'staff development' which in effect means taking courses from training-and-development 'how-to' people where you learn to role-play the job you have in reality been doing ever since graduate school. Certainly it is good to have better technique with the overhead projector. But recent expansion in this area of staff development suggests that this new 'expertise' is to a large degree merely marking out its territory with excessive zeal to establish positions for its many 'trainers'. My suspicion is strengthened when I turn to the emergence of the all-consuming national body, the New Zealand Qualifications Authority (NZQA), its skills-based assessment, and its struggle to bring tertiary institutions into its ambit.

NZQA – the measure of all things

I first became aware of the significance of the NZQA while a research fellow and tutor in the Education Department, University of Auckland, in 1992–3. I went to the Education Department because of my interest in the acculturation of New Zealand children via outside school experience. No sooner did my research proposal on that topic take shape than I realized that the NZQA, and the new educational policies initiated by the Labour government (Ministry of Education 1990; NZQA 1991), had plans for a seamless web of learning that included a skills-based assessment of things learned outside of formal schooling, and educational research was used to back this up.

> [R]esearch has shown that the family remains an important ingredient in influencing education and developmental outcomes, probably a more important one than the school . . . both vocational educators and corporate spokespersons have begun to call attention to the vacuum of information concerning how young people learn about work and develop work habits – much of which presumably occurs away from confines of the classroom, outside of school. . . . [Another] basis of interest in developing a more systematic understanding of non-school time is theoretical. To treat life outside of school as residual is to ignore the habituation and learning that are part of every moment of lived experience in everyday life, about three-quarters of which is spent outside of school.
>
> (Dannefer *et al*. 1991: 250)

The Ministry of Education went so far as to ask: 'What would the pupils have learned anyway without the efforts of the school, teacher or district?' (1990: 31)

At first glance there seemed to be an opportunity to develop my research interests in how New Zealand children are 'acculturated via everyday life' in conjunction with ideas spearheading educational change in New Zealand. As one does, I tried to incorporate these interests in an application for a grant from the New Zealand Ministry of Education. But I was clearly on the horns of a dilemma between the comparative, holistic approach in anthropology, where learning is seen to extend beyond the confines of institutionalized Western models, and the realization that this holistic approach could in turn be co-opted by the state until there is no such privilege as aimless leisure or any pedagogy too unique to be absorbed and measured by the Ministry.

On the one hand, the egalitarianism of a 'seamless web of learning', where the astute physics and mathematical cunning of a game of marbles can be seen as an expertise of sorts, or where pre-school language 'nests' run by and for Maori are officially recognized and supported, are appealing to an anthropologist. I was intrigued by initiatives in various New Zealand colleges where there is 'extensive use of community resources by school and school resources by community' and where interactions with community groups such as producing a local newspaper or building jumps at the pony club become 'the vehicle for learning rather than the focus of it' (Nightingale 1990: 33). Nightingale also reports a greater effort to 'work with a variety of other agencies' (1990: 43). These can include Polytechnics, Link, Access, Maccess and Industry Training Courses. On the other hand, extending the definition of formal education into the informal pleasures of what remains of private life in after-school hours carries with it the power to judge the outcome of what was once thought to be leisure. Although as an ethnographer the social anthropologist may analyse society in a holistic manner and see all aspects of society as interrelated, in Western advanced capitalism some semblance of private life, not under the direct socializing control of the state, is one of the few arenas in which people can experience some sense of agency. What will happen to a simple game of marbles under the adult gaze of the New Zealand Qualifications Authority?

Along with moves which tend to incorporate the community into the school programme are innovations in evaluation and assessment such as the 'Records of Achievement' trial. This is part of a move 'towards measuring student performance against described levels of achievement' (1990: appendix). Some of those involved in this trial commented that too little recognition was given to outside school learning. This introduces new questions about what constitutes 'success', 'achievement', 'skill' and 'competence' in a wide field of learning, including a greater range of outside school experiences. These questions are compounded when one considers the multicultural differences and philosophical complexity of New Zealand society. In the case of Maori education, because the elements of content, context and control are defined by Maori, these moves will have an effect on a distinctive aspect of the educational configuration in New Zealand. Although the Maori education movement is fundamental to our bi-cultural commitments as a nation, our society is in fact made up of many cultural configurations and these include educational variables. From such configurations develop the 'systems of symbols and meaning in terms of which a particular group of people make sense of their world, communicate with each other and plan and live their lives' (Metge 1988: 26). As Metge points out there may be elements in diverse cultures which seem similar but have different meanings in context. It is the reinterpretation of context – be it Maori or out-side school settings in general – that can produce distortion when incorporated into a national system of schooling which depends on a uniformity of practice, content and assessment procedures.

Initiatives such as the achievement-based assessment model which identifies the skills required, but leaves open the route by which they are obtained, is one way to shift from the concept of uniform practice towards an emphasis on the achievement goals. I share Metge's concerns in regard to the potential to distort Maori knowledge. Should New Zealand proceed down that road there is the added concern that parents release their children into the schooling system in the expectation that the education they will receive is the best that can be offered. It is not enough to allow unlimited access to these children from whatever agency claims to offer a significant body of knowledge. Nor, to re-emphasize my earlier point, is it necessarily in the best interests of the child for outside school experiences to be subjected to the scrutiny of the classroom with the potential for an increasing incorporation of what once was 'private life' into a public institution. As long as education is compulsory and monitored by the state, these issues will remain.

Methods of assessment are being developed in New Zealand schools, such as pupil profiles, which increasingly recognize outside school experience. This trend is evident internationally:

> Silberman expands the concept of 'teacher' or 'educator' to include not only school, college and university instructors but also parents, community leaders, media directors, journalists, sponsors and leaders of community organizations (for example Boy Scouts, Girl Scouts, and Junior Achievement), religious educators (pastors, priests, rabbis and church school teachers), lawyers, doctors and dentists, business and corporate executives and trainers, textbook writers and publishers, military leaders and instructors, and others who intentionally and as part of their roles or occupations teach others. United States society, then, contains numerous educative agencies and educators, all of which have curricula that have been as intentionally planned as those of the public schools. Public education, conceived

broadly as the education of the American public, includes many educative agencies, only one of which is the public school system.

(van Scotter *et al.* 1991: 120)

One of the problems with skills-based assessment which seems not to distinguish between one 'educator' and another is that the intentions (and values) of the assessor are part of the 'invisible hemming tape' in the seamless web. Withers (1997) draws attention to the selective nature of these forms of assessment and variations in the intentions of any particular student profile. He notes that some assessors stress competition whereas others stress non-competitive practices. This spectrum of values alone would find many degrees of support in a wide range of community settings which involve children in learning experiences.

The New Zealand Qualifications Authority deals directly with such issues.

Many adults have knowledge, skills and experience they wish to have credited towards a qualification. . . . Before this learning can be recognized it must be assessed against the competencies required for the qualification. . . . This assessment must be equitable and easy to obtain. It must be rigorous and open to scrutiny so that standards are upheld.

(NZQA 1991: 64)

Prior learning, in the view of the NZQA, has a very wide definition, with consideration given to work-based learning, experiential learning, overseas qualifications and attestation. It is of course NZQA that will recognize 'competencies', and application for recognition must be paid for.

My research application to explore the implications of these issues was not successful – there are always many reasons for lack of success in a funding round – but it is certain that the timing was all wrong to question the direction of change spearheaded by a government intent on restructuring everything in its path. At the same time, I began to realize that tertiary institutions were next in the reformists' sights.

Madonna meets the Frankfurt School

Part of the difficulty in formulating a critique of the restructuring of education in New Zealand is the apparent egalitarianism that lies behind it. Yet that egalitarianism is often deeply embedded within an ideological postmodernism that imagines a world without history. In terms of education, this implies a sweeping away of traditional boundaries between disciplines, dismantling institutions which have built up many years of experience in a particular field, and relying on current practice as a sufficient (or 'efficient') dialectic to theory.

During 1993, the NZQA made a concerted effort to win the tertiary institutions in New Zealand over to the new education framework, and specifically to the new skills-based assessment. At a meeting held at the Auckland College of Education, it was proposed that even highly academic subjects, such as philosophy, the social sciences and classics could be broken down into various 'skills'. This was seen to be important because then the academics, as well as the students, could be audited and assessed to see if these skills had indeed been taught and learned, and thus the departments and universities could be in turn audited and their success rate clearly indicated. We were told that, for example, teaching critical theory could be assessed in this way.

A paper was distributed called 'Putting Praxis into Practice' (Webb n.d.) which I later renamed for my own edification 'Madonna meets the Frankfurt School'. As a critical theorist myself I was appalled at the way in which, by a rapid change of costume, make-up, and presentation, Webb was able to turn Critical Theory into 'being critical', 'adopting a critical stance', 'a critical approach', and then dismiss critical theory as a potentially oppressive 'preconception of an ideal form'.

After an initial discussion of critical theory, the author moves into his theme 'praxis into practice' and presto! the critical 'stance' becomes 'all the "received" wisdom, the historical rationales, the inertia associated with doing things in certain ways falls open to discussion' and 'it is no longer feasible to think of a lecturer choosing an "efficient" teaching method to get over a subject matter, as efficiency or instrumentalism give way to a moral or "value orientation"'. Certainly, critical theory as developed by Adorno and the Frankfurt School did have a value orientation but the assumption that one could dismiss history was not part of it. However, gradually, it becomes clear in the essay that what concerns the writer most is how to adapt critical 'theory' as a teaching method – and how to specify practices which can be measured in order to show that a critical 'approach' is being applied in the classroom. 'Emancipation', he says, 'comes through rational discourse and reform; the message is the medium and the medium is the message.' Thus we get a checklist of measurable behaviours in the 'anti-received-wisdom stance' which includes such things as:

- through rational choice . . . decisions are made to lecture, hold tutorials etc. and not because of tradition
- discussion is bounded by value positions, is rational, is subject to critical analysis, is held in open forum of the class
- egalitarian principles hold sway
- active participation
- consensus and democratic decision-making
- decisions will be emancipatory
- help [class members] to take responsibility for their own destinies
- classroom = society and acting in society

The assertion is made that the current lecture format 'tends to suggest a social organization which is autocratic and dictatorial' and 'students are disenfranchised from participatory decision making'. He also suggests that assessment should be negotiated with the students.

Many of these ideas seem to me to be consistent less with critical theory and more with the current New Zealand government restructuring of social organization and institutions in this country. Health is now seen to be the responsibility of the individual, so that, for example, mental hospitals are closing and their 'clients' kept on drugs and released into the 'community'; prisons are being privatized and their 'clients' are banded and returned to the 'community'; the fire service is being downsized and the fighting of fires is being returned to the 'community', where volunteers localize the protection of homes and where the occupants have been empowered to install their own fire prevention systems. Now education, having empowered the schools by replacing experienced educationalists in the old government Department of Education with localized parent-run school boards and broken down the barriers to skill-assessment so that the whole of life can be measured, has extended this neo-egalitarianism to the universities.

However, Webb's obvious confusion throughout his paper is revealed in his conclusions when he quotes Ellsworth (1989: 306) as saying, 'Strategies such as student empowerment and dialogue give the illusion of equality while in fact leaving the authoritarian nature of the teacher/student relationship intact.' Indeed, Webb himself goes on to say, 'By looking to critical theory for procedural prescriptions, we may be attempting to mould the vibrant world of human endeavour and conflict into an artificial and sanitised pre-conception of an ideal form, which may ultimately be as oppressive as theocratic, positivistic or Marxist alternatives.'

So where does that leave us if we try to apply the NZQA model of assessment and skills based on a kind of points system?

In his critique of government proposals for policy on university education, Dutton (1997), who teaches philosophy of art at the Canterbury University, notes an unholy mix with alarm. The policy of casting universities into the free marketplace of competition by reducing government funding goes along with encouraging students, spurred by higher fees and huge student loans (with accumulative interest), to stir the competitive soup by flocking to institutions where they find the least resistance to 'fast food' courses and quickie degrees.

> This isn't competition creating excellence, but a dumbing down to lure students – viewed now as dollar-bearing 'clients' – through the gates. Of course, it's never described as lowering standards, but as 'offering exciting new inter-disciplinary alternatives'. (Oppose such dumbing and you'll be dismissed as 'conservative', 'complacent', or 'Luddite'.)
>
> (1997: 3)

Dutton does not believe that the NZQA should be the 'arbiter of university quality'.

> This would be a disaster. Despite its heavy cost to the taxpayer, NZQA continues to experience difficulties in producing competent exams at the high school level. Its procedures are best designed to define minimum criteria courses in practical subjects such as panel beating . . . NZQA has neither the qualifications nor the authority to assess university teaching and scholarship.
>
> (1997: 3)

What the hairdresser saw

My only quibble with Dutton is that he assumed that panel beaters, and other practical folk, would be quite happy with the NZQA framework. In an article called 'Framework or Gallows? Is our education on death row?' in *New Zealand Hair and Beauty* (1995), the publishing editor wrote: 'It was Benjamin Disraeli back in 1874 who said, "Upon the education of the people of this country the fate of this country depends"'. He identified serious flaws in the new education framework (Just 1995):

> [S]et up by the 1990 Education Amendment Act to ensure consistency and oversee standards in qualifications, the New Zealand Qualifications Authority has added another level of bureaucracy to our education process. Instead of forming a national framework for all recognised qualifications, it is creating a framework of 'units of learning' into which qualifications are being forced to fit.

He says that

> one of the major problems faced by those trainers and educators trying to grapple with this grand design of a national framework (unique in the whole world . . . no other country has put trade and vocational, school, and tertiary academic qualifications under one authority like this) is that the NZQA keeps changing the rules . . . moving the goal posts. There is a certain, almost arrogant self-righteousness among many of the staff (I was told by one young bureaucrat that we would quickly drop all our international beauty therapy qualifications because the NZQA diploma would become the best in the world!).

What is at risk is an established practice in New Zealand where

> beauty therapy has had established training schools providing sound courses leading to internationally recognised qualifications for many years. Overseas examiners from leading organisations and schools in Europe and beyond have come to this country and validated the quality of the work being done.

The reason that some in the beauty industry have spent four years 'working to establish a beauty therapy diploma qualification on the national framework' is because 'otherwise beauty therapy students would no longer receive the limited student benefits or loans currently available'.

Like the mysterious dissection of critical theory, those working on a beauty therapy qualification 'have been obliged to dissect beauty therapy and the training courses into the magic "units of learning". A large series of "learning outcomes" is defined for each unit . . . a detailed set of standards to be met.' One problem with this is that some units of learning required by beauty therapists are already registered with the NZQA, such as massage, by physiotherapy and massage practitioners, and 'Beauty therapists will therefore not be permitted to have their own specific units . . . structured to their specific needs . . . they must use the ones already registered' (Just, 1995). This is how the seamless web, and units of skill achievement, and outside school learning, and breaking down the barriers of established canons, and so forth, all come together – and the impact is felt by hairdressers and academics, and no doubt by panel beaters, alike. The magazine editor bemoans the blurring of vocational and academic education, but at the same time he believes all education requires qualities of mind that are 'difficult to measure with neatly structured unit standards, yet ultimately they determine an individual's future success in a world where the only certainty is that change will get faster'.

In April 1994 the now retired Dean of the now restructured former Social Sciences Faculty at Massey University reported:

An even more disturbing policy of the Ministry and Government is that not only does government determine from our record and the bids we put in how many EFTS (equivalent full time students) it will fund, but it is now indicating clearly which areas it has preference for and which it does not. . . . [I]t is not prepared to fund additional Humanities, Business or General Arts subjects within the Social Sciences. We note that these are popular areas with students, but even if there are students wishing to enter, if the university accepts them it has to be as non-funded efts. One might pause to think that this is more than the thin end of a wedge in direction by central government of university education. In modern times only China and the Soviet Union in their worst periods have dictated to universities what they shall teach. *The pioneers of the nineteenth century who came to New Zealand to escape the hierarchical dictation of Britain dominated by the aristocracy must now be turning in their proverbial graves* [my italics]. If NZQA has its way and brings us directly under control of its authority, the government of New Zealand will have succeeded in making this the first democracy in which university education is both financially, and in terms of policy, directed by central government and its policies.

(Shouksmith 1994)

[Grim] reaping

Perhaps the last word should go to the NZQA itself. In their own publication, *Learn (The Magazine for Education and Training Professionals)*, an article called 'Reaping the Benefits of Training' provides food for thought for anthropologists, particularly those interested in ritual and mortuary practices. Wright (1994) says,

> The Funeral Service industry has joined the long list of New Zealand industries who are revamping their training and qualifications as part of the new Qualifications Framework. To the uninitiated this might seem unusual, but like any area of enterprise, the funeral service industry is highly competitive. For the country's 150 funeral service companies training can play a big role in achieving market growth. The transition to learning assessed against the new national standards will be overseen by the new funeral service Industry Training Organisation (ITO). The first step is a needs analysis to establish what unit standards the industry requires. . . . In time, the ITO will look at using or adapting unit standards developed in related areas such as grief counseling, management skills, or anatomy and chemistry.

There is also acknowledgment of an increasing emphasis in the industry on training to meet the needs of different cultures:

> Death has no cultural or socio-economic bounds. Our current syllabus includes a vast array of cultures. There is a high ethnic or cultural dimension to our work. In Auckland, for example, the size of the Chinese or Vietnamese or Japanese communities [means that] each have their own needs.

It is interesting that at the same time that the New Zealand government and the NZQA downsize the social science funding in universities, other 'industries' are preparing to register their own 'ethnicity' and 'cultural' modules within the qualifications framework. If they get in first, does anthropology have to abide by their unit specifications for skills assessment?

Most recently, the Ministry of Education has circulated for comment descriptions of university subjects so that a New Zealand Standard Classification of Education can be prepared for 'the delivery of the Universal tertiary tuition allowance and to form the subject basis of a new national qualifications framework' (Appel 1999). The 1999 draft document, 'The New Zealand Standard Classification of Education' (Min. of Educ.) classed social anthropology in the general category of 'Studies of Human Society'. Social anthropology was described in such a manner that one might have supposed the definition was taken from a nineteenth-century text:

> Courses that provide or further develop the abilities of individuals with an understanding of the historic and prehistoric origins of humans, their cultural development, social customs, and beliefs. Principal subject matter usually includes some of the following: comparative anthropology, kinship systems in primitive societies, culture and personality in primitive societies, social organisation of pre-literate societies, economic anthropology, religion in primitive societies, languages, comparative ethnology, methods of cultural anthropology.
>
> (Min. of Educ. 1999)

Fortunately meetings are being held with university academics where there is an opportunity to comment on the draft document; the Professor of Social Anthropology at Massey University, for instance, has objected to the use of terms such as 'primitive' and the out-dated description of the subject matter.[3]

Categorizing the subject matter of the discipline is a worrisome enterprise at best, but when it is associated with the notion of the NZQA's Standard Classification of Unit Standards, the element of assessment and control becomes a serious potential threat to academic freedom. The draft document assures us that the 'National Qualifications Framework of the future will include all qualifications offered in New Zealand, which have been quality assured by an authorised quality validation body (QVB)'. Yet, to remain outside such documents is not an option. Unless, that is, universities reinvent themselves and once again become only the occasional home to wandering scholars with their bread in their sleeves.

Notes

1 Here and elsewhere, newspaper paragraphing is ignored.
2 Meade had attended a British Council course for vice-chancellors and deans entitled 'Academic Staff Development: A strategy for higher education' at the University of Sheffield in 1991.
3 Social anthropology at Massey includes ethnography and film, medical anthropology, urban anthropology, and covers a wide range of topics based on staff research in *contemporary* Northern Ireland, Sri Lanka, Andaman Islands, Bali, Malta, Bougainville, Italy, India, the Cook Islands and New Zealand.

References

Appel, E. (1999) Letter to Massey University Vice Chancellor, Ministry of Education, Wellington.

Dannefer, D., Frederick, C. and Munson, H. (1991) 'Involvement in Task Activities Outside of School', *Research in the Sociology of Education and Socialization* 7: 249–81.

Dutton, D. (1997) 'Quality and Competition – What Kind of Competition Do We Need in Universities?', *New Zealand Education Review*, 3 September, p. 8.

Ellsworth, E. (1989) 'Why Doesn't this Feel Empowering? Working through the Repressive Myths of Critical Pedagogy', *Harvard Educational Review*, 59: 297–324.

Fox, A. (1997) Forward to P. Meade, 'Challenges Facing Universities: Quality, Leadership and the Management of Change', University of Otago: Dunedin.

Girvan, D.W. (1993) 'Challenged Indeed', *The Times*, 22 December, London.

Just, E. (1995) 'Framework or Gallows? Is Our Education on Death Row?', *New Zealand Hair and Beauty*, Auckland.

Meade, P. (1997) 'Challenges Facing Universities: Quality, Leadership and the Management of Change', University of Otago: Dunedin.

Metge, J. (1988) 'Culture and Learning – Education for a Multi-Cultural Society' in Renwick, *et al. Government Review of Te Kohanga Reo*, Ministry of Education, Wellington.

Ministry of Education (1990) 'Tomorrow's Schools', Wellington.

—— (1997) 'A Future Tertiary Education Policy for New Zealand: Tertiary Education Review', Wellington.

—— (1999) 'The New Zealand Standard Classification of Education', Draft Document, Wellington.

New Zealand Qualifications Authority (1991) 'Designing the Framework:

A Discussion Document About Restructuring National Qualifications', Wellington.

Nightingale, D. (1990) 'School Leaver Documentation Developmental Project', Ministry of Education, Wellington.

Patten, J. (1993) 'Only Quality can save universities', *The Times*, 6 December, London.

Shouksmith, G. (1994) 'Dean's Report, April', Social Sciences Faculty, Massey University: Palmerston North.

Strathern, M. (1997) '"Improving Ratings": Audit in the British University System', *European Review* 5(3): 305–21.

van Scotter, R., Haas, R., Haas, J., Kroft, R. and Schott, J. (1991) *Social Foundations of Education*, Boston: Allyn & Bacon.

Webb, G. (n.d.) 'Putting Praxis into Practice' (unpub. manuscript), University of Otago.

Withers, G. (1997) 'One extreme to the other – a report on Profile Reports', Research information for teachers, Wellington: New Zealand Council for Educational Research.

Wright, D. (1994) 'Reaping the Benefits of Training' in *Learn: The Magazine For Education and Training Professionals*, April/May.

Chapter 4

Accountability, anthropology and the European Commission

Maryon McDonald

The material on which this chapter draws has been gained through fieldwork inside the European Commission and the European Parliament, mainly during the years 1992–4 and 1998, just prior to the eruptions of 1999. In 1999, the European Commission apparently excelled itself, reaching the supposed acme of confirmation of one of its most common public stereotypes – as a corrupt, overpaid, complacent and irresponsible organization. This is what a report published in early 1999 and requested by the European Parliament, together with the press commentary surrounding it, seemed to suggest. Under apparent pressure from a European Parliament that was seeking a high profile and a new public image of its own just prior to the 1999 elections, the entire College of Commissioners then resigned as a result.

Thereafter, external commentary on the Commission, encouraged by spokespersons from within the Commission itself, took shape within familiar demands of 'accountability'. There were in fact two critical reports produced during 1999 at the request of the Parliament.[1] Both suggested that reforms were essential and phrased them within managerialist notions of accountability. Both reports were written by a Committee dominated by professional auditors. The first report brought certain Commissioners to task for a lack of probity, acknowledging in the process the authors' own debt to the standards established for public service by the 1995 work of the Nolan Committee in the UK. The second report claimed to be talking of the Commission services more generally and, from within a framework of value-for-money audit and a more general managerialism, noted the general inadequacy of the Commission's internal 'culture'. These reports, initially demanded by sections of the European Parliament to substantiate accusations of 'corruption', of 'fraud, mismanagement and nepotism' in the Commission, interestingly turned out to use, advocate and support the same language of reform which had already been tried to the point of near-exasperation by some officials inside the Commission itself.

The Commission had already been trying to reform itself internally for almost four years, since the inception of the Santer Commission and the arrival of the new Member States (Finland, Sweden, Austria). In 1997 I was contracted by services within the Commission to give, at the end of 1998 and during 1999, some anthropological insight into the reforms – and what seemed to be internal resistance to them. This chapter does not pretend to offer anything more than a few aspects of this work, with some of the often bubbling discussion of that time presented here in citation. The material is not fully contextualized, however, for reasons that include a complexity of internal Commission concerns about anonymity, and constraints of length. The account I offer is itself inevitably accountable.

In 1998 the question of reform was so heated inside the Commission that one section of the services went on strike from February to March, and on 30 April officials more generally went on strike for a day, with further strikes threatened. The subsequent and sudden *débâcle* of 1999, with the College of Commissioners resigning in the face of external criticism for apparently failing to reform, did not stop internal resistance altogether but certainly made it quieter. In this world of self-conscious intrigue, the European Parliament as the *vox populi* of Europe had been mobilized and made to speak the language of managerial reform. It was now important to be seen to go along with it. 'Northern Europe has won', one Commission official told me, shaking his head. 'The triumph of the US!' commented another. 'This isn't Europe – it's Anglo-Saxon tyranny.'

Accountability

Before returning to such internal comments of the Commission officials, we need to understand something of the wider arena of accountability into which the Commission has been summoned.

Democratic accountability is perhaps the longest-lived and best-known image of accountability. However, the European Commission was never intended to fit models of democratic accountability as we might now understand them. Dominant amongst those now seen as its 'founding fathers' was expertise in top-down planning, largely in France, and the Commission officials of the 1950s and 1960s were heralded as a 'technocratic elite' answerable only to the 'European ideal'. This ideal necessarily transcended nationalism. Whilst each nation had expended a great deal of energy on inventing its own 'people' and its own 'public', there was no obviously self-defining 'European people' or 'European public' out there to answer the Commission back. They existed solely as a cipher, a metaphor for going beyond nations and nationalism.

The European Parliament has progressively given itself the task of trying to rectify what has become known as the 'democratic deficit'. This has not been easy. Elections to the European Parliament, notorious for their relatively poor turn-out, have been fought on largely national issues within each national context. Moreover, the Parliament works through other directions and models of accountability. Not only does each Member State of the EU offer a different model of the accountability of its executive and different notions of what accountability to the people might or should involve, but within the Parliament also the MEPs – encouraged by list systems – tend to feel themselves to be answerable above all to their national parties. In important respects, the search for a uniform 'European' election system for all Member States – resulting in 1998 in list systems for all – has merely increased the hold of national parties on their members. Any censure of the Commission has been riven and tempered by national and party allegiances, both within Parliament and beyond it, such that the only obvious solution to the most recent criticism was in the end, in March 1999, for Commissioners of all parties and all nationalities to resign en bloc.

Any sense of accountability within the European Parliament is constructed through contexts in which different understandings of Europe and nation and the relations between them, plus national and party loyalties, lobby or client-group responsibilities, competing traditions of coalition and Westminster-style oppositional government, all make demands that further negate any simple sense of representation of, or responsibility to, a people or constituency. Within the Commission, similarly, officials have felt themselves torn in different directions (Abélès, Bellier and McDonald 1993; Lord 1998). The European Union institutions, moreover, do not offer any straightforward model of a distinct legislature and executive in conformity with political theory's dominant models of democratic accountability. Within the Commission itself, issues of governance are being actively re-thought with such points in mind: there is an awareness that insistence on established models of representative democracy has denied the Commission legitimacy, but some Commission officials have found comfort and inspiration in the fact that governments in Europe no longer work in practice – if they ever really did – in the way these models have supposed (Lebessis 1996). In Europe more generally, an apparent shift in some quarters from left/right party allegiances to single-issue politics (manifest in environmentalist groups, for example), together with deregulation and decentralization, changes in processes of policy construction, and discussions surrounding an apparent 'retreat of the state', have created a new space in which legitimacy has seemed up for grabs, and questions of accountability have changed shape and loomed large. Such a situation could undoubtedly benefit an organization such as the Commission, offering a new space in which to construct its own legitimacy – the lack of which had been sorely felt internally, and increasingly so since the populism of the late 1960s (McDonald 1997). However, whilst a few officials inside the Commission have been critically rethinking such issues, the dominant models of ideal governance in Europe more generally have tended to remain or become variations on a Weberian state. Within such models, old notions of legitimacy have found new life in new but more positivistic 'accountability' ideals and practices, including in those called 'new public management' or 'managerialism'. It is within these dominant models that the Commission seemed externally to reach, in the apparently failed reforms, the critical reports and then the resignations of 1999, the acme of its illegitimacy.

A great deal has now been written on questions of audit culture and the genesis and spread of these current ideas of accountability.[2] I will not repeat these points here. In general, the available historiography of this new accountability – an historiography in part inspired by and informing a critical resistance to it – suggests that the developing, corporate and national accounting practices of the eighteenth and nineteenth centuries co-existed with, and were informed by, pedagogical practices of examination, writing and quantification and that these eventually facilitated the construction of not only visible, calculable, governable spaces but also, within modern management theory, governable persons who were ideally reflexive, calculating selves. Discipline and accountancy, financial and human accountability, were merged. Inevitably perhaps, this baggage was eventually transposed to the European Community and above all to the Commission as its lack of fit with national structures of accountability was becoming all the more apparent. The initial emphasis has been on external audit, but this has been linked to a growing demand for more efficient internal auditing and more general managerial reform.

For the European Commission, external audit has been above all financial audit, but embedded within notions of 'sound financial management' or *bonne gestion financière*. Auditing practices grew up around the Commission in the 1980s and 1990s as a means (ostensibly) by which Member States of the EU could be sure that public money was being well spent. This has been felt to be especially important within those Member States deemed to be net contributors to the Community budget. The Court of Auditors was founded in the late 1970s under pressure from the UK particularly, and existed for many years in uneasy tension with the Commission. In general, the external auditing of public bodies and their use of public money has been accepted as a norm of good government, but the Court was seemingly expected to watch over the Commission above all, and was never intended to be an intrusive body holding the entire complex of relations to account. There has often been resentment of 'interference' when Member States have found themselves under scrutiny (Levy 1996).

A broader value-for-money auditing, a mode of auditing evident now in national contexts of the northern European net contributors, has since become increasingly important in the mode of auditing adopted by the Court of Auditors. From 1995 onwards, with the new Santer Commission in place and the new Member States in the EU, the reports of the Court of Auditors began to be given a serious hearing within the Commission in a way they had not always previously (Laffan 1997, 1999). In practice, however, value-for-money auditing is highly problematic at a trans-European level given the diversity of evaluative preferences and practices involved, and the diversity of bodies and models more generally has made any auditing of the public spending involved in Community programmes or projects extremely complex (Levy 1996, 1997). For the Commission, the shift from an apparent frenzy of legislation or policy-making in the late 1980s and early 1990s, with the establishment of the Internal Market under Delors, towards the effective manage-ment, including control and evaluation, of all the legislation or policies and programmes hitherto constructed, has not been an easy one. For both practical reasons (the Commission is, relative to other bodies and the tasks required, a small organization)[3] and for reasons to do with comitology, partnership ideals, and other aspects of EU governance,[4] the management and implementation aspects of policy have relied increasingly on the facilities of Member States. It would seem to be here that problems arise particularly. In this complexity of state organizations, auditing has relied on auditors who have relied on auditors, and the fact that figures have sometimes been a matter of negotiation – both inside the Commission and outside it – gives rise to suspicion. It is no great surprise to anthropologists (and to some accountants, see Morgan 1988) that, in this sense as well as in a more fundamental way, the practice of accountancy in any form of audit 'constructs' reality. Value-for-money auditing simply writes this large. Within the EU, it would seem to be a combination of well-intentioned positivism and sometimes competing perceptions of political insanity or astuteness that have been largely determinant in shouting 'corruption' at any one point and at any one time in the complex relations involved.

The reforms

When the services of the Commission went on strike in February and then April 1998, the principal and most immediate sources of concern seemed to be a project of managerial reform that had begun in 1995, launched by the new Nordic Commissioners responsible for personnel and budgetary matters and for questions of fraud. In 1995, an initiative entitled SEM 2000 had been launched to encourage 'Sound and Efficient Management' in financial matters. This was encouraged by the Court of Auditors but also by the Council and by parting, written criticisms from the out-going German Commissioner who had been responsible for budgetary matters and combating fraud under Delors' presidency (Laffan 1997). The SEM 2000 programme envisaged the up-grading of budgetary responsibilities and the gradual but partial decentralization in the Commission services of financial management. Then, in 1997, a broader programme called MAP 2000 was launched as an on-going project aiming at the 'Modernisation of Administration and Personnel Policy'. This project initially had two phases. The first phase largely involved a decentralization of certain administrative responsibilities from a Personnel Directorate General (known as DG IX) to the other Departments (or Directorates General, DGs). Following this, there was to be decentralization within each Department or DG – with the measures summarized as 'cutting red tape', empowerment and *responsibilisation*; and others concerning mobility, training, information technology, and programming and planning. New measures were also proposed in matters of recruitment, promotions, discipline and equal opportunities. 'Cost awareness' measures (e.g. on the use of the telephone) will be further developed, DG IX will eventually become more responsive to its 'customers' (the rest of the Commission) and communication is to be improved.

Hard on the heels of these two projects came, in an announcement in 1997 and in practice in 1998, a project entitled *Dessiner la Commission de Demain*, initially known in English as Decode for short and then announced in one meeting by a witty, French-speaking senior official as DCD or '*décédé*'. The English translation of Tomorrow's Commission soon took over. This project has been described by officials immediately involved as an internal 'snapshot screening' intended to see, in the first instance, just what the main tasks and activities of all the Commission's units are, and thereafter to 'pave the way for a rationalized, more effective new Commission'. By June 1998, these three projects – SEM 2000, MAP 2000 and Tomorrow's Commission – had clearly become, in internal statements, three steps of one and the same reform project. In March 1998, prior to the strike of all the services and claimed by a number of officials as the last straw, it had also been discovered that a report existed which sought to reform the staff regulations or statutes. It was then claimed by the powerful staff unions that the Commissioner for Personnel had initially denied the existence of this report when challenged. The report touched on a wide range of questions from recruitment to retirement and pensions, and included issues to do with salary, sanctions and allowances, and seemed to be suggesting managerialist cuts and performance or productivity incentives. The whole reform package then became for many a metaphor for all that the Commission should not be. 'Those people think the Commission is Coca-Cola!' a vociferous union member warned me.

'They are out to get us' has been another and not unrelated reaction within the services. The 'they' here can change according to context and is variously the Member States, the US, the UK, northern Europe more generally, DG IX, or quite simply 'the

Nordics' (*les nordiques*). There has undoubtedly been a strong and angry reaction to the reform proposals. On the one hand have been those who have felt that the whole project would not go far enough. SEM 2000, they point out, had already left service DGs intact that oversee financial control, and it was through these Departments that 'camouflage' was effected by Member States who did not wish 'irregularities' concerning them to come to light. Having officials and MEPs alike 'plugged into their capitals' for their own advancement meant that this camouflage was not difficult. Member States had no real interest in a well-organized and decentralized Commission. They wanted to exploit '*le flou*' – but 'the Commission will get the blame'. We shall return to this perception of '*le flou*' in a moment. On the other hand are those officials – more numerous and vociferous – who have feared that decentralization, making individual and lower-ranking officials visible and responsible, would mean they were simply 'not covered' in their decisions any more by the old hierarchy and might even be 'sent to the Parliament as a sacrifice'. At the same time, '*l'empowerment*' has seemed curiously 'selfish' to many and, rather than liberating the self in the way post-1960s rhetoric seemed to promise, the concentration on the reflexive construction and re-construction of self within the new managerialist language of 'career' can feel like 'yet another thing to have to think about'. 'It's so *tiring*.'

A context of uncertainty

Although perceived as serious, the concerns of 1998 are by no means the first time that Commission services have lived with a sense of crisis affecting their daily lives. Officials have felt themselves to be living in what was plaintively described in one internal meeting as a constant state of 'rolling uncertainty'. There seem to be two aspects to this uncertainty, a feature of life in the Commission that has been stressed to me many times, often summed up as *le flou*. The first is felt to be a structural uncertainty, a pre-existing condition of life in the Commission. The second is an historically induced uncertainty linked to changes in the broader context in which the Commission exists. These two aspects are dealt with below.

1.   Firstly, an important and general anthropological point is that when different conceptual and behavioural proprieties meet, as they

do in an institution such as the Commission, then there is often an inevitable apprehension of incongruence. The systems do not match, do not 'fit', giving a sense of disorder. Second, such apprehensions are often made sense of in national terms – it is there that difference is most commonly noticed and in such terms that it is readily understood. Definition and self-definition, we know, are always relational and contextual; cultures are not homogenous wholes but relationally constructed; and nations do not consist of essences or given national characters. The Commission is not a world in which different national cultures simply bang into each other. Rather, nations or nationalities provide the conceptual boundaries by which difference is most easily constructed and recognized, and then the whole do-it-yourself kit of national difference – with 'culture' part of that kit – comes into play. Third, difference is also widely understood, at the same time, in terms of the ideas which came with nineteenth-century nationalisms and which we generally know, for short, as the ideas of positivism and romanticism. These three points are not meant to imply any stage-by-stage process of thought but a simultaneity of definition and experience, a unity of theory and observation (McDonald 1993).

Putting the third point more simply, it would seem that people across Europe often unthinkingly make sense of difference in terms of dichotomies such as rationality/irrationality ('we' are rational, 'they' are irrational), or reason/emotions, realism/idealism, practicality/impracticality, and so on, dualities which in daily life can easily and contextually evoke each other. For example, it is in terms of such dualities that differences between the sexes have also been popularly understood, and even the two sides of the human brain (there is said by some to be a part for 'reason', another for 'emotions'), and much else besides. These are the very dualities in terms of which differences between northern and southern Europe have often been asserted or described, while in other contexts they describe differences between different countries – Britain and France, for instance.

Such differences – commonly known as stereotypes – would seem to be subtly confirmed in moments of everyday life in the Commission, with the French regularly appearing emotional to the British, for instance, and the British appearing coldly rational to the French (McDonald 1989, 1993 and 1997). The perceived managerialist ethos of MAP 2000 has seemed to give further empirical substance to such divisions, to the point that one self-consciously 'southern' official upset by the proposed changes claimed any talk of management as proof that his demanding Head of Unit was being both 'typically British' and un-European and 'would walk over a dead body'. The British boss, in the meantime, claimed – as others had done before him – to come from a tradition in the British civil service wherein everyone is ideally part of a team, sharing information, collegial, all on the same side. When the British come to the Commission, and especially those with a British civil service background, it can feel like anarchy. British officials and officials from northern Europe more generally commonly talk of what they perceive to be the general 'anarchy', 'shambles' and 'disorganization' of the Commission. The systems do not match, to the point that there can appear to be 'no rules at all'. But then the British always knew the Continent was like that, and the North of Europe has long known this of the South. All emotion and no rationality. 'All ideas and no practicality'.

In such a view, reform of the Commission is essential. At the same time, it has come as no surprise that the greatest enthusiasm for reforms has seemingly emanated from *les nordiques*. Both a desire for reform and some aspects of apparent resistance to it are, in part, encapsulated in this complex of mutual perception.

In very general terms, there was often a North/South divide apparent in some form in the Commission when I first started work there in 1992 and this division would now seem to have been given new life by the 1995 enlargement and the whole MAP 2000 programme. The attribution of North/South changes contextually, but the countries generally in the North would be Britain, Ireland, Netherlands, Denmark, Germany, Luxembourg, sometimes Belgium, and now Sweden, Finland and Austria also; and those in the South would include France, Spain, Italy, Greece and Portugal. On certain points, Belgium becomes definitionally the South. France's inclusion in the South is owed, in part, to the unusually long tenure of President Delors. All such divisions or demarcations can move around and are not, of course, simple national or geo-graphical divisions. They are metaphorical statements in which moral and political perceptions and preoccupations both take up, and are distributed in various ways across, geographical and ethno-logical space. Some do not talk of North or South, but of *Nordiques* and *Latins*, for example, or of *Nordiques* and *Méridionaux*. 'Anglo-Saxons' and 'Latins' have been added to this ethnological armoury in managerial discussion and disagreement.[5]

Among those deemed to be from the North in the Commission, there has long seemed to be a greater, or perhaps louder, sense of unease. This is partly because the idiom of a rational, ideal-type bureaucracy has been theirs and this discourse has been able to define 'problems' with public credence or legitimacy. It is also now because those same problems have been redefined as a lack of management, with management often perceived to be itself of broadly northern and anglophone legitimacy.

In the meeting of different systems in the Commission, there is an incongruence, at once conceptual and practical, of the frontiers between administration/politics, public/private, public/personal. Apparently political, private or personal matters seem to appear where, for those from the North, they should not. This intrusion or mismatch is inherent to perceptions of disorder, a sense of unease and uncertainty. I was repeatedly told of 'contradictory forces', of 'unpredictability', a 'lack of trust'. There seemed for some to be no coherence in time (including no obvious, shared filing system or erratic minutes) and no coherence in space (no co-ordination, no collegiality, no readily shared information). There seemed to be only idealism, which differences in conventions of text-writing could seem to confirm ('look at their *notes!*'), and I was told that there was only competition, sabotage and power. Everything can seem linked to the person (sensitivity, honour, arcane personal networks, *hommes clés* . . .).

It is perhaps important to interject here that there were many officials for whom, whatever their background, there were some modes of co-ordination, for whom there was structure, and simple ways of getting information. Make friends, I was told. Be sole master of your dossiers. There is lots of autonomy. There is plenty of space in which to do creative and exciting things. It is 'democratic'. If there's a problem, send it up the 'hierarchy'. That's what the hierarchy is there for. It's not difficult. For many from the North, however, it has seemed difficult and there has seemed to be a problem. I heard many times that there were no job descriptions and that the hierarchy was there only to check up on you or to be used to get rid of problems, or to spoon-feed you. 'You are treated like a child.' A hierarchy has to check even your simplest letters: 'you cannot take responsibility'. There are no clear rules. It is 'like trying to re-create your job every day'. It is continual 'self-starting'. And where are the frontiers? How far can you go? 'It's a cruel place.' Such comments were not limited to those deemed by themselves or others to be from northern Europe. I learnt from officials of a variety of backgrounds that the Commission was *'un panier de crabes'*. People were waiting to take your dossier from you, there were no obvious lines of demarcation and no one to appeal to. 'Nothing is clear'.

Within all this, the ideals of the relative impartiality of an administrative system, a system ideally independent of politics and the personal, seemed to be encountering systems in which the political and the personal play an important role. The feeling that personal networks dominate was, and is, encouraged by the operation of patronage systems of various kinds. In this connection it is known, from self-comparative studies of northern and southern Europe, that patronage systems of various kinds operate relatively openly in parts of southern Europe as an important, if not the only, moral system. There is not space to give details here, or to distinguish as one should between the different proprieties involved (and there have, of course, been many classic anthropological studies[6]). Some of the actions of those from southern Europe do not always, they know, have the formal sanction of official rules and official approval, whether at home or in the Commission; they do, however, have an informal sanction, their own pride and virtue, a pride and morality which cannot easily be given expression in the idiom of an ideal model of an impartial and rational administration favoured by those from the North. There is no easily neutral language available in which to discuss such proprieties and expressing one system in terms of another brings traducement. Where those from the South see loyalty, honour and pride, for example, those from the North can see immorality and corruption. It only takes one case of rule-breaking corruption in southern parts to be revealed for a whole world of empirical truth to seem to be confirmed, and a world of honourable obligation and commitment to be traduced. On similar cases in northern Europe, there is relative silence.

In the Commission as outside it, patronage systems have a self-evident importance for those who operate them: indebtedness can be created as a matter of pride and honour, and debts similarly repaid with loyalty and support. During the period of intense activity in the Commission in the late 1980s and early 1990s, when I first began fieldwork, 'patronage networks' of various kinds were said to be operative 'from the President's *cabinet* down' and gained in importance as a major way of getting work done. Trust and predictability were gained for those able to maintain their position within such networks, and reciprocation assured.

There were internal criticisms of the patronage systems, criticisms coming from those who actively participated in them, but these tended to be criticisms which sustained them. ('He's *our* Commissioner', I was told, 'and he's done nothing for my husband!') It is a common feature of the way many patronage systems are sustained that each party seeks more honour or more help and favours. At the same time, there is awareness amongst all parties that this is not the only available moral system, both in their own terms and in the context of living and working alongside people from other backgrounds. Moving between the moralities available has been quite common. When someone else gets the job, task, help or promotion and you don't, then you can openly condemn the *piston, magouille, imbroglio* or *enchufe* at work; as to your own success, however, well this happens *par hasard* or *par accident*.

Since the second enlargement of the EU in 1995, it has been largely officials from new Member States who have been the critical voice of northern Europe, asserting their own summary and sometimes stinging diagnoses: 'The Commission is childish, male-dominated, very southern and very French.' Or: 'There is a serious lack of management here – no transparency, no information, no proper rewards or sanctions, no planning, and no clear idea of who is meant to be doing what.' And: 'They are all so sensitive, it's all so unpredictable and personal.' Within all the apparent unpredictability of the Commission there has been moral pressure on all sides, with 'a lack of trust' seeming warranted all round, but the moral pressure has tended to be especially on those from southern Europe on whom the weight of old stereotypes often falls. In some respects, this pressure now feels to some officials as if it has increased: 'They want change because they imagine we're all just lazy and corrupt.'

2.   Apart from the sense of inherent unpredictability, there is also an externally-induced sense of uncertainty which can be dated historically. 'You need a bit of history,' I was told. Too often, it is felt, new arrivals rubbish what went before. Whilst those promoting reform might justifiably contest such an image, it nevertheless has its own force as a summary statement of a sentiment that important realities are in danger of being ignored or misrepresented.

The story I have been told begins with the early era up to about the first enlargement. These were largely the days of 'a single Europe' in which 'we were all working together, and we knew why we were doing what we were doing'. The days of the relatively small, fledgling Commission were 'our peace movement'. Nationalism, which had resulted so horrifically in the Second World War, was self-evidently something to battle against. The workforce was smaller and geographically more concentrated. Long hours were worked unquestioningly. 'We drank coffee together, ate sandwiches into the night . . .'.

However, during the late 1960s 'the world was changing – but we didn't really feel many aspects of it here until the early 1970s.' During this period, external events such as decolonization, together with demographic changes and the studentification of the populations of Europe, encouraged the invention of a 'generation gap', the re-invention of 'youth', and the invention of 'cultural diversity' as we now understand it – as something to be appreciated and even encouraged, celebrated. Many ideas that had been at the heart of the EEC project – modernity, progress, reason and positivism generally – began to be put in question (McDonald 1996). 'Top-down' was to give way to 'bottom-up', the 'elite' to the 'people', the 'technocracy' of the state apparatus to the 'citizen', and the centre to decentralization. The world was relativized and denaturalized, and one enduring example of this was a conceptual and discursive shift from talk of 'sex differences' to an understanding of 'gender'. Equal opportunities legislation really got going. At the same time, the management theory industry took off, in the anglophone world particularly – and did so within a new framework that retained the old positivist methodology but also rode on post-1960s preoccupations, putting the 'self', 'autonomy' and 'empowerment' centre-stage.[7]

Cultural diversity, gender issues, management: these and other related ideas have been associated by some officials with the first enlargement of the Community and the entry of the new nationalities, 'especially the British and the Danes', into the Commission itself. For some longer-serving officials: 'you can date many of our present troubles from that time'. The first post-enlargement influx of officials from the new Member States brought the English language, brought talk of 'management', and brought new ways of doing things. The new arrivals sometimes had 'different ideas of Europe', and some were also 'critical of the functioning of the

Commission'. It was then under a Danish Commissioner, in the mid-1980s, that internal management courses began, but seemingly with no broadly enthusiastic up-take.

By this time, attention was largely focused elsewhere. The Internal Market programme gathered momentum and it felt imperative to 'work hard and fast'. 'It was exciting. We were really making a difference.' There was 'no time for management-talk'. All-night negotiating sessions were not uncommon, and can now be looked back on with nostalgia. Constructing and mastering dossiers and getting them through the Council were the priority. That is the real thrill of working in the Commission. 'And we did it. Whatever anyone says, the Commission works and works well.'

It is acknowledged that the activities of officials were not always greeted with such enthusiasm outside the Commission. The unprecedented flurry of directives constructing the Internal Market brought external resentment of a perceived interference from Brussels. However, as the Commission's public profile increased, and as criticism and misrepresentation increased also, 'we became used to it' and the old grand narratives were still available: history was being made. This confidence faded thereafter. The Maastricht Treaty referenda that followed were carried out in a context in which, with the Internal Market legislation, Brussels interference already seemed established fact. Going beyond nationalism had once seemed self-evidently right, but it now appeared to be interference and threat. The Danes seemingly said 'No'. A senior official once close to Delors' cabinet explained: 'We didn't really expect that. We just didn't expect it.' But: 'The Commission really became a target after that. Criticism from Member States is not necessarily a reason to change things.'

In the US and in parts of Europe in the meantime, the phenomenon which has become known as 'new public management' or 'managerialism' was developing. This has involved the transferral of private sector managerial techniques to the public sector. Concerns about national economies (and the cost and financing of the welfare state), a consonant growth of the New Right in some countries, with ideas of 'rolling back the state', together with the higher expectations generated by increased education, and the continuing growth of 'management theory', have been amongst the factors generally felt to have permitted and encouraged this trend. Although most Member States have now been touched by it in some way in their own national, public administrations, it is the

UK and the Nordic countries which are generally said, by analysts of this phenomenon, to be the furthest down this road.[8] The ideas involved began to enter the Commission in systematic form from 1995 onwards, culminating in MAP 2000.

MAP 2000 has arrived when some were 'still demoralized after the end of the excitement of the Delors era' and 'unsure where the Commission is going'. It came when hard work had been exacted, it came with an influx of new officials, it came in an intellectual context sometimes known as postmodernism when 'in some ways, the ground was shifting beneath our feet anyway', and it seemingly came for many 'without transparency' and as 'an announcement from on high, without consultation'. A Union official explained to me that 'we live with uncertainty here. All they are doing with these reforms and the way they are doing them is increasing the uncertainty.'

Contrasting with all this, however, is an internal historiography in which all the uncertainty in the Commission is simply due to 'lack of rational organization' and 'lack of management'. The reform project will move the Commission 'from anarchy and messianism to rationality'. Those who oppose the reforms are 'in the Dark Ages'. It would seem that 'they simply want to hang on to privileges – they imagine the Commission is so different, so special'. Moreover, Danish officials were never so popular in some quarters in the Commission as they were after the Danish Maastricht referendum result: 'Many sensed that the Danes had got it right.'

The kind of structural uncertainty described becomes, within these rather different histories, one point on a trajectory from 'a young organization' to a 'mature administration'. Officials would have to learn to take responsibility: 'it's a bit like growing up'. At the same time, the clarity of motivation has gone 'and it's sad that we have to learn it from management courses now'. Similarly, the rewards of working at the Commission are not obvious any more. Even the old Euro plates on cars, once a mark of distinction, are eschewed: 'they get vandalized'.

'There is the public sector and there is the private sector . . .'

Dominant ideas in Europe of what state governance is all about have long drawn on a division of public and private. The state sector is the model public sector. In its ideal forms, it is variously not the market; or it is not 'civil society'; or it is not the world of personal relationships, of kin or family; or not the world of individualism; or not the vagaries of competitiveness, irrationality or preference. In this view, any state governance is ideally the world of rationality, impartiality, independence or the rule of law before whom all citizens are equal. Even in parts of Europe in which patronage systems are strong and rife, this ideal persists and dominates, if only as an elusive realm of the impersonal by reference to which public employees can divest themselves of responsibility in relation to someone to whom a debt is not owed or someone external to the relevant personal networks ('I would help you but the rules don't allow it . . .')[9].

There are many versions of this state ideal in Europe, with different elements being salient or realized in different ways. The French state has offered one influential version of this ideal model, in which an historical battle against the Church, for example, has created a strong notion of an ideally inaccessible, impervious and vigilant public space hedged around its edges with an ever-threatening irrationality: *l'arbitraire*. Within this model, the elite corps of state *fonctionnaires* traditionally take their expertise out to industry rather than the other way round, and in France as in other countries modelled on its governance, the highly-educated, sometimes self-consciously intellectual and specialist nature of the state functionary means that management is often felt to be alien and unbecoming. 'We were taken on as *des conceptuels* – now we're being asked to be merely *des gestionnaires.*' With all this in mind, it is perhaps no surprise that in a key unit meeting in the Commission services in which the introduction of managerial techniques was proposed by one official with industrial experience, an official of French civil service background interjected very angrily, cutting the speaker short: 'Listen, there is the public sector and there is the private sector. Those who want that management should stay in the private sector.' Each side could find irrationality in the other and the discussion got no further.

There have been many examples of this kind. It is widely said that 'the Commission is French'; it was explained to me that 'the model is French and cannot reform itself'. However, the model of the French state has spread widely and has outlived its daily practice within France itself. In a wider context, MAP 2000 would seem to be muddling recensions of the public/private dichotomy and doing so in a way that some find morally and politically offensive and deeply disappointing. 'They are doing this in the Commission, of all places.' 'This is Europe. We expect rationality.' 'Do they know what Europe means to those who have lived through *l'arbitraire* of dictatorship?'

For most, however, it is the language of systems and of business and the market that is simply inappropriate, and the shift in some of the Commission services towards English from French – previously the dominant working language – that has accompanied the introduction of the reforms is simultaneously resented and highlighted: *'On ne parle plus du travail, on doit parler du "productivity" ou de "input" ou "output". On ne parle plus d'une personne. C'est un "career profile"'*. But even within the English language: 'How can there be talk of productivity and performance-related pay? We do not have simple "products" and we do not have a profit-loss account.' The context in which the Commission works cannot be expressed in this way: 'Imagine not getting Council agreement after years of hard work – and then being punished with less pay as well!' But there is also felt to be a more sinister aspect: 'This is the language of downsizing'. When the conceptual floodgates of *l'arbitraire* open, and take in job losses and the whim and revenge of Member States on the way, then: 'This could be the end of the Commission and the end of Europe.'

Officials who support the Map 2000 reforms feel that such fears rest on misguided assumptions. They have been insistent that the Commission 'does not belong to its officials – it belongs to the European taxpayer' and that Europe's citizens 'are our customers. They won't buy if we don't produce a good product.' The Commission is required to show its 'customers' that they are getting 'value for money', and it is hoped that MAP 2000 measures will encourage officials to realize they are paid from 'public money and are accountable'.

There is undoubtedly some support for this language in those parts of the services for whom such language is also that of their client group. 'There is a world out there talking this language – it's the language of the real world.' Others resent it as reductionist, and what is perceived to be an economistic value-for-money language also encourages fears that a hire-and-fire ethic is at work. 'There is a very real problem of independence at stake here.' Higher salaries, it is argued, and the non-payment of Belgian taxes further guarantee that independence. There are large structural funds to be disbursed. There are sensitive issues of competition policy to deal with. There are also seemingly 'many difficult and messy infringement cases', for example, including against Belgium. 'We have to be neutral and immune.' One long-serving Italian official, angry at the apparent harm that the new public management might do to the commitment of officials of his generation and motivation, summed up a common sentiment : 'We are being moved away from the European ideal to something resembling Coca-Cola: does anyone seriously think we are going to be motivated by this?'

The idea that the appropriation of private sector management in this ideally 'public' arena is a threat to both Europe and the Commission is given further substance by a fear that the key decentralization feature of MAP 2000 will open the doors to both increased national interest and increased 'chaos'. National interests and chaos can seem to be one and the same thing, in a domain of non-Europe consonant with *l'arbitraire*. Such a fear is given empirical dress and feels very real for some officials from their experience in committees or working groups. The mediating role of the Commission readily appears like a supranational role and, without it or without very great effort from Commission officials, it is clear that in many areas decisions could simply not be reached. 'There could be no Europe without us.' 'It would be chaos in those meetings without some body such as the Commission.'

The fear that chaos would break out with decentralization is also encouraged by the fact that this is an institution already felt to be pervious to unpredictable preference. For better or worse, national issues and identification are already seen to be encouraged in the Commission by external pressures, including lobbyists, the Council and, to some extent, the Parliament; by some features of the modes of recruitment and promotion, by the cabinet system, and national officials on secondment. These aspects seem to structure important contradictions into the heart of the organization (Abélès, Bellier and McDonald 1993; McDonald 1996, 1997). People who come in through a *concours*, who have been in the Commission for years, who feel they have struggled to build something called Europe, can suddenly find themselves passed over for promotion, ostensibly on national lines. Moments of anger and disillusionment have been rife on these points – to the extent that one senior official explained: 'One certain way to failure here is to be European.'

However, the conceptual dichotomy which produces this sentiment – in which 'Europe' and 'nation' are distinct and mutually defining – is now seen to be problematic by other officials. It is a view within which Europe and nation are conceptually opposed and this opposition given moral and political dress: 'But the relationship with Member States is not a zero sum game in this way,' explained one senior official promoting reform in the Commission. 'That view is simply old-fashioned.' For those either opposing or expressing serious misgivings about the reforms on offer, however, there is a very real fear that decentralization will give 'free rein to national preferences' and that 'we will be subjected to the capriciousness of Member States or of individual Director Generals'. Suggestions that Director Generals might be employed in future on flexible, short-term contracts have encouraged this concern. Each DG would eventually be free, it is said, to make its own appointments; 'they could interpret the statutes as they wished'. Suspicions that the accountability of some senior officials and Commissioners is already to their respective national contexts rather than to Europe are congruent with this fear and lend substance to it. The reforms in this view, therefore, could turn Europe into all that it is not meant to be.

Within all this, different ideas of Europe and of European governance are at work. Officials promoting reform stress, within the history already referred to, that 'times have changed', that 'the Commission must learn its lesson' and 'move with the times'. 'Europe is not a fight against Member States.' 'The Commission is not a future government of Europe.' Whilst many within the Commission would hold fast to a contrary view, these officials tend to be adamant: 'If you talked of a United States of Europe now, people would just laugh at you.'

Traducement

Social anthropology has been well used to having to battle against positivisms, and the audit culture of new public management into which the academy has been incorporated can feel in many respects like one more such battle to fight. Whether looking at auditor or auditee, manager or the managed, issues of misrepresentation and traducement loom large. The apparent 'crisis of representation' (e.g. Nencel and Pels 1991) which some anthropology has belatedly been through has merely underlined an ambition to offer a language in which the realities of those under study are not traduced.

In a chapter of this length about a self-consciously complex organisation in a self-consciously troubled time, and written within the constraints of other accountabilities, it can feel as if that ambition has been virtually shelved. What I have tried to do is limited: first, to give an indication of where and how a long-standing anthropological sensitivity to traducement can be used to pick out and understand the sentiments of those under study, and, second, to suggest that anthropology can offer a language in which such issues can be re-thought. In the Commission, for example, it is important that questions of difference and of stereotype can be thought and talked about without appearing to be simply 'prejudiced' or un-European. Similarly, opposition to current reforms, for example, is not captured for the anthropologist – although it might be for the reformer – in notions of complacency, backwardness, laziness, inefficiency, and so on.

We have seen how enthusiasm for reform and opposition to it are in many ways encapsulated within a whole symbolic complex through which those definitionally from the South in particular can feel their realities traduced. Similarly, both a determination to reform and any opposition to the reforms can all too easily, each in their own way, be traduced by the other, wither on the tongue. The anthropologist, in such circumstances, can pretend to give voice to the ineffable.

The reforms under way in the Commission were intended, in many ways, to seek clarity before the next enlargement of the EU. This will not be an easy task, even if the idea is attractive. There has long been a search within the Commission for a domain of implacable rationality that will still the vagaries of *la magouille*, if only as a domain to which appeal can be made when needed (such as the staff statutes) or that can symbolically pose when required as the ineluctable rules but for which one would be the patron of everyone's indebtedness. The new decentralized procedures are not of this kind, and inevitably raise internal fears of instantiating a hitherto unknown 'corruption' of the very sort which their proponents – including by now the European Parliament and the Member States of Europe – have enthusiastically seen them as curing. At the same time, we have seen that there has been a strong sense amongst officials that an inappropriate language is at work, or that the reforms are demeaning or reductionist, or that daily life in the Commission is incapable of expression in the terms offered. This sense was further heightened in 1998 when the staff appraisal (or *notations*) exercise was shifted from a qualitative to a quantitative exercise. A beguiling positivism was erected in the form of a points system (from 1 to 50) by which all staff performance could be measured. Staff unions and the Personnel Department had all agreed that this seemed 'objective' and would avoid any linguistic impediments that might otherwise creep into a qualitative report in which 'every word could count'. However, a ceiling was imposed of 30 points, informed by memories of a previous qualitative system in which staff were 'excellent' if you wished to get rid of them: someone else would give them a job. There was to be no such exaggeration this time. But the system then only re-translated into a qualitative system, as it inevitably had to do, as awarding only a maximum of mediocrity. The whole exercise was felt to be demoralizing and contributed greatly to the strike.

The realization that the 'real' qualities of staff could not be expressed in a language of numbers – or any associated performance measures in which their lives are prejudged – has found echoes of possible traducement elsewhere. Representation, and the whole technology of accountability, is problematic. Managerial 'planning' cannot work, it is said, in a context with so many daily '*choses imprévisibles*'. Similarly, the Tomorrow's Commission exercise is welcomed by some as potentially making the Commission's main activities and internal divisions of labour visible for the first time, thereby potentially eradicating tiring turf battles, easing co-ordination, clarifying the procedures of best practice, and rendering the Commission governable in a way it has not been before. At the same time, a representational scheme of limited tasks and activities cannot possibly be an account, it is felt, 'of what I actually do most of the time'. When the value-for-money language of accountability that imbues MAP 2000 is added, together with the language of systems (input/output) and of business and the markets (products, productivity, and so on), the terms on offer cannot easily pretend to be an account of the non-productive productivity of reflection, brainstorming, making friends, weekly unit meetings, or lunching with a lobbyist, to give just a few examples, of life in the services.[10] Forcing all activities through the language of such accountability inevitably feels as if it is variously missing, traducing, or misrepresenting much of the infrastructure of everyday working life.

Amidst all the discussion and strife that has gripped the Commission on these matters during 1998 and 1999, there are those who have long since found their own quiet solutions. After a long seminar in which discussion raged on these matters, and in which new procedures were discussed, one official sat back and listed all the things she had still to do that day, with rationality and the ineffable each conjuring up the other: 'Whatever the rules are, I don't know them. The important thing on everything here is *le feeling de la maison*. You know when something is sensitive and then you deal with it accordingly.' It was fine to 'speak "management-speak" ' but it was also important to get on with 'real life'.

Notes

1 The first report was published in March 1999, after which the Commission resigned; the second was published in August 1999 (formally dated September), just prior to the new Commission formally taking up office in the September: see Committee of Independent Experts (CIE) 1999a and 1999b.

2 For some of the main points, see Hoskin 1996; Hoskin and Mace 1988; Miller 1992; Miller and O'Leary 1987 and 1990; Miller and Rose 1990; Munro and Mouritsen 1996; Power 1994; Rose 1988; Strathern 1997. Much of this critical literature is anglophone but heavily influenced by the work of Foucault and his insights drawn, in part, from a critique of the French modes of governance in which he lived.

3 By 1999, available figures (taken from the *Official Journal* and cited in CIE 1999b) showed a total of 16,511 full-time permanent staff working for the Commission.

4 For a general overview, see Edwards and Spence (eds) 1994; Nugent 1997; Corbett, Jacobs and Shackleton 1995; Lord 1998; Hix 1999. In the words of one of these commentators, the 'Commission is responsible for initiating policy proposals and monitoring the implementation of policies once they have been adopted. . . .' (Hix 1999: 7). All legislation passes through the Parliament – for consultation, amendment or veto – and the Council formally makes the final decision. 'Comitology' refers to the controversial system of committees by which 'national experts' intervene in various ways in the Commission's proposed implementation measures.

5 The Commissioner responsible for the reforms addressed a seminar of officials in 1998 only to be openly dismissed by more than one critic as putting forth 'Anglo-Saxon' ideas, a term the Commissioner himself dismissed. Only southern Europeans, he said to the French-speaking critics who used it, seemed to know what that meant. It is indeed a term commonly used in the French language and is very common in the Commission; some aspects of its more general history are worth noting. It took moral shape largely in the nineteenth century when the Celt was invented as the morally privileged contrary of all that industrial, male-dominated, rational society was not. The morally unprivileged half – required thereby to bear the warts of all that the Celt was not – was invented, through English self-critics, as the Anglo-Saxon. In France, this then became a term by which all that was morally repugnant and un-French (un-Gaulish, un-Celtic) could be

defined. The moral discourse of Anglo-Saxon and Celtic has since been used in the French language to distinguish English/American on the one hand from all things French on the other, and as for France, so too thereafter for all other countries in southern Europe. The *Nordiques* and *Méidionaux* , and *'Anglo-saxon'* and *'Latin'*, distinctions feed off the same morality as Anglo-Saxon and Celtic, or English and Irish. The categorical dustbin of all that emotion, the soul, and all things nice are not, 'Anglo-Saxon' is not something that many would really want to be. Further details of the invention and career of the term Anglo-Saxon can be found in Chapman 1978; McDonald 1989.

6 Examples of the best-known studies would include: Blok 1981; du Boulay 1974; Campbell 1964; Davis 1977; Gellner 1977; Gellner and Waterbury 1977; Gilmore 1987 (ed.); Giovanni 1981; Herzfeld 1980, 1985, 1992; Loizos 1975; Peristiany 1965; Pitt-Rivers 1954, 1977.

7 For further details, see Pollitt 1993; Rose 1996.

8 For these analyses, see Farnham *et al.* 1996; Pollitt 1993; Ridley 1996; Walsh 1995.

9 For examples, see Herzfeld 1992.

10 Strathern (1997) has similarly talked of some of the problems of audit in the UK in relation to the non-productive productivity of university life.

Bibliography

Abélès, M., Bellier, I. and McDonald, M. (1993) *Approche Anthropologique de la Commission Européenne*, unpublished report, Brussels: European Commission.

Blok, A. (1981) 'Rams and Billy Goats: a key to the Mediterranean code of honour', *Man* 16 (3): 427–40.

Boulay, J. du (1974) *Portrait of a Greek Mountain Village*, Oxford: Clarendon Press.

Campbell, J. (1964) *Honour, Family and Patronage*, Oxford: Clarendon Press.

Chapman, M. (1978) *The Gaelic Vision in Scottish Culture*, London: Croom Helm.

CIE (1999a) *First Report on Allegations regarding Fraud, Mismanagement and Nepotism in the European Commission* (Committee of Independent Experts), Brussels: European Parliament.

—— (1999b) *Second Report on Reform of the Commission. Analysis of current practice and proposals for tackling mismanagement, irregularities and fraud*, volume I, (Committee of Independent Experts), Brussels: European Parliament.

Claisse, A. and Meininger, M.-C. (1994) *Fonctions Publiques en Europe*, Paris: Montchrestien, coll. 'Clefs'.

Corbett, R., Jacobs, F. and Shackleton, M. (1995) *The European Parliament* (third ed.), London: Pearson.

Davis, J. (1977) *People of the Mediterranean*, London: Routledge.

Dilley, R. (ed.) (1992) *Contesting Markets*, Edinburgh: Edinburgh University Press.

Edwards, G. and Spence, D. (eds) (1994) *The European Commission*, Harlow: Longman.

Farnham, D., Horton, S., Barlow, J. and Hondeghem, A. (eds) (1996) *New Public Managers in Europe. Public Servants in Transition*, London: Macmillan.

Gellner, E. (1977) 'Patron and Clients', in E. Gellner and J. Waterbury (eds) *Patrons and Clients*, London: Duckworth.

Gellner, E. and Waterbury, J. (eds) (1977) *Patrons and Clients*, London: Duckworth.

Gilmore, D. (1987) (ed.) *Honour and Shame and the Unity of the Mediterranean*, Washington: American Anthropological Association, special publication no. 22.

Giovanni, M. (1981) 'Woman: a Dominant Symbol Within the Cultural System of a Sicilian town', *Man* 16 (3): 408–26.

Gupta, A. (1995) 'Blurred Boundaries: the Discourse of Corruption, the Culture of Politics and the Imagined State', *American Ethnologist* 22 (2): 375–402.

Herzfeld, M. (1980) 'Honour and Shame: Problems in the Comparative Analysis of Moral Systems', *Man* 15 (2): 339–51.

—— (1985) *The Poetics of Manhood*, Oxford: Clarendon.

—— (1992) *The Social Production of Indifference. Exploring the Symbolic Roots of Western Bureaucracy*, Oxford and New York: Berg.

Hix, S. (1999) *The Political System of the European Union*, Basingstoke: Macmillan.

Hoskin, K. (1996) 'The "Awful Idea of Accountability": Inscribing People into the Measurement of Objects', in R. Munro and J. Mouritsen (eds) *Accountability. Power, Ethos and the Technologies of Managing*, London: International Thomson Publishing.

—— and Mace, R. (1988) 'The Genesis of Accountability: the West Point Connections', *Accounting, Organizations and Society* 13 (1): 37–73.

Laffan, B. (1997) 'From Policy Entrepreneur to Policy Manager: the Challenge Facing the European Commission', *Journal of European Public Policy* 4 (3): 422–38.

—— (1999) 'Becoming a "Living Institution": The Evolution of the Court of Auditors', *Journal of Common Market Studies* 37(2): 251–68.

Lebessis, N. (1996) *Governance. Progress Report*, unpublished report, Brussels: European Commission.

Levy, R. (1996) 'Managing Value-for-Money Audit in the European Union: The Challenge of Diversity', *Journal of Common Market Studies* 34 (4): 509–29.

—— (1997) 'Managing the Managers: The Commission's Role in the Implementation of Spending Programmes', in N. Nugent (ed.) *At the*

Heart of the Union. Studies of the European Commission, Basingstoke: Macmillan.

Loizos, P. (1975) *The Greek Gift: Politics in a Cypriot Village*, Oxford : Blackwell.

Lord, C. (1998) *Democracy in the European Union*, Sheffield: Sheffield Academic Press.

McDonald, M. (1989) *'We are not French!' Language, Culture and Identity in Brittany*, London and New York: Routledge.

—— (1993) 'The Construction of Difference: an Anthropological Approach to Stereotypes', in S. Macdonald (ed.) *Inside European Identities*, Oxford: Berg.

—— (1996) '"Unity in diversity": Some Tensions in the Construction of Europe', *Social Anthropology* 4 (1): 47–60.

—— (1997) 'Identities in the European Commission' in N. Nugent (ed.) *At the Heart of the Union. Studies of the European Commission*, Basingstoke: Macmillan.

—— (1998) *Anthropological Study of the European Commission*, unpublished report, Brussels: European Commission.

Miller, P. (1992) 'Accounting and Objectivity: the Invention of Calculating Selves and Calculable Spaces', *Annals of Scholarship* 9 (1–2): 61–86.

—— and O'Leary, T. (1987) 'Accounting and the construction of the governable person', *Accounting, Organizations and Society* 12 (3): 235–65.

—— and O'Leary, T. (1990) 'Making Accountancy Practical', *Accounting, Organizations and Society* 15 (5): 479–98.

—— and Rose, N. (1990) 'Governing Economic Life', *Economy and Society*, 19 (1): 1–31.

Morgan, G. (1988) 'Accounting as Reality Construction: Towards a New Epistemology for Accounting Practice', *Accounting, Organizations and Society* 13 (5): 477–85.

Muller, P. (ed.) (1992) *L'Administration française est-elle en crise?*, Paris: L'Harmattan.

Munro, R. and Mouritsen, J. (eds) (1996) *Accountability. Power, Ethos and the Technologies of Managing*, London: International Thomson Publishing.

Nencel, L. and Pels, P. (eds) (1991) *Constructing Knowledge*, London: Sage.

Nugent, N. (ed.) (1997) *At the Heart of the Union. Studies of the European Commission*, Basingstoke: Macmillan.

Peristiany, J. (1965) *Honour and Shame: the values of Mediterranean society*, London: Weidenfeld and Nicolson.

Pitt-Rivers, J. (1954) *People of the Sierra*, New York: Criterion Books.

—— (1977) *The Fate of Schechem, or the Politics of Sex*, Cambridge: Cambridge University Press.

Pollitt, C. (1993) *Managerialism and the Public Services* (2nd edition), Oxford: Blackwell.

Power, M. (1994) *The Audit Explosion*, London: Demos.

Ridley, F. (1996) 'The New Public Management in Europe: Comparative Perspectives', *Public Policy and Administration* 11 (1): 16–29.

Rose, N. (1988) 'Calculable minds and manageable individuals', *History of the Human Sciences* 1 (2): 179–200.

—— (1996) *Inventing Our Selves*, Cambridge: Cambridge University Press.

Strathern, M. (1997) '"Improving Ratings": Audit in the British University System', *European Review* 5(3): 305–21.

Walsh, K. (1995) *Public Services and Market Mechanisms*, Basingstoke: Macmillan.

Part III

Chapter 5

The trickster's dilemma

Ethics and the technologies of the anthropological self

Peter Pels

> What I am afraid of about humanism is that it presents a
> certain form of our ethics as a universal model for any kind of
> freedom. I think that there are more secrets, more possible
> freedoms, and more inventions in our future than we can
> imagine in humanism . . .
>
> Foucault (in Martin 1988: 15)

As several chapters in this volume attest, auditing and accounting
have become the operational signs of the global spread of neo-
liberal values. On the one hand, they accompany high hopes about
a transformation of transnational relationships in the direction of
good governance and an increasing transparency of the organization of state and civil society; on the other, they generate the fear
that this transformation of liberal morality cloaks a novel order of
increasing global inequalities. If, as Power argued, auditing threatens
to replace the monitoring of quality with the monitoring of systems
to monitor quality (1994: 6), this may remind us of an earlier
critique of liberalism: its tendency to replace political discussion by
the systems that are supposed to safeguard democratic representation, depoliticizing relationships that are in fact fraught with
conflict (Schmitt 1993; Habermas 1989). Elsewhere (1999a: 111)
I have argued that the recent resurgence of interest in the ethics of
anthropology must also be seen against the background of the
spread of neo-liberal ideals, and that this raises similar doubts about
the way in which anthropological morals may cover up new structures of exploitation. Here, I want to continue that investigation
into the cultural and historical background of anthropological
morality, precisely because it can bring out some of the dilemmas
peculiar to the constitution of the liberal self. In particular, I think

that the anthropologist's 'duplex' position (Pels 1999a), situated, like a trickster, in between different moralities and epistemes, discovers some of the impossibilities of maintaining the liberal desire for individual autonomy of choice and opinion at a distance from political struggle over existing inequalities in the world.

Such a desire to create a subject position divorced from political struggle also characterizes the attempt to lay down ethical guidelines for anthropological conduct, and this political aloofness partly explains why attempts to generate ethical discussion among anthropologists often has received little feedback (Levy 1993: 25) or met with scepticism, even disapproval ('Why waste time on that?').[1] I will try to explain that attitude by interpreting ethics, understood in terms of a set of quasi-legal rules, as part of a specific technology of the (professional) self.

I hope to show that, first, this professional technology of self is directed at a specific ideal of anthropological *publicity*, and second, that this public persona is only one of the ways in which anthropologists have constituted themselves as subjects. The following section considers how this use of 'ethics' has changed under the influence of the new technologies of domination that characterize the spread of neo-liberal market models and auditing techniques. Novel uses of 'ethics' shift the balance between public and backstage professional performance towards the latter, and lead us to distinguish between 'ethics', 'ethic' and technologies of self. Next, I show the cultural and historical background of such distinctions in a specifically *liberal* constitution of self, a schizoid modern self that is both the object of improvement and the subject that does the improving. This humanist subjectivity, by constituting itself as its own measure, is thereby both liberated and isolated from its surroundings. The liberal self is in turn the background against which to see the emergence of a professional ethic or sense of service and its romantic notion of 'ethics', a professional self that is manifested in early twentieth-century anthropology in a very peculiar way. Having established, I hope, that the anthropological subject shares the liberal self's isolation and its consequent denial of its political engagements, I then locate this isolation in the professional ethics of anthropology, its discourse on method, the genre of the ethnographic confessional, as well as the production of disinfected dialogue through a discussion of what I regard as one of the terminal ethnographies of the twentieth century, Castaneda's *The Teachings of Don Juan* (1968). In conclusion, I argue that to guard against the negative effects of the depoliticization of research by ethics and method, anthropologists may have to consider agonistic confessions, the historicizing and politicization of methodology, and the possibility of an emergent ethics, one that is no longer tied to a stable community but arises from contingent negotiations. The consciousness of political engagement, however, also brings forward the trickster's dilemma: owing public allegiance to both research sponsors and research subjects, anthropologists can no longer desire to show either of them a 'true' face.

Anthropological ethics as a technology of self

To understand what it means to treat anthropology's professional ethics[2] as a technology of the self, I first have to sketch what it means to understand a set of cultural standards as just such. I start from the assumption that 'technology' refers to a regulation of human practice that comes in a certain objectified form, as a set of objects (tools, machines, buildings), as a set of more or less explicit rules, as a ritual or an exemplar of conduct, or as a disciplinary apparatus (of course, a technology usually combines two or more of these). It is crucial to realize that its status as an objectification of a human practice implies that a technology can be transferred from situation to situation without necessarily changing its form – although each transfer can change its identity and meaning. Foucault (1988: 18–19) distinguished four major types of technologies through which human beings objectify their practical reason (and thereby understand themselves): technologies of production (to make and change things), of sign systems, of power (objectivizing the subject), and of the self. Technologies of the self, he wrote (ibid):

> permit individuals to effect by their own means or with the help of others a certain number of operations on their own bodies and souls, thoughts, conduct, and way of being, so as to transform themselves in order to attain a certain state of happiness, purity, wisdom, perfection or immortality.

The four types rarely operate separately, an important point to bear in mind. Foucault himself mostly focused on the latter two, and especially in his later years paid much attention to what he called 'governmentality', the contact between technologies of dominating others and those of constituting the self, granting that in his earlier work he may have concentrated too exclusively on the former.

Given Foucault's description, we can distinguish three aspects of a technology of the self: the set of technological operations, the self operated on (bodies, souls, thoughts, conduct), and the purified self that ought to be the result of the operations. In implementing a certain technology of the self, the subject is constituted by a movement through all three aspects. Foucault was fond of using confession as a example (partly because he thought 'Western man has become a confessing animal' [quoted by Gutman 1988: 104]), and the practice of confession clearly shows this tripartite constitution of the subject, for it is a 'ritual of discourse in which the speaking subject (who embodies the "technological" operation) is also the subject of the statement' (the 'self' operated upon), which, through absolution, constitutes the purified subject. This triad can be made to correspond to the triad of Aristotelian ethics based on the assumption of an untutored humanity (the 'self' operated upon) that had to be elevated by rational ethics (the 'technological operation') to a realization of its potential essence (the purified subject; MacIntyre 1984: 52–3). Thus, it seems reasonable to investigate the notion of ethics as (part of a) technology of self.

What would this mean when applied to those professional codes of conduct drawn up in anthropology from the late 1960s onwards? When we look at the text of the Principles of Professional Responsibility (PPR) drawn up in the early 1970s by the American Anthropological Association (Fluehr-Lobban 1991: 247–52), it becomes clear that the 'purified subject' aimed at, the ideal professional anthropologist, is someone whose first and paramount responsibility is to 'protect the physical, social, and psychological welfare and to honor the dignity and privacy of those studied'. Subsequently, anthropologists were deemed to be responsible to the public, to their discipline, to their students, to sponsors, and lastly, to their own and host governments – not necessarily in that order, for the only explicit hierarchy of responsibility is given by the paramountcy of the interests of the people studied.

The PPR does not give a clear indication of the self 'operated upon' – the 'untutored humanity' among anthropologists – except by default, as when one recognizes the extraordinary stress laid in all articles of responsiblity (those about relations with students excepted) on the avoidance of secrecy in the contracting, practice and dissemination of the results of research. This can, of course, be explained by the direct influence of the protest against counter-insurgency research at the time of Project Camelot and the war in Vietnam, Thailand and Cambodia (Fluehr-Lobban 1991: 24ff.), and displays an older anxiety about the potential use of anthropologists as spies. Thus, the anthropological self that has to be tutored is a potentially *duplicitous* self, one that may keep hidden what ought to be in public view.

Lastly, we may wonder what are the precise 'technological operations' that this technology of the professional self was to apply to 'untutored' anthropologists. The objectification of ethics in a set of explicit rules was meant to guard, according to the Western folk theory of professionalism formulated in the early twentieth century, the competence and honour of the professional, that is, to help discipline the members of the profession so its clients could trust the technical and moral quality of the service rendered (Carr-Saunders and Wilson 1933: 302, 394; Taeusch 1933: 472). Here, however, the text of the 1970s PPR displays some ambivalence: its epilogue circumscribes the anthropologist's ethical and scientific responsibility by saying that

> [it] is a human, not superhuman responsibility. To err is human, to forgive humane. This statement of principles of professional responsibility is not designed to punish, but to provide guidelines which can minimize the occasions upon which there is a need to forgive.
>
> (Fluehr-Lobban 1991: 252)

The emphasis on 'forgiveness' rather than 'punishment' reveals the extent to which the American Anthropological Association, like most other anthropological associations, and despite certain attempts to make such associations more exclusively professional,[3] was more of a learned society than a professional association with official sanction to punish infractions of its code of conduct. This did not mean that the peer control envisaged within a professional association was not part of the technology of the self of the PPR: on the contrary, the passage on forgiveness was immediately followed by one affirming that any of the 'legitimate powers of the Association' could be used to enquire into suspicions of irresponsible conduct of colleagues. Thus, despite the emphasis on forgiveness rather than punishment, one can still identify the PPR as a statement functioning within a technology of self that was meant to ensure ethical conduct by the joint operation of a set of explicit, quasi-legal principles, that stressed the commitment of the anthropological subject to publicity in all aspects of professional life, and that could be reinforced by professional peer control.

The specificity of anthropological ethics as compared to other instances of this technology of the self is apparent, therefore, in the relative weakness – as compared (say) to medical or legal associations – of the professionals' capacity to discipline colleagues. Publicity has a different, more radical, meaning among anthropologists because they do not have the equivalent of the doctor's, lawyer's or priest's right to confidentiality: the right to refuse to disclose what clients have communicated to them (Givens 1993: 37). This is related to the fact that anthropological associations cannot license general practioners. Instead, most British anthropologists have long regarded a 'general' anthropological practitioner as a 'no longer anthropologist' (Wright 1995: 66–7), implying that 'pure' academic anthropology legtimates the discipline and that 'applied' anthropology is only derivative (Evans-Pritchard 1946). This may have been less pronounced in the United States, but Britsh, American and Dutch anthropology seem to have shared, until recently, the identification of anthropological work with 'pure' academic research (Fluehr-Lobban 1991: 22; Wright 1995).[4] As I have argued elsewhere (Pels 1999a), this indicates another, rival, set of values, which anthropologists – like other professionals – set next to their sense of service: the morality of science and its ideal of truth, to be attained by methodology and public discussion. This morality of truth grounds the claim to authority of anthropologists to deliver a 'public service' (see Fluehr-Lobban 1991: 244; Malinowski 1929; Wilson 1940). As argued below, this set of values indicates the existence of technologies of the anthropological self other than professional ethics.

If we compare the latter stance of public service to the hierarchy of values in the early 1970s PPR, however, we recognize a peculiar conundrum that is absent from other forms of the use of professional ethics: an ambivalence about the primary audience to be addressed in order to constitute oneself as an anthropological subject. While anthropologists before this time were predominantly concerned with a public service adressed to an audience of research sponsors and government, the first ethical code made the interests of the people studied paramount. It brought into the open anthropologists' ambivalence about who actually should be the client of their expertise – research sponsors or research subjects.

This brings to the fore at least two other ways of constituting the anthropological self and other that coexist with the apparatus of professional control, and which help to explain the relative weakness of the latter. The first is the practice of public relations with powerful research sponsors, which implies a constitution of self through the effective communication of a positive image; its dominant technological operation would seem to be the grant application. The second is the constitution of self through the effective communication with the people researched by the methods and techniques of ethnography and fieldwork ('rapport'). The first constitutes the anthropologist by means of the values espoused by the sponsoring organization, the second by means of de-identifying the anthropologist with his or her personal background. The ambiguity is summarized (but not resolved) by the invocation of 'welfare' in the first article of the PPR: although anthropologists' primary responsibility is towards the welfare of the people researched, the notion itself refers back to the situation in which anthropologists presented themselves to research sponsors as the 'welfare experts' to be employed by (predominantly) colonial governments. One should be aware of the fact that even when anthropologists' first interest is to sell themselves to research sponsors, they also (help to) formulate the 'paramountcy' of the interests of the people (to be) researched.[5]

Anthropological ethics in the age of audit

Few anthropologists, whether in business or in government employ, will lack experience with the recent changes in managing the anthropological profession and accounting for its efficiency, and this volume documents ways in which they signify important changes in governmentality. Power argues that this 'fundamental shift in patterns of governance' (1994: 5) is related to the spread of a new form of public management essentially derived from private sector administration (1994: 15), signalled by the transfer of the idea of auditing from its original practice of financial control to far wider realms of application. Audit aims at increasing transparency of organizations by a 'control of control':

> Audits are often not directly concerned with the quality of performance, whether environmental, educational or financial, but rather with the systems in place to govern quality. This

'policing of policing' distinguishes the audit explosion from an older tradition of engineering-based quality control and its statistically grounded methods.

(Power 1994: 6)

Paradoxically, the stated goal of making the inner workings of organizations more visible goes together with a positioning of the audit process itself as an increasingly private and invisible expert activity (1994: 26). Audit, moreover, actively constructs the environments in which it operates, making them more 'auditable' at the same time that it renders itself thereby invulnerable to its own failure (1994: 7–8). Academics are familiar with the ways in which student questionnaires are meant to make teaching more auditable, in which research is increasingly reformed by the measures used to assess it, and in which research programmes constrain research in order to make it more auditable even before it has started. The grant proposal, formerly seen as an incidental instrument to produce funding, has now come to occupy a much larger chunk of the professional horizon.

The political outcome of this is uncertain: audits can support and enhance the quality of an organization's performance as well as discipline it (Power 1994: 4). Its novelty is equally debatable for, as we shall see, forms of qualitative 'accounting' have an impressive pedigree in the history of liberal technologies of the self. However, audit is important to our discussion of anthropological ethics because it allows us to specify a way in which ethics is being reformed so as to function as an alternative, qualitative form of the assessment of anthropological performance. To understand that, it is crucial to realize that recent economic literature argues that 'it will be rational for the auditee to contract *voluntarily* to undergo an independent audit in order to make good offices visible' and reduce the risk that principals – employers, funding agencies, government – remain unaware of 'moral hazards' and insufficient performance because there are information asymmetries between them and the agents monitored (Power 1994: 11). Recent changes in the use and formulation of ethical codes in social science correspond to that development: codes of ethical conduct are increasingly voluntary means to publicly reduce the anxieties that research sponsors and employers may have about research performance. Paradoxically, and in line with the critique of audit advanced by Power, this development can be shown to result in a *decreasing* public visibility of anthropological research performance itself.

These developments are directly related to the increase in non-academic employment among British and American anthropologists from the mid-1970s onwards (Goldschmidt 1979: 8; Wright 1995: 68, 89 n4). I encountered this situation in 1993 myself when asked to sit on a commission reviewing the code of conduct of the Dutch Association for Social Sciences (NVMC). This code, dating from 1975, was perhaps the first to be drafted for anthropologists after the US American PPR and it was closely modelled on the PPR, except that it was meant for both sociologists and anthropologists. As in the USA and United Kingdom, a revision of the code was thought necessary when the Association changed its profile into that of a more general social science organization, significantly also meant to cater for the interests of non-academically employed social scientists. Most members of the commission had a sociological background, and both my predecessor anthropologist in the commission and myself had a number of difficulties with their suggestions for revision. One of the most important contributors to the discussion, a man employed at a business school who was also one of the main initiators of proposals for a new code, maintained that we needed a 'postmodern' code to fit our times. The new code did not rate the interest of the people studied as highly as before. It was meant as a guideline for conduct and as a teaching device (just as the proposals circulated in AAA circles from 1984 onwards), but much stress was laid on the function of a code to show an appropriate, dependable public image of social scientists to potential sponsors and employers, something clearly reflecting the interests of some of the new, non-academically employed scholars within the Association. Although I found many of the new insights deriving from a more articulate presence of practical social science refreshing and important, I did not think a code would be the way to defend them properly.[6]

Discussions with a similar background occurred in the American Anthropological Association in the 1980s, leading eventually to a condemnation of proposals for revision by one leader of the discussion in the 1960s as 'Reaganethics' and a licence for 'unfettered free-enterprise research' (Berreman 1991: 52, 59). This assessment did not sufficiently take into account the fact that some of the premises of the early 1970s PPR had become outdated not only because of the increase of anthropologists in private employ but also because critical anthropology's plea for 'studying up' and criticizing the regimes of power within which anthropologists work had generated different ethical concerns (Pels 1999a: 112; see also the comments by Nader (1999) and Sluka (1999)). But it remains true that some of the 1980s proposals for reform indicated a shift towards a more public-relations oriented code of ethics. This became apparent from the 1984 proposal for a new code (Fluehr-Lobban 1991: 265–69), which dropped the obligation not to exploit informants, the duty of publicity, and the clauses about the illegitimacy of clandestine research. While 'business firms' were added to the environments in which anthropologists work, the code proposal dropped the paramountcy of the interests of the people studied as well as the clauses about the power of the Association to take measures against infractors.

If we think of the 1970s code as a technology of the professional self, then it seems that the 1984 proposals suggested abolishing it, for the notion of the 'untutored' anthropologist (one who kept secret what should be made public) and the reference to sanctioning infractors of the code (even if only by their colleagues' 'forgiveness') both disappeared from the proposal. Eventually, the 1984 proposals were defeated by determined opposition from members of the Association (such as Berreman). Instead, a compromise version of the PPR was proposed in 1990; nonetheless this also dropped the paramountcy of the interests of people studied for a much more modest formulation, and removed the prohibition on secret and clandestine research (Fluehr-Lobban 1991: 274–9).

I share some of the worries of Berreman and others about these developments, and they may well signify the demise of the – already limited – use of ethical codes in anthropology. We have seen, however, that twentieth-century anthropological morality moves in a tenuous balance between the clientage of research sponsors on the one hand and the clientage of research subjects on the other. There is a sense in which ethical codes in the age of audit start to function differently towards research subjects as well. This shows the other side of the present uses of ethical codes in organizations: as contracts rather than means of advertising. The semi-contractual sense of obligation that ethics may produce potentially empowers the people being researched by spelling out conditions of the researcher's use of research findings. In the case of a Dutch colleague working in Oceania, for example, the élite members of the group studied tried to prevent the researcher from publishing his findings, with the argument that it harmed the interests of the group concerned (drawing upon the first article of the early 1970s PPR, among other things); the opinion of the researcher was that they wanted to do this because his text explicitly described this élite's attempts towards cultural control of the whole group, while also describing how they maintained a relation of inequality with less privileged members of the group through this form of control.[7]

Thus, ethical guidelines for anthropologists seem to function in new ways, all modifying the relationship between public and backstage performance towards a more determined emphasis on the latter. In the public-relations sense of presenting an ethical code to potential employers, the demand for full publicity (characteristic of the orginal PPR's articles) is thought to obstruct the full employability of anthropologists by new, private sponsors. But in the semi-contractual sense of guaranteeing obligation towards people studied the code may function to prohibit the publication of research findings unpleasant to the latter. In this sense, the use of an ethical code towards both sponsors and subjects displays the paradox pointed out by Power in his analysis of audit: in setting the code between anthropologist and sponsor, or anthropologist and people studied, a measure meant to produce a more transparent relationship actually works to keep more facets of the inner workings of anthropological research from public view. The professional's dedication to publicity seems to give way to a more concerted effort to screen off the internal politics of anthropological work.

I think it crucial for an understanding of anthropological ethics to focus more intently on this changing ratio of inner working and public presentation, and to do so by going back to the historical formation of the ethics of professional responsibility in anthropology. But first we have to be conscious of what the recent developments in revising ethical codes in anthropology mean for our understanding of ethics as a technology of the self. A first conclusion is that 'ethics' as a set of quasi-legal statements seems to function in different technologies of self. Recent revisions of the PPR may not have abolished the statement that one may still use the 'powers of the Association' to enquire into the propriety of colleagues' conduct, but the mechanism for such inquiry (the Committee on Ethics) has been effectively abolished. The AAA seems, therefore, to have given up on the operative technology of the anthropological self as it was envisaged in the late 1960s and early 1970s. More important, the notion of an 'untutored' self which needs reform has disappeared now that there is no longer a reference in the code to anthropologists who keep secret what ought to be public.[8] The ethical code, therefore, seems to serve different technologies of self: one stressing professional duties towards publicity, another more in line with the ethos of self-auditing of recent shifts in organizational governance. The latter seems to take up a place alongside the grant proposal as a technology of producing a marketable self.

Thus, we reach a point at which we have to distinguish between 'ethics' as a set of quasi-legal principles, the 'ethic' (in the sense of Weber's 'Protestant ethic') in which a set of principles is deployed, and the technologies of self that make both 'ethics' and 'ethic' operative. The first, as we have seen, can be deployed in different technologies of self. In fact, it is a common assumption of Western folk theories that ethics can be made to mask unstated sets of self-interests. In contrast, a technology of the self always has a notion of the good, of the purified self towards which the technology of the self will reform the untutored subject.[9] As such, an 'ethic' also has to be distinguished from a technology of the self: it is mostly objectified in its exemplars or explicit notions of the purified self, and may therefore acquire a different meaning when transposed to another technology of the self. This is in fact what happened to the exhortation to anthropologists in the PPR to be candid and publicly accountable: when moved from a technology of the professional self to one of qualitative audit, it changed its meaning from a statement of public professional duty to a screening (in both senses of the word) of the inner working of an organization of professionals. If we keep these distinctions between ethics, ethic and technology of the self in mind, we are in a better position to understand the way in which twentieth-century anthropological moralities were constructed from the late nineteenth century onwards. They allow us to ask: *what kind of ethic needs 'ethics'?* I suggest that it is a specifically liberal ethic which needs 'ethics', and that its possibilities and difficulties arise from a specifically liberal constitution of the self.

The double life and moral isolation of the liberal self

This section runs rough-shod over several centuries of European history in an attempt to understand some of the preconditions of the constitution of the ethic of professional service, to be dealt with in the next section. In particular, this section should give historical and cultural background to the isolated 'ethics' that appeared as an an explicit code of conduct in the past thirty years. I suggest that liberal ethics is characterized by a specific doubling of the self basic to the constitution of humanism, that is, of 'man' as his own moral measure. Moreover, I hope to show that this doubling is impossible without morally isolating the self from the collectivity at which it directs itself. Such moral isolation divorces the self from any shared moral practice except that of a quasi-legal, objectified and alienated set of 'ethics'. Much of this analysis of liberal ethics is inspired by MacIntyre's argument that European history has seen the loss of the third element in the triad of Aristotelian ethics, the ideal towards which each person should strive, leaving the other two elements, 'untutored humanity' and rational ethics, isolated and structurally opposed to each other. The following section suggests that, in anthropology, this humanist absence of a third source of independent moral measures took on a very specific and essentially ambiguous form.

Campbell's brilliant revision of Weber's classic has shown that the middle-class personality did not derive from 'the Protestant ethic', singular, but was composed of a Puritan and a Romantic one (Campbell 1987). The Puritan ethic (which Weber wrongly dubbed '*the* Protestant ethic', for the Romantic ethic has equally strong Protestant roots) was the ancestor of nineteenth century rationalism and utilitarianism. The Romantic ethic only emerged in its full-fledged form, in the twin appearances of consumerist hedonism and Bohemian critique, in opposition to this rationalism and utilitarianism. If I may simplify Campbell's argument rather drastically, one could say that he follows Weber in portraying the Puritan or Calvinist ethic as one which stressed work and produc-tion, which suspected the self and denied it the possibility of intentionally improving itself, and which reduced the signs of moral righteousness to those of economic success. In contrast, the Romantic ethic derived from a Pietist ethic in which the appro-priate showing of charity and feelings of pity and compassion were taken as signs of salvation. This produced an 'ethic of feeling' in the eighteenth century that directly foreshadowed the Romantic ethic, which rejected the existing utilitarian world of economic calculation and worked towards moral excellence by the liberation provided by sentiments of the imagination (Campbell 1987: 178). Thus, romantic 'ethics' stood opposed to the utilitarian morality of *laissez-faire* economics, and as Schmitt (1996: 71) noted, both worked in tandem to liberally annihilate the political. If one follows Berreman's diagnosis, one may say that the shift, in anthropological ethics, from professionalism to audit is yet another instance of the swing of the liberal pendulum from a romantic primacy of the ethical to a utilitarian primacy of the economic.

This contradictory balance in liberalism between the ethical and the economical is supported by a specific constitution of the liberal self as an isolated individual, something best understood through an early example of one of the most important Western technologies of self: confession. Rousseau's *Confessions*, completed in 1765, 'reveals and celebrates the atomistic, autonomous self' by insisting on a 'primacy of feeling', and in that sense it may be taken as one of the first announcements of the ethic of romanticism (Gutman 1988: 100–1). Rousseau's intentions were partly to make a secular confession of sins, to unburden himself of his shame by an honest revelation of his inner thoughts, and in this sense he also stands in a tradition of Puritan confessions that 'make up the balance' of one's sins in writing a diary 'account' (Paden 1988: 69, 71) – the book-keeping and calculating metaphors showing that the qualitative forms of audit can boast an impressive historical parentage. But Rousseau also constitutes his self by this confession: it is not just a confession of sins, but 'the enumeration of each and every experience that has made one what and who one is' (Gutman 1988: 107). Rousseau's confessions, unlike, say, Augustine's, celebrate his self by a narrative of experiences constituting the individual – a notion of *Bildung*, of growth and life, that Foucault identified as crucial to the modern episteme. Apart from constituting his self as an objective, positive fact, however, Rousseau also condemns it to a peculiar, and typically romantic, isolation: he accounts for himself by saying that his imagination envisages a better world in which to live, thus constituting the extant world as other, as essentially inhospitable to his real and ideal individuality, while appealing to his public by arguing that his imagined world is a better place to live in (1988: 110). His individuality, therefore, is constituted by a internal division between the self as an objective product of the world, and the self as the author of an imaginary better world. Rousseau's confession makes him simultaneously into an objective self, and a subjective imagination that can measure and work upon this self: a double life that harbours the romantic spirit of rebellion, residing in the constant desire for liberation from the existing world (1988: 118).

According to Campbell (1987: 219, 223), this double life of a rebellious self that morally justifies itself by its imagination, juxtaposed to a self formed by a utilitarian world of objective fact and natural or economic law, is characteristic of the middle-class personality. Liberal selves, therefore, can choose between two possible ways of defining an escape from political contingencies: when criticizing the objective facts of capitalist society, they romantically imagine an ethics to reform it; and when criticizing the subjective imaginary of romantic ideals, they fall back on utilitarian arguments about how the world is factually constituted (this indicates the two ways of liberally formulating 'universal' ethical standards: by either 'human' or 'natural' rights). This internally divided and potentially contradictory way of constituting man as his own measure has led to the typically modern problematic of ethics, where explicitly stated standards are always under threat of being criticized as masking objective self-interests, and objective interests need to be reformed by explicit quasi-legal standards of ethics (MacIntyre 1984: 86). According to classical liberal theory, until a definitive statement of human/natural rights has been reached, politics has to be replaced by the free and public discussion of private individuals about the relative weight of different notions of rights. Often, the unstated assumption was that only those already constituted as responsible – that is, privately constituted by sufficient property or education – could take part in this public discussion (Habermas 1989: 85). For such standards to be amenable to public discussion and rational choice, they have to be explicitly formulated as quasi-, or better, supra-legal legitimations.

But if legalistic morals and choice constitute a specifically liberal sense of freedom (which, according to MacIntyre, can also be interpreted as a loss of ethical direction), they are always subverted by the necessity to impose that freedom on those who have not yet mastered the liberal sense of self (cf. Parekh 1995).[10] This is the background against which to interpret the rise of an elite of welfare professionals and its – often illiberal – sense of superior expertise. Both anti-liberals such as Schmitt (1993) and nostalgic liberals such as his pupil Habermas (1989) have identified the late nineteenth century as the moment at which classical liberalism's sense of freedom of depoliticized discussion turns into the management of public opinion by the mass politics of a newly interventionist state. This turn to public relations, the management of political imagery, was partly carried by an emerging class of civil service professionals, whose constitution of a professional ethics seems to be a translation of a romantic ethic of individual moral isolation to a new authority of disciplinary expertise not amenable to public discussion. The authority of the independent professional emerged in particular during the nineteenth century (Johnson 1973: 126), and in fact the first romantic rebels or Bohemians were often sons of a fairly affluent class of professionals (Campbell 1987: 195–6). The professional ethics that were to have an impact on anthropology were more associated with a later phase of the development of professionalism, one that was firmly tied to the increase of state control and embodied in particular by the professionalization of the civil and colonial services (cf. Johnson 1973: 126). In this context, the 'backstage' of professional expertise – an interior screened off from the general public – decisively influenced the ethical constitution of self in the social sciences.[11]

'Public service' and the backstage of professional expertise

One can trace the development of the ethic of professional 'public service' by noting how the London School of Economics (a major breeding ground of a new class of professional civil servants, including Beveridge, architect of British metropolitan and colonial welfare arrangements [Mackenzie and Mackenzie 1977: 356]) emerged from the ethos of the leadership of the Fabian Society. Started as an action group of romantic spiritualists such as Podmore and Besant, the Fabian Society, although retaining its 'ethical socialism', moved towards the more sceptical creed of managerial efficiency of Shaw, the Webbs and Wallas. The Fabians displayed a strong romantic temperament in trying to dissociate themselves from a society in which 'the competitive system [had] broken down' and which therefore had to be 'reconstructed in accordance with the highest moral principles' (Mackenzie and Mackenzie 1977: 25). Increasingly, these moral principles came to be defined as the property of a class of knowledgeable experts, defined in turn by their mastery of the routines of public administration and local government and of statistical social research. This group tried to 'permeate' the bulwarks of power by means of this expertise, retaining the romantic horror of convention and conservatism, and aiming at the reform of conservative thinking not through the imagination but through confronting it with the cold truth that would unmask its covert destruction of human happiness (1977: 173). This was the background of the Webbs' initiative to found the LSE: 'reforming society is no light matter and must be undertaken by experts specially trained for the purpose' (1977: 61, 215). The LSE became a fulcrum of the construction of the welfare state ideologies of professionalism (through R.H. Tawney: Freidson 1984: 2), of the autonomy of the intelligentsia (Mannheim 1936), and of rationalizing colonial administration (Malinowski 1929, 1930).

Some years after the start of the LSE, the Webbs drew three like-minded anthropologists from Cambridge into the School. Haddon had long been a socialist critic of British imperial aggression (Stocking 1993) and made regular pleas for the combined rational-ization and humanization of colonial rule (Haddon 1891, 1897, 1921). Rivers started a single-minded scholarly career before moving through similar pleas for a more ethical colonial policy to succeeding Sidney Webb as Labour candidate of the London university constituency (Slobodin 1978: 79–80). Together with Seligmann, fellow-member of the Torres Straits expedition, they not only initiated the practice of intensive fieldwork, but also came as part-time teachers from Cambridge to the LSE, to educate, among others, Malinowski and Radcliffe-Brown. Just as the Webbs and Wallas thought to permeate the civil service through working upwards from the system of municipal local government (Mackenzie and Mackenzie 1977: 108–10), so did Rivers argue for educating young colonial officials in anthropology. This was so they could work themselves up through the colonial hierarchy until anthropology had permeated to the proconsular level, where the governors themselves would then work towards the material and moral welfare of 'subject peoples' (Rivers 1917: 325). This plea for anthropological training was orchestrated in co-operation with a number of former British Indian officials who shared more or less the same language and method (Risley 1890, 1911; Temple 1914). Together with Lord Lugard, a later favourite of the Labour government (when Sidney Webb was its Colonial Secretary), they pleaded that a moral approach would be to let subject peoples 'develop on their own lines' as much as possible (Haddon 1921: 52, 61; Lugard 1921; Rivers 1917: 305). As Haddon said, that would be a truly civilized 'charity' (1921: 62).

The shared moral elevation of the trainers of a new breed of civil and colonial servants was successful, to some extent, in the circles of the LSE's civil service training, but the anthropologists struggled long and unsuccessfully for government support until, again, the LSE became their springboard in the late 1920s with Rockefeller finance (Stocking 1985).[12] More importantly, this meant that both groups co-operated in transforming the isolated and morally elevated romantic self into the persona of the professional civil servant, a process that culminated in Malinowski's lament that he was now forced to exchange the romantic antiquarianism of a previous anthropology by the 'sense of power given by the formulation of scientific laws' (1930: 408). Sharing an ethics of 'service' to government bureaucracies, Malinowski's teachers as well as the LSE Fabians also complicated that sense of service by claiming to have to educate the governmental bureaucracy so it could better serve the underprivileged groups in society. Haddon told colonial administrators to 'Know, Then, Thyself' (1921: 36), and he was echoed by Rivers, who accused colonial rulers of being too satisfied with their own imperfect knowledge (1917: 307).

The anthropologists thus presented themselves, like the Romantics, as their own measure, being able to both judge and remedy an imperfect world. At first, they did this, like the Webbs and their fellows, by claiming the authority of advanced technologies of domination, and particularly of the novel, large-scale methods of the statistical survey (which, at that time, was still predominantly a counting and classifying, rather than calculating operation; Risley 1911; Rivers 1917: 323). However, this landed them in paradox, for if their theory proclaimed their superiority over colonial servants to judge what was good colonial government, they also avowed that determining policy was not their province (Haddon 1921: 35). Coupled to the fact that the new methods of survey research were rapidly spreading in colonial bureaucracies, this may help to explain why Malinowski's teachers were largely unsuccessful in their pleas for support for anthropology.

The dilemma is typical of the ethic of a professional civil servant: to the extent that he is a servant who 'value-freely' serves the status quo, he denies the rebellious independence that is part of the claim to expertise; but when the ethical imperative inherent in this expertise is put forward, the independence claimed through the status of being a value-free servant is denied. This dilemma can also be found in the statements about practical anthropology by

Malinowski and his pupils (Malinowski 1929, 1930; Wilson 1940). It is a specific version of the general liberal dilemma, that there will always be a moment at which liberalism will illiberally turn against those whom it perceives as not (yet) liberal (enough), in order to convert them into its own image (Parekh 1995). With Malinowski however, the technology of the self that carried this liberal dilemma would change, shifting the isolation of the self of the critical professional civil servant who was completely at home neither in his own ethical superiority nor in his practical service, to a different set of practices. This change was a methodological shift: from Haddon's and Rivers' emphasis on the large-scale surveys which encompassed what they called 'intensive' work, to their pupils' more exclusive reliance on the latter. This meant the reintroduction of confession, as a technology of the self, to the constitution of the anthropological subject.

In a sense, all scientific methodologies are technologies of the self, for they are meant to constitute a subject that is universal and transparent, a non-presence that can serve as a perfectly neutral carrier of truth. As the dilemma of Haddon, Rivers, Malinowski and Wilson shows, this discursive non-presence is at odds with the superior moral presence of the social critic. 'Method', here, is also a form of social distinction, a way to isolate the expert's Fact from the critic's Value. However, the distinction by means of the survey methods employed by Haddon, Rivers and their friends in the colonial service did not work in practice because the surveys were products of the colonial service itself, developed and practised by colonial servants long before anthropology became institutionalized and before the anthropologist Galton started to develop them into the more quantitative forms of statistics we know today (Pels 1999b, 2000, n.d.). In the early twentieth century, the development of quantitative statistics became the stronger language of social science, pushing the more qualitative elements of ethnography to the margin (Asad 1994). At the same time, however, the Ethnographer acquired an new expert identity, one that *did* provide distinction vis-á-vis the colonial establishment: the identity of the professional fieldworker. It is only in a discipline that has to constitute the self as *both* a measuring instrument *and* a detached observer – in other words, one that relies on ethnographic fieldwork – that confession becomes a structural part of the methodological discourse of the 'expert'.

Let us go through the well-thumbed pages of the introduction to *Argonauts of the Western Pacific* once more, and note that, not unlike Rousseau, Malinowski claims to present a methodical self more 'candid and above board' than that shown by other field-workers up to now, so that the 'searchlight of methodic sincerity' can shine over an account of the 'actual experiences' that led to the conclusions he has drawn (1922: 2–3). He gives us a picture of the untutored self or 'untrained mind' of the 'average practical man' (1922: 5) and sets himself up as the purified Ethnographer, who works on his self by methodology, adopting 'real scientific aims', putting himself into 'good conditions of work', that is, as far away from other white men as possible, and disciplining himself through the operation of 'collecting, manipulating and fixing' data in writing, such that even the 'personal equation' becomes visible (1922: 6, 20). Here, the individual constitutes himself in isolation, not just in the imagination, but by actual travel, an isolation from his own society which he presents in a kind of bragging confession (which, as we know now, was itself isolated from his imperfect self, appearing in yet another piece of confessional writing, his diary [Malinowski 1989]). This isolation was maintained for a long time in subsequent ethnography by the division between an all-too brief introductory preface (couched in the 'I–you' interaction of writer and reader) and a correspondingly long ethnography of others (the 'they' of the ethnographic present; cf. Fabian 1983: 85). It was only with the publication of Bohannan's confessional (Bowen 1954) that the confession genre got its book-length elaboration in professional anthropology; although that does not deny that it was a structural presence from the publication of *Argonauts* onwards.

Malinowski's introduction stands out, then, in the way it isolates the Ethnographer from his surroundings, emphasizing that his self needs to be tutored away from his own, white society. The 'native' is largely absent from this introductory account as well, appearing as marginal nuisance ('surfeit of native' [1922: 6]) or at the most as an abstract and passive 'native point of view'. The introduction to *Argonauts* is the antithesis of the ethnography itself, a preparation of self for a reading public by means of confession, which construes the Ethnographer in such a way that he can legitimately pose as a neutral channel of information about 'them'. It remained the major exemplar of the genre until, from 1954, more strictly autobio-graphical confessions began to emerge, where the Ethnographer did not appear in an invulnerable and purified way (e.g. Bowen 1954, Read 1960, Powdermaker 1966). The contrast between the constitution of self as a kind of neutral non-presence in *Argonauts* and the vulnerable presence of the person of the ethnographer in the later confessions indicates the double life of the liberal self, its simultaneous posing as an untutored self and as the standard towards which it needs to be tutored. But both forms of the genre show that anthropology, from about the time of the adoption of fieldwork as the outward sign of anthropological professionalism,[13] created its own specific interiority, a space hidden from public scrutiny by a 'conspiracy of silence' (Berreman 1962: 4).[14] It is not so much that fieldwork operations were a professional secret, a kind of emperor's clothes better hidden from lay views; nor that fieldwork was a superior kind of methodological expertise that anthropologists kept to themselves. Rather, the conspiracy of silence around fieldwork constituted a private sphere within the public performance of the profession, a liberal division of the anthropologist's self against his or her everyday self, which became especially clear in relation to students to whom the fieldwork moment was made to appear as a kind of initiation, a public secret that hid the actual work on the self from the explicitly stated canons of the profession.

Ethics, methodology and the politics of the field

Thus, from the 1930s onwards, the confessional discourse on method served as a kind of screen, a form of visibility on which the anthropological expert's self-image was projected for the audiences of sponsors, students and other non-initiates. Methodology, being 'prophylactic in its essence' (Andreski 1973: 115), screened off existing political relations with the people researched to portray the anthropologist as a neutral expert or authoritative teacher. In the 1960s, this immaculate conception of expertise, based on neutralizing and depoliticizing the presence of the anthropologist in the field, was increasingly questioned by the book-length ethnographic confessional and more analytic approaches of the fieldwork relationship (Berreman 1962; Bowen 1954; Read 1960; Powdermaker 1966). It seems no coincidence that, at the same time, and sometimes by the same scholars, the ethics of anthropological research were explicitly put on the agenda. Ethics, like methodology, distils responsible fieldwork from the murky politics of fieldwork. Like methodology, ethics works to isolate research ideals from the political relationships in which they necessarily have to operate. As I have argued elsewhere, there is a discursive parallelism between 'ethics' and 'truth': both evoke statements that are supposed to be immune to politics, yet need politics to exist (Pels 1999a: 104). By identifying the prophylactic nature of ethics and methodology, we can now see that the parallelism extends to the liberal technologies of self used to produce ethical and truthful statements. Both are representations of research relationships that have filtered out the political nature of these relationships; both, therefore, *perform* as well as represent fieldwork for non-expert audiences.

Professional ethics and methodology alike exemplify the liberal tendency to neutralize and depoliticize political relationships by constituting the self in isolation from the political interactions in which it necessarily has to operate. In the case of methodology, a first step was made when Malinowski, in his fieldwork confessional introducing *Argonauts,* portrayed the 'average practical man' – which, in effect, included the representatives of the powers that be – as an untutored self that did not have a legitimate place in the fieldwork relationship; his second step being, of course, the part-erasure of his own presence in the field by relegating much of it to his fieldwork diary. However, this could not exorcize the ambivalence about the political relationships in which anthropologists were caught, by claiming both expertise on policy effectiveness and at the same time subordinating themselves to the policy-makers to whom their 'value-free' expertise was offered. Ethics became more central to anthropological identity when, in the 1960s, the subservience to policies made by others was called into doubt, a position that is clear from the clause in the 1967 AAA Statement on ethics that '[e]xcept in the event of a declaration of war by the Congress, academic institutions should not undertake activities or accept contracts in anthropology that are not related to their normal functions of teaching, research, and public service' (Fluehr-Lobban 1991: 244). As Schmitt argued, the *jus belli* is the supreme example of the modern state's political autonomy, a declaration of sovereignty to which any legal, ethical or economic consideration will become subordinate (Schmitt 1996: 45–6). Thus, we may read this statement as an attempt by anthropologists to restrict to a minimum the political appeal that the nation-state of which they are citizens can make on them. It was prompted by the fear that the reputation of anthropology would be tarnished by its involvement in counter-insurgency work in Latin America or Southeast Asia, but in the era of decolonization the inequalities and politics of fieldwork were of course a more general concern. Ethics was a way to protect, however weakly, anthropologists from these political relationships.[15]

It is essential to set this development within anthropology in context: the context not only of increasing suspicion, in what was then called the Third World, towards anthropological research, but also of the demise of modernization theory (Wallerstein 1976) and the grudging recognition that the Third World might have different trajectories of development from those offered from the 'West' (for example, Spiro 1966). Just as modernization theory had presupposed a historical subject – the West – at the centre, that could formulate directions of 'development' in relative isolation from the target societies that were to be developed, just so anthropology tried to maintain, in the figure of the 'pure' academic researcher who occasionally stooped to 'applied' anthropology, a similar isolation of expertise – often directly related to the establishment that was empowered by the discourse of 'development' and modernization. The formulation of the Principles of Professional Responsibility, with its declaration of the paramountcy of the welfare of the people studied, needs to be understood against the background of the demise of (supremely liberalist) modernization theory and its relative isolation of the West as historical subject. It seems no coincidence, therefore, that the same period also saw a comparable attempt to undo the isolation of the self constituted by (confessional) methodology.

This development can, I think, be approached by discussing Castaneda's *The Teachings of Don Juan* (1968), published shortly after the first explicit statement on ethics by AAA members (1967: see Fluehr-Lobban 1991: 243–46) and the appearance of the most sensational fieldwork confession (Malinowski 1989 [1967]). Although, for obvious reasons (see below), Castaneda's book has rarely been acknowledged as such, it is possible to regard it as an early critique of the depoliticized and isolated methodical subject, one that provided the way for the critical and 'dialogical' conceptions of anthropological fieldwork advocated explicitly in the decade to follow (Dwyer 1977; Fabian 1971; Scholte 1974; Tedlock 1979). More important, perhaps, its subsequent career can also be taken as an example why the dialogical conception of fieldwork *did not work* in the experimental ethnography that would emerge in the neo-liberal 1980s. As such, Castaneda's work can be taken as giving the lie (literally) to both the liberal isolation of the self in ethnography, and its reconstitution in terms of a new romantic ethics of dialogue that was supposed to replace it during the heyday of neo-liberalism.

The story is familiar: the young Peruvian Castaneda came to California and became acquainted with psychical research, New Age mysticism, Huxley's *The Doors of Perception* and psychedelic mushrooms (Castaneda 1997). He enrolled in anthropology at UCLA and started to produce the personality of Don Juan Matus, a 'Yaqui man of knowledge' or sorcerer who introduced him to a 'nonordinary reality' that satisfied all the wants of the late 1960s and early 1970s New Age audience, which bought bestseller after bestseller. Despite early doubts about the authenticity of Don Juan and of Castaneda's fieldwork by some of his supervisors (Beals 1978; but see also Spicer 1969), Castaneda earned a PhD in anthropology from UCLA for a manuscript that was his third bestseller, *Journey to Ixtlan* (1972), 'plus an abstract in academic language' (Murray 1979: 190). Despite widespread suspicions, Castaneda's work was seen as inspiring by many anthropologists (Douglas 1973; Goldschmidt 1968; Silverman 1975; Wilk 1978; Willis 1985: 479) and it was not until recently, a few years before his death, that Castaneda's status as 'illusionist' or 'con and mystic' was definitely established (Castaneda 1997; Fikes 1993; De Jong 1998).

One could say that, as in all largely autobiographical anthropological stories, the proportion of confessional versus objective ethnography of *Argonauts* has been reversed in Castaneda's first text, but with a subtle difference: it is not an experience that constitutes the self as much as one that records its change under the influence of a powerful 'other', the Native American guru Don Juan. As one of the positive reactions to Castaneda's books had it, Castaneda 'accepted the reality of his experience rather than the reality of his enculturation' (Wilk 1977: 85), while another said the importance of Castaneda's work was the practice of 'thinking together' (Silverman 1975). This celebrated a romantic reversal of the isolation of the self: now, anthropological methodology confessed its weakness in the face of, and need for reform by, the superior modes of perception of the 'Yaqui' sorcerer. In that sense, and also if one looks at the bulk of the text of *The Teachings* and the other books, Castaneda's work can be interpreted as the harbinger of 'dialogical' anthropology: an ethnography that not merely records the other, but also allows him to change the cosmology of the observing self. As Goldschmidt (1968: viii), then chair of the UCLA anthropology department, put it in introducing Castaneda's book:

> The central importance of entering into worlds other than our own – and hence of anthropology itself – lies in the fact that the experience leads us to understand that our own world is also a cultural construct. By experiencing other worlds, then, we see our own for what it is and are thereby enabled also to see fleetingly what the real world, the one between our own cultural construct and those other worlds, must in fact be like.

Thus, ethnography is also allegory, as later theorists of a dialogical anthropology argued as well (Goldschmidt 1968: vii; cf. Clifford 1986). This seems to validate Castaneda's work as a kind of fulfilment of a hidden promise of anthropology, and it seems that the hiding of that promise was done by existing anthropological theory and methodology. Silverman read Castaneda as providing an alternative understanding of methodology in sociology (1975: 35ff.). Like Wilk, he argued for a primacy of (communal) experience that went before and beyond methodology and validated itself and the methods used (Silverman 1975: 39; Wilk 1978: 363). Even anthropologists who were not happy with Castaneda's 'minimal concern for methodology' recognized the value of 'the experiential approach' (Maquet 1978: 362–3). One might look upon the 50–page 'structural analysis' that follows the 200 pages of dialogical ethnography of *The Teachings* as a tongue-in-cheek reference to this subversion of the necessarily ethnocentric primacy of theory and methodology in anthropology.[16] The implication seemed to be that methodology had to be discarded as a technology of the anthropological subject, for it interfered with the 'subjectivization' of the researcher by a (powerful) other. Comparing this to the first article of the PPR, it seems that Castaneda indeed portrayed the interests of the researched as paramount.

But this debunking of the prophylactic function of methodology in favour of prolific experience runs into the objection that Castaneda *imagined* this powerful other, that is, he appears to have constructed him from a potpourri of Aldous Huxley, New Age gurus, and Huichol shamans in the isolation of study and library rather than in the dialogue of the field (Castaneda 1997; Fikes 1993). On the one hand, this led to accusations of unethical behaviour: to some, Castaneda should have been 'defrocked', and, even if not, his PhD retracted and the AAA called upon to publicly investigate his fraud (Murray 1979: 191). On the other, others argued from early on that the invention of Don Juan did not matter: even if believing in his real existence was always an 'act of faith' (Beals 1978: 359), his personality was an important addition to general literature (Roszak 1971: 732), or to that of social science in particular (Douglas 1975: Silverman 1975). Crapanzano (1973: 472), one of the more percipient investigators of the dialogical turn in anthropology argued that, indeed, the presence of the texts of Castaneda showed how anthropological methodology and writing attempted to evade the full brunt of the political confrontation with otherness:

> Professional anthropology, traditionally and somewhat naively, tries to evade the experience, to bracket off the 'I', in order to arrive at an 'objective account' of the 'culture', the 'social organisation', the 'religion' of the people under study. Insofar as it fails to acknowledge that the 'I' can only be bracketed off for heuristic or rhetorical purposes, . . . it remains a discipline in bad faith.

But instead of joining the ranks of Castaneda's defenders, Crapanzano went on to argue that Castaneda's books displayed a 'quest structure' that may explain their popularity but also 'inevitably distort[s] the reality which is that of everyday life and which is in fact the subject matter of anthropology' (1973: 473). (This argument was repeated in a discussion between an Africanist sorcerer's apprentice and his critic [Stoller and Olkes 1987; Olivier de Sardan 1992].) This quest structure is an important part of Western New Age narratives of conversion to esoteric truths under the tutelage of a guru. Thus, the attack on the artificial methodological isolation of the anthropological subject is itself based on a typical genre of romanticism, a confession that *performs* a revelation of otherness. As in Rousseau's confessions, the acceptance of this performing subject as an actual revelation of self is based on an act of faith in the subject's self-construction (Gutman 1988: 112).

Castaneda's work shows that a form of liberal isolation emerges not only from performances of methodical or ethical responsibility, but from the practice of ethnographic confessional writing as such. His *Teachings* show that ethnography is, by definition, based on an act of faith in its self-presentation. In our written reports, the 'possessive past' of 'having been there', converted to or immersed in another way of life, is the substitute for ethnography's incapacity 'to carry [its] appropriate contexts with [it]' (Stewart 1994: 55). This absence of other-than-textual grounds for authenticity creates the space for ethnographic betrayal and forgery (Fabian 1983: 94). Thus we come to a recognition of the slippage between the sense of authenticity of self and other produced by a confession like Castaneda's (for, in the end, he confesses to have run away from the tasks facing a 'man of knowledge': Castaneda 1968: 198; cf. also Stoller and Olkes 1987: 229), and the facticity of the experiences on which it says it is based. To be sure, this facticity is itself autobiographic (Fabian 1983: 89), which shows that in anthropology objectivity can never but be confessional, based on an act of faith in the self thus constituted. This is in itself a damning indictment of ethnographic experimentation, or the reform of self through text, for it shows that the experimentation with the ethnographic genre can itself function as a prophylactic of the political relations of fieldwork, by, as Said wrote, producing 'scrubbed and desinfected interlocutors' (Said 1989: 211; cf. Fabian 1991: 193–4). To bring this back to a wider historical context, it is only necessary to acknowledge the argument that many neo-liberal strategies towards the recognition of dialogue in development – in terms of 'indigenous knowledge systems' or 'participatory development' – can equally serve as manipulative tricks to safeguard the interests of people in power (Esteva 1992: 7–8).

Can we put politics back in?

This discussion of methodology and confession as technologies of the anthropological self leads to the conclusion that, whether they function as public performance or as the constitution of a hidden sphere of expertise and experience (and ethics in the time of audit does both), they may hamper our own understanding of the politics of the way we work. One can ask whether there is a way to process ethnographic experience that does not fall victim to the liberal isolation of the self that lies at the heart of this. To be sure, there are a number of standard professional power relationships that individual anthropologists cannot escape without cost: the power of the publishing industry, which entrenches authorship in such a way that it is difficult if not impossible to change it by means of textual experiments (Fabian 1991: 193–4; Pool 1991); the power of the academic industry and its standards of 'pure' research, which may allow native 'voices' but has difficulty with finding ways of granting them political agency; the inequalities that, on a global scale, condition the interaction of contexts in which anthropologists produce texts. Moreover, there are indications that anthropology is currently going through a process a *deprofessionalization*: anthropologists seem to lose much of their former legitimacy as independently operating and academically trained welfare experts by the combined effects of changing conditions of employment under neo-liberal market models and the increasingly vocal dissent of people researched. If, at the height of its career, during the late colonial period, the anthropological profession was caught in an ambiguous relationship of servicing the powers that be on the one hand, while representing the interests of the people studied on the other, its ambiguities are now compounded insofar as the independence of the expert in 'culture' is being eroded by the democratization of the use of 'culture' on both sides.

Of course, this is not a situation that lends itself to facile conclusions. However, there are three existing directions of investigation which might be added to the creative ways of coping with this situation (for example: Wright 1995), based on the three forms discussed above: confession, methodology and ethics.

First, we need to think about the possibility of producing *agonistic confessions*. Ethnography may only be able to undo the isolated persona of its authority and reintroduce the politics of anthropological work by explicating the practical management of the aporia of research. If we want to move beyond the deconstructions of the anthropological subject that have been the (most worthwhile) occupation of anthropologists until recently, we may want to explore an ethnography of the fieldwork situation that, instead of leading to disciplinary introspection, may provide excellent material for an anthropology of modernity. After all, the powerful languages of the academy and of other dominant global institutions are very often deconstructed by the people researched – a situation that, as I argued elsewhere, does not only produce knowledge about the ethnographer's personal failures but, much more important, gives positive indications of how the regimes of representation and the politics of perception common to modernity are reinterpreted, transformed or resisted by people encountered in the practice of research (Van Dijk and Pels 1996). Thus, the failures of a fieldwork encounter may provide a site and topos for the anthropology of modernity (cf. Escobar 1995: 11) that remains, I feel, insufficiently explored, and should be crucial to any attempt to make anthropology relevant to present-day postcolonial encounters.

Second, we need to *historicize methodology*. A sizeable literature has begun to explore how methodology itself functions as a modern political device in the practical history of anthropology (among others, Cohn 1987; Dirks 1993, 1999; Fabian 1983; Ludden 1993; Pels 1999b). The most obvious implication of these findings is that, methodologically speaking, we are no longer able to reduce our research engagements to a dyad of ethnographer and people researched: as the critique of anthropology since the 1960s has made clear, anthropology cannot be understood without situating it in different locations of the production of knowledge, where 'third parties' that establish authoritative values have varying, but usually dominant, capacities of determining the outcome (for an overview, see Pels and Salemink 1999). Locating anthropological work once more in the triad of powers that be, ethnographer, and people ethnographized will serve to return our methodological arguments to the question for whom method is being invoked. It raises, therefore, the issue of the politics of method, providing yet another site for the ethnographic investigation of modernity.

Lastly, we need an investigation of the possibility of an *emergent ethics*, one which is no longer tied to a specific community (such as a professional association) but which locates ethical discussion in the negotiation of individual or communal interests that is characteristic of the practice of fieldwork. Instead of relying on quasi-legal and quasi-professional sets of standards, of which we already have a number anyway, this would bring forward the moral practice inherent in ethnography as an exemplar, to instruct and guide non-anthropologists in ways of moral negotiation. Anthropologists' professional situations seem to shift from a former emphasis on legitimate intervention in, or adequate representation of, societies studied, towards one in which the expertise of negotiating between people studied and powers that be becomes more prominent (Pels 1999a: 112). In such situations, a relational and contingent constitution of the anthropological subject seems more appropriate than that of the isolated liberal self that 'humanistically' sets itself up as the source of value.

To recapitulate, ethnographers might agonistically confess how they failed to intellectually and physically realize the values (of sponsor or academy) they brought into research, in relation to those to which they were subjected by people researched; they can do this by recounting the politics of method used to make room for those antagonistic values; and by relating the emergent compromises or antagonisms that this confrontation produced. This would, I feel, maintain the promise of the critical discussion of anthropological ethics which characterized the production of the ethical codes of the 1960s and 1970s, without stultifying the discussion in the way that the specific technology of self of quasi-legal ethics has done.

Afterword: the trickster's privacy

And yet, has this conclusion any realistic potential? Recall one argument running through part of this chapter: the constitution of an anthropological 'interior', a private self which is familiar during fieldwork but which often has to be hidden, to make room for the pragmatic performances of disciplinary competences, whether directed at teachers, funding agencies or employers. What about our privacy, the interior that safeguarded our independence if not our expertise, when we confess to political struggle rather than distanced observation, particularize our methodologies, and show we are moral bricoleurs? Does not this mean that, when we put politics back in, it comes back with a vengeance? For the implication of resituating anthropological research in the triad of powers that be, researcher and researched may be that, as individual researchers, we can never find an audience to which we can show a 'true' face: 'impression management' towards both sponsors and people researched will be the only way to continue our existence as (paid and accepted) ethnographers. There is, clearly, a contingent limit to showing what one's politics is about. Maybe that has been the case all along; maybe anthropologists have always been forced to maintain the secret that, in the end, they can never be completely trusted by anyone, because there are no overarching values to which any of their projected audiences can definitely hold them. Contrary to what is usually maintained by liberal political theory, the guarding of secrets can be a supremely moral practice. But which form of publicity will convince the audiences on whom we depend that that is the case?

The answer to that question lies in our practice and its efficacy in the future. However, we may be on the wrong track if we define this publicity in defensive terms, of merely telling sponsors and people researched that our ethics and methods are, after all, responsible and effective. In a world where audit and accountability spell the further increase of the power of the languages of quantification and statistics (cf. Asad 1994), the best defence may be attack – an attack on the illusions of quantitative measures and models that have been devised in splendid isolation and are easily appropriated by the powers that be; and concomitantly, a moral critique of those methods that, I feel, can be demonstrated to be far less ethically *responsible* than the qualitative negotiations of ethnography. Thus, we can work on an ethnography of modernity that is, at the same time, a critical engagement with our present.

Acknowledgements

This chapter was presented at a panel on 'Ethics and other technologies of self', American Anthropological Association meetings, Philadelphia, 1998; I thank the participants for their constructive comments. Some of the arguments presented in Pels 1999a are also included here.

Notes

1 This is, of course, surprising given the broad base of the critical discussions that preceded the drawing up of the first professional code of conduct, the AAA's 'Principles of Professional Responsibility' (see below).
2 Studied here on the basis of British, American and Dutch examples.
3 For example, the British ASA, the start of which can be seen as an attempt to separate out academic anthropologists from the more broadly 'amateur' Royal Anthropological Society (Leach, quoted in Wright 1995: 67).
4 As Nader argues, however, the question of the professionalization of anthropology requires further thinking and research (see her comment to Pels 1999a).
5 See the remarks on the co-operation between Malinowski, Lugard and the missionary Oldham in Bennett (1960) and Cell (1989).
6 Eventually, this led to a division of opinions: the sociologists adopted a new code on the model of a recent code drafted for the American Sociological Association, and the anthropologists followed my advice in refraining from drafting a new code and putting more energy into the attempt to include ethical discussion in anthropological education.

7 In the interests of the parties concerned, I refrain from providing more details.
8 In the 1967 Statement on Problems of Anthropological Research and Ethics that preceded the formulation of the PPR, this untutored anthropological self was made even more specific by the mention of people 'falsely [claiming] to be anthropologists' (Fluehr-Lobban 1991: 246).
9 Even if this notion of the good' is amoral, as is the case with the scientific ideal of truth.
10 This shows the Christian background of liberal ethics: a similar distinction between the freedom of religious belief of Europeans and the duty to missionize those who had not yet achieved such freedom of religious choice in the colonies was a fundamental aspect of the transformation of modern religion and the concomitant definition of a liberal public sphere (Van der Veer 1995; Van Rooden 1995).
11 This development did not occur without social struggle, concentrating, in part, on the rise of the medical establishment to power (Pels 2000).
12 Which shows that the new welfare ideologies also appealed to the US American administrators of Rockefeller Foundation money.
13 Which, one should add, was parasitic on the adoption, by Haddon and Rivers, of the fieldwork method as such (Stocking 1983).
14 Or, alternatively, a conspiracy of eloquence, as when Kroeber pulled out the fattest ethnography from his shelf telling his student, 'Go forth and do likewise' (Nader 1970: 98).
15 Here note that the involvement of anthropologists in the Allied effort during World War Two shows that this ethical protection could be easily superseded by political objectives (Robben 1999: 122).
16 Bob Scholte, personal communication. Douglas (1975: 194–5) interpreted the 'structural scheme' as drafted by Castaneda's teachers and as an unsuccessful struggle by the latter against the wisdom of Don Juan.

References

Andreski, St (1973) *Social Sciences as Sorcery*, Harmondsworth: Penguin Books.

Asad, T. (1994) 'Ethnographic Representation, Statistics and Modern Power', *Social Research* 61: 55–88.

Beals, R. (1978) 'Sonoran Fantasy or Coming of Age?', *American Anthropologist* 80: 355–62.

Bennett, G. (1960) 'Paramountcy to Partnership: J.H. Oldham and Africa', *Africa* 30: 356–60.

Berreman, G. D. (1962) *Behind Many Masks. Ethnography and Impression Management in a Himalayan Village*, Ithaca, NY: Society for Applied Anthropology.

—— (1991) 'Ethics versus "Realism" in Anthropology', in C. Fluehr-Lobban (ed.) *Ethics and the Profession of Anthropology. Dialogue for a New Era*, Philadelphia: University of Pennsylvania Press.

Bowen, E. Smith (pseudonym of L. Bohannan) (1954) *Return to Laughter. An Anthropological Novel*, New York: Doubleday & Co.

Campbell, C. (1987) *The Romantic Ethic and the Spirit of Modern Consumerism*, Oxford/Cambridge, Mass.: Blackwell.

Carr-Saunders, A. M., and P. A. Wilson (1933) *The Professions*, Oxford: Clarendon Press.

Castaneda, C. (1968) *The Teachings of Don Juan. A Yaqui Way of Knowledge*, New York: Ballantine Books [1969].

—— (1972) *Journey to Ixtlan. The Lessons of Don Juan*, New York: Pocket Books [1974].

Castaneda, M. R. (1997) *A Magical Journey with Carlos Castaneda*, Victoria: Millenia Press.

Cell, J. W. (1989) 'Lord Hailey and the Making of the African Survey', *African Affairs* 88: 481–505.

Clifford, J. (1986) 'On Ethnographic Allegory', in J. Clifford and G. Marcus (eds) *Writing Culture. The Poetics and Politics of Ethnography*, Berkeley: University of California Press.

Cohn, B. (1987) 'The Census, Social Structure and Objectification in South Asia', in B. Cohn, *An Anthropologist Among the Historians and Other Essays*, Delhi: Oxford University Press.

Crapanzano, V. (1973) 'Popular Anthropology', *Partisan Review* XL: 471–82.

De Jong, S. (1998) 'Getroebleerd zoeker' ('Troubled seeker'; obituary of Carlos Castaneda), *NRC-Handelsblad*, 19 June 1998: 6.

Dirks, N. B. (1993) 'Colonial Histories and Native Informants: Biography of an Archive', in C. Breckenridge and P. van der Veer (eds) *Orientalism and the Postcolonial Predicament*, Philadelphia: University of Pennsylvania Press.

—— (1999) 'The Crimes of Colonialism. Anthropology and the Textualization of India', in P. Pels and O. Salemink (eds) *Colonial Subjects. Essays in the Practical History of Anthropology*, Ann Arbor: University of Michigan Press.

Douglas, M. (1975) 'The Authenticity of Castaneda', in M. Douglas, *Implicit Meanings*, London: Routledge and Kegan Paul.

Dwyer, K. (1977) 'On the Dialogic of Fieldwork', *Dialectical Anthropology* 2: 143–51.

Escobar, A. (1995) *Encountering Development. The Making and Unmaking of the Third World*, Princeton: Princeton University Press.

Esteva, G. (1992) 'Development', in W. Sachs (ed.) *The Development Dictionary. A Guide to Knowledge as Power*, London and New Jersey: Zed Books.

Evans-Pritchard, E. E. (1946) 'Applied Anthropology', *Africa* XVI: 92–8.

Fabian, J. (1971) 'Language, History and Anthropology', *Philosophy of the Social Sciences* 1: 19–47.

—— (1983) *Time and the Other. How Anthropology Makes its Object*, New York: Columbia University Press.

—— (1991) 'Dilemmas of Critical Anthropology', in L. Nencel and P. Pels (eds) *Constructing Knowledge*, London: Sage.

Fikes, J. C. (1993) *Carlos Castaneda, Academic Opportunism and the Psychedelic Sixties*, Victoria: Millenia Press.

Fluehr-Lobban, C. (1991) (ed.) *Ethics and the Profession of Anthropology. Dialogue for a New Era*, Philadelphia: University of Pennsylvania Press.

Freidson, E. (1984) 'The Changing Nature of Professional Control', *Annual Review of Sociology* 10: 1–20.

Foucault, M. (1988) 'Technologies of the Self', in L.H. Martin, H. Gutman, P. H. Hutton (eds) *Technologies of the Self. A Seminar with Michel Foucault*, Amherst: The University of Massachusetts Press.

Givens, D. B. (1993) 'Ethics of Confidentiality', *AAA Newsletter* 34/7: 37.

Goldschmidt, W. (1968) 'Foreword', in C. Castaneda, *The Teachings of Don Juan. A Yaqui way of knowledge*, vii-viii, New York: Ballantine Books [1969].

—— (1979) (ed.) *The Uses of Anthropology*. Washington: American Anthropological Association, special publication no. 11.

Gutman, H. (1988) 'Rousseau's Confessions: A Technology of the Self', in L.H. Martin, H. Gutman, P.H. Hutton (eds) *Technologies of the Self. A Seminar with Michel Foucault*, 99–120. Amherst: The University of Massachusetts Press.

Habermas, J. (1989) *The Structural Transformation of the Public Sphere*. Cambridge: Polity Press.

Haddon, A. C. (1891) 'Indian Ethnography', *Nature* XLIII: 270–3.

—— (1897) 'A plea for a Bureau of Ethnology for the British Empire', *Nature* Oct. 14: 574–5.

—— (1921) *The Practical Value of Ethnology*, Conway Memorial Lecture, London: Watts & Co.

Johnson, T. J. (1973) 'The Professions', in G. Hurd (ed.) *Human Societies. An Introduction to Sociology*, London: Routledge and Kegan Paul.

Levy, J. E. (1993) 'Anthropologists and Ethical Challenges: Open Discussions at the 1993 Annual Meeting', *AAA Newsletter* 34/7: 25.

Ludden, D. (1993) 'Orientalist Empiricism', in C. Breckenridge and P. van der Veer (eds), *Orientalism and the Postcolonial Predicament*, Philadelphia: The University of Pennsylvania Press.

Lugard, Lord F. D. (1921) *The Dual Mandate in British Tropical Africa*, London: Cass (reprint 1965).

MacIntyre, A. (1984) *After Virtue. A Study in Moral Theory*, 2nd ed., Notre Dame: University of Notre Dame Press.

Mackenzie, N., and Mackenzie, J. (1977) *The First Fabians*, London: Weidenfeld and Nicolson.

Malinowski, B. (1922) *Argonauts of the Western Pacific*. London: Routledge and Kegan Paul.

—— (1929) 'Practical Anthropology', *Africa* 2: 22–38.

—— (1930) 'The Rationalization of Anthropology and Administration', *Africa* 3: 405–23.

—— (1989) *A Diary in the Strict Sense of the Term*, Stanford: Stanford University Press (first publ. 1967; 2nd ed. with a new introduction by Raymond Firth).

Mannheim, K. (1936) *Ideology and Utopia*, London: Routledge and Kegan Paul.

Maquet, J. (1978) 'Castaneda: Warrior or Scholar?', *American Anthropologist* 80: 362–3.

Martin, R. (1988) 'Truth, Power, Self: An interview with Michel Foucault', in L.H. Martin, H. Gutman, P.H. Hutton (eds), *Technologies of the Self. A Seminar with Michel Foucault*, 9–15, Amherst: The University of Massachusetts Press.

Murray, S. O. (1979) 'The Scientific Reception of Castaneda', *Contemporary Sociology* , 8/2: 189–92.

Nader, L. (1970) 'From Anguish to Exultation', in P. Golde (ed.) *Women in the Field*, Chicago: Aldine.

—— (1999) 'CA comment on Pels 1999a', *Current Anthropology* 40(2): 121–2.

Olivier de Sardan, J.-P. (1992) 'Occultism and the Ethnographic "I". The exoticizing of magic from Durkheim to "postmodern" anthropology', *Critique of Anthropology*, 12: 5–25.

Paden, W. E. (1988) 'Theaters of Humility and Suspicion: Desert Saints and New England Puritans', in L.H. Martin, H. Gutman, P.H. Hutton (eds) *Technologies of the Self. A Seminar with Michel Foucault*, Amherst: The University of Massachusetts Press.

Parekh, B. (1995) 'Liberalism and Colonialism: A critique of Locke and Mill', in J. Nederveen Pieterse and B. Parekh (eds) *The Decolonization of the Imagination. Culture, Knowledge and Power*, London: Zed Books.

Pels, P. (1999a) 'Professions of Duplexity: A Prehistory of Ethical Codes in Anthropology', *Current Anthropology* 40(2): 101–36 (with CA comments).

—— (1999b) 'The Rise and Fall of the Indian Aborigines: Orientalism, Anglicism and the Emergence of an Ethnology of India', in P. Pels and O. Salemink (eds) *Colonial Subjects. Essays in the Practical History of Anthropology*, Ann Arbor: University of Michigan Press.

—— (2000) 'Occult Truths: Race, Conjecture and Theosophy in Victorian Anthropology', in R. Handler and G.W. Stocking (eds) *Excluded Ancestors Inventible Traditions: Essays Towards a More Inclusive History of Anthropology*, History of Anthropology vol. 9, Madison: University of Wisconsin Press.

—— (n.d.) 'Colonial Service. British Anthropologists and Colonial Administrators, 1890–1946', paper presented at workshop on the history of European anthropology, 3rd EASA Conference, Oslo, June 1994.

Pels, P. and Salemink, O. (1999) 'Introduction: Locating the Colonial Subjects of Anthropology', in P. Pels and O. Salemink (eds) *Colonial Subjects. Essays in the Practical History of Anthropology*, Ann Arbor: University of Michigan Press.

Pool, R. (1991) 'Postmodern Ethnography?', *Critique of Anthropology* 11/4: 309–31.

Powdermaker, H. (1966) *Stranger and Friend. The Way of An Anthropologist*, London: Secker and Warburg.

Power, M. (1994) *The Audit Explosion*, London: Demos.

Read, K. (1960) *The High Valley*, New York: Charles Scribner's Sons.

Risley, H. H. (1890) 'The Study of Ethnology in India', *Journal of the Royal Anthropological Institute* 20: 235–63.

—— (1911) 'Presidential Address: The Methods of Research', *Journal of the Royal Anthropological Institute* 41: 8–19.

Rivers, W. H. R. (1917) 'The Government of Subject Peoples', in A.C. Seward (ed.) *Science and the Nation*, Cambridge: Cambridge University Press.

Robben, A. C. G. M. (1999) CA comment, *Current Anthropology* 40/2: 122.

Roszak, T. (1971) 'Plugged-Up Fools', *New Society*, 14 October 1971: 732–3.

Said, E. (1989) 'Representing the Colonized: Anthropology's Interlocutors', *Critical Inquiry* 15: 205–25.

Schmitt, C. (1993) 'The Age of Depoliticization and Neutralization', *Telos* 96: 130–42.

—— (1996) 'The Concept of the Political', in C. Schmitt, *The Concept of the Political*, ed. G. Schwab, 19–79, Chicago: The University of Chicago Press [orig. 1932].

Scholte, B. (1974) 'Towards a Critical and Reflexive Anthropology', in D. Hymes (ed.) *Reinventing Anthropology*, New York: Vintage Books.

Silverman, D. (1975) *Reading Castaneda: A Prologue to the Social Sciences*, Boston, London and Henley: Routledge and Kegan Paul.

Slobodin, R. (1978) *W.H.R. Rivers*. New York: Columbia University Press.

Sluka, J. (1999) 'CA comment on Pels 1999a', *Current Anthropology* 40(2): 124–6.

Spicer, E. (1969) Review of Castaneda 1968, *American Anthropologist* 71: 320–2.

Spiro, H. J. (1966) (ed.) *Africa. The Primacy of Politics*, New York: Random House.

Stewart, S. (1994) 'Psalmanazar's Others', in S. Stewart, *Crimes of Writing. Problems in the Containment of Representation,* Durham and London: Duke University Press.

Stocking, G. W. (1983) 'The Ethnographer's Magic: Fieldwork in British Anthropology from Tylor to Malinowski', in: G.W. Stocking (ed.) *Observers Observed. Essays on Ethnographic Fieldwork,* History of Anthropology, vol. 1, Madison: University of Wisconsin Press.

—— (1985) 'Philanthropoids and Vanishing Cultures: Rockefeller Funding and the End of the Museum Era in Anglo-American Anthropology', in: G.W. Stocking (ed.) *Objects and Others. Essays on Museums and Material Culture,* History of Anthropology, vol. 3, Madison: University of Wisconsin Press.

—— (1993) 'The Red-Paint of British Aggression, the Gospel of Ten-per-Cent, and the Cost of Maintaining our Ascendancy: A. C. Haddon on the Need for an Imperial Bureau of Ethnology', 1891, *History of Anthropology Newsletter* XX/1: 3–15.

Stoller, P. and Olkes, C. (1987) *In Sorcery's Shadow. A Memoir of Apprenticeship among the Songhay of Niger,* Chicago: University of Chicago Press.

Taeusch, C.F. (1933) 'Professional Ethics', in E.R.A. Seligman (ed.) *Encyclopedia of the Social Sciences,* New York: Macmillan.

Tedlock, D. (1979) 'The Analogical Tradition and the Emergence of a Dialogical Anthropology', *Journal of Anthropological Research* 35: 387–400.

Temple, Sir R. C. (1914) *Anthropology as a Practical Science,* London.

Van Dijk, R. and Pels P. (1996) 'Contested Authorities and the Politics of Perception: Deconstructing the Study of African Religion', in R. P. Werbner and T. O. Ranger (eds) *Postcolonial Identities in Africa,* London: Zed Books.

Van Rooden, P. (1995) 'Nineteenth-Century Representations of Missionary Conversion and the Transformation of Western Christianity', in P.v.d.Veer (ed.) *Conversion to Modernities: The Globalization of Christianity,* New York and London: Routledge.

Van der Veer, P. (1995) 'Introduction', in P.v.d.Veer (ed.) *Conversion to Modernities: The Globalization of Christianity,* New York & London: Routledge.

Wallerstein, I. (1976) 'Modernization: Requiescat in Pace', in I. Wallerstein (ed.) *The Capitalist World Economy. Essays,* Cambridge: Cambridge University Press, 1979.

Wilk, St (1977) 'Castaneda: Coming of Age in Sonora', *American Anthropologist* 79: 84–91.

—— (1978) 'On the Experiential Approach in Anthropology: A Reply to Maquet', *American Anthropologist* 80: 363–4.

Willis, R. (1985) 'Magic', in A. and J. Kuper (eds) *The Social Science*

Encyclopedia, London, Boston and Henley: Routledge & Kegan Paul.

Wilson, G. (1940) 'Anthropology as "Public Service"', *Africa* 13: 43–61.

Wright, S. (1995) 'Anthropology: Still the Uncomfortable Discipline?', in C. Shore and A. Ahmed (eds) *The Future of Anthropology. Its Relevance to the Contemporary World*, London: Athlone.

Chapter 6

Audited accountability and the imperative of responsibility

Beyond the primacy of the political

Ananta Giri

> The reflective spiral of the reciprocal observation of the other's self-observations does not escape the circle in which both external observation and self-observation are always a system's own observation; it does not penetrate the darkness of mutual opacity. . . . Luhmann's depiction of the self-legitimation of a politics anchored in a state apparatus begins to fall apart if systems theory is confronted with the task of 'conceiving the theory of the state from the perspective of an ethically responsible and responsive society'.
>
> Habermas 1996: 347, 342

> All that matters for the realization of society is that the component autopoietic systems should satisfy certain relations regardless of the actual structures (internal processes) through which they realize them. Accordingly, hypocrisy plays an important role in the realization of human societies, permitting human beings under stress to feign having certain properties which they abandon as soon as the stress is removed. This is why in a human society a social change takes place as a permanent phenomenon only to the extent that it is a cultural change: a revolution is a revolution only if it is an ethical revolution.
>
> Maturana 1980: xxvii

Accountability has multiple meanings, and I take it not merely as a question of procedural validation but as intimately linked to the calling of responsibility. It refers not only to being accountable for what one is expected to do or perform but to one's responsibility beyond legal minimalism, to the growth of oneself and the other and thus contributing to the creation of dignified relationships in society. Here, accountability requires a deeper ontological grounding, self-attunement and cultivation of an engaged attentiveness to the other; it is not merely procedural and epistemological, even though in the complexifying context of social systems in the process of modernization and now the postmodernization of life procedures have a role to play in fostering a climate of accountability. But what happens when procedures of accountability seem a substitute for our preparation for a life of ethical responsibility? This is the major challenge posed to us by the current onslaught of 'audit explosion' in advanced societies where audit and assessment seem to be the ubiquitous tools of accountability. At the contemporary juncture, 'accountancy becomes linked to a more general idea of accountability, and with it an expansion of the domain of auditing' (Strathern 1997: 309). Audit 'represents a very particular conception of accountability' (Power 1994: 8). 'Audits are needed when accountability can no longer be sustained by informal relations of trust alone but must be formalized, made visible and subject to independent validation' (1994: 11).

The present chapter is concerned with this contemporary logic of audited accountability. As someone not yet subject to systemic auditing to the extent colleagues in countries such as the UK and other European countries are, I wish to create a critical portrait of audited accountability as a 'discursive formation' (cf. Foucault 1972). In creating this portrait, I build upon my reading of both its defence as well critique and on my conversations with fellow social anthropologists in the UK who share their experiential perceptions of it. Such a multi-dimensional discursive portrait of audited accountability shows us its limits. One primary limitation of audit is that it is too much tied to the logic and language of a priori systems and lacks the ability to recognize emergent forms of creativity and accountability.

The audit culture could almost be drawing on the language of self-organization and autopoiesis of biological systems, but only to forget that if in the autopoiesis of the biological systems cognition plays an important role, then in the world of self-making (what 'autopoiesis' literally means), in the field of culture and society, both cognition and recognition play an important part. As Habermas (1996: 342) tells us, what goes on in the name of societal autopoiesis is the reign of 'the darkness of mutual opacity' in which 'both external observation and self-observation are always a system's own observation'. In this context, there is a need for audit to recognize creativity, performance and practice beyond the formulated eye of the system. It must now learn a new language which, to begin with, is a language of shared understanding beyond its own 'specialized semantics' (1996: 342). This does not just mean a return to the world of everyday language but attentiveness to the 'metalanguage' (Habermas 1996) inherent in ordinary language and the 'metadomain' (Maturana 1980) entailed in any act of cognition. I submit that there is now a need to recognize the creative world of emergence for which the systemic 'self-observation' of the audit culture is a very poor resource.

I further advocate that the contemporary language of audit culture, namely the language of self-observation, must be linked to the language of self-rule, self-responsibility and self-governance. Yet this linking has to be done not in the sense of a structural coupling but in a transformational praxis of *Swaraj*, or *self-rule*, proposed by Gandhi. *Swaraj* in Gandhi means not only political freedom but spiritual enlightenment; it means not only self-rule but also self-restraint and an unconditional ethical obligation of the self to the other. Gandhi's *Swaraj* is akin to Kant's idea of autonomy, and both help us not only to prepare ourselves for our imperatives of responsibilities but also transform our anthropological imagination. I conclude with the argument that anthropology now needs to break away from the modernist preoccupation with politics and the view that political awareness is the only key to emancipation of itself as a discipline and the people it works with. Now it needs to develop a moral language to talk about accountability and the imperative of responsibility. For the language both of contemporary audit and of the so-called critical anthropology is inadequate to make sense of the calling of moral responsibility – a responsibility emerging out of the conversations and dialogues between us as interacting subjects (the ethnographer and the informants, or for that matter between the auditor and the auditee) – and for this it now needs to make a dialogue with morality and not only with politics. In order to rescue anthropology from the powerful audit explosion of contemporary systems of money and power, anthropologists must learn how to fight back not only with the weapon of politics of which they are such weak performers anyway (despite their illusive sense of potency) but also with the categorical imperative of morality of Kant and Gandhi's soulforce of *Satyagraha*.

Audited accountability

The recent (1997) Dearing Committee report on higher education in the UK states almost as a guiding principle that the academic community should recognize that the autonomy of institutions can be sustained only within a framework of collective responsibility for standards, supported by the active involvement of professional bodies. According to the report, 'There is now greater emphasis on recognition of the individual as customer or consumer. People's expectations of publicly funded services have arisen and they no longer accept unquestioningly what is offered' (1997: 64, 4.59). The Committee further observes that four skills are key to the future success of graduate students: (a) communication skills; (b) numeracy; (c) the use of information technology, and (d) learning how to learn. We can immediately note here that the whole exercise is technical and governed by a technological fix. Among these skills, there is no acknowledgement of the need to cultivate appropriate virtues and appropriate moral and ethical commitments, commitments which enable us to use technology for creating dignified relations in society and a more habitable world for all of us (see MacIntyre 1999).

The report talks of collective responsibility but is this co-operative or not? To find an answer to this, let us read the following lines of Durham University's analytical account of its Continuation Audit:

> most academics feel that the University's quality assurance procedures are too much 'top down'. This in part reflects the pressure on the central administration to undertake the work associated with the University's regular quality and standard assurance and the extra burden associated with TQA. It would be desirable to be able to develop a more integrated approach with departments which would involve more visits to departments to help develop their systems and approaches. A more developmental role would be preferable to the current perception of an office which simply issues decrees. Nevertheless, the staffing position and the likely continuing squeeze on resources make it unlikely that this approach will be achievable in the immediate future.
>
> (1998: 41)

The university's statement regarding the procedure and process of audit draws three important points. First, Durham was pressured to undertake this audit exercise and in that sense it was compulsive, not co-operative. Second, the university itself recognizes that it could play a more developmental role in its interaction with departments and we must add, in its interaction with individual members of the faculty. This extension would help us realize that the unit of observation is not only the system (whether universities/departments) but the individual and the self. Third, the university does not take seriously its own expected and perceived role as a developmental agent and puts it aside on excuses such as financial squeeze. If performing one's role as an agent of development is crucial to the whole exercise of audit and the performance evaluation of teaching and research, then cannot money be arranged for this? One could argue that both the Higher Education Funding Council for England and the university have a moral responsibility to ensure this.

It is further written in University of Durham's analysis:

> The University has not found the Higher Education charter, published in 1993, to be a particularly helpful document . . . Nevertheless, in response to the publication of the Charter, the University reviewed the way in which its own procedures satisfied the requirements of the Charter and introduced a number of changes in response to this publication.
>
> (1998: 52)

Yet if the university did not find the charter of the Higher Education Funding Council helpful why could not it argue with the Council and create a charter agreeable to both parties? This was not possible because the parties were not partners and what Habermas (1993) calls a 'co-operative search for truth' was not at all a concern with the more powerful party in this interaction (HEFCE). The less powerful partner of interaction had to change its procedure without which it may not have been recognized as a university at all. And here Strathern (1997: 311) helps us understand the whole problem of recognition and one's evaporation into a cloud of non-being: 'The university's workings must be described through a set of social elements already recognizable to the auditors – if they are not there then somehow the university is not there.' Speaking of her own knowledge of Cambridge University's subjection to the process of (adminstrative) audit, Strathern writes:

> It seems to me, as an ethnographer, quite extraordinary that there was no inquiry into *how* the University worked . . . The auditors' interest is not in producing an 'organizational model' in the sense of a model of an ongoing organization with its own chracteristics, but in producing a model that would show how well Cambridge is organized to achieve its goals. And the evaluation of 'how well' is already taken care of by preexisting measures.
>
> (1997: 312, original emphasis)

Thus in the processes of interactions which constitute the regime of accountability, there is no scope for real self-description. When it is not available to powerful units such as the universities, we can only imagine the plights of individuals who belong to them.

Moreover, when universities are not able to describe their own order of existence, their ability to describe the creative world of emergence can only be guessed. Yet the description of one's realm of 'is' and 'ought' – the world of reality and possibility – is quite crucial to the generation of a critical consciousness. However, the very fact that there is in this crucial area no move from description to critical dialogue in the contemporary audit culture is not accidental. Power (1994: 19) helps us understand this:

> In audit what is being assured is the quality of control systems rather than the quality of first order operations. In such a context accountability is discharged by demonstrating the existence of such systems of control, not by demonstrating good teaching, caring, manufacturing or banking.

In this context, it is no wonder then that 'system-based audits can easily become a kind of ritual, concerned with process rather than substance, and governed by a "compliance mentality" which draws organizations away from their primary purposes' (1994: 19–20).

Ritual creates heightened energy and audit elicits a self-description of the organization in terms of constant activation, 'as though it were in a state of perpetual self-awareness, animation and explicitness' (Strathern 1997: 318). But such a mode privileges hyperaction and discourse and has no patience for quiet action and listening to the wisdom of silence (see Giri 1998a). It has been a problem with the constitution of modernity that it fails to realize the silence which exists at the mid-point of utterances. The contemporary audit culture continues this but it needs to realize that 'interaction between persons is an acute form of elicitation, and works best on a periodic base. People fall silent before they speak, and that relation is crucial to the very maintenance of relations' (Strathern n.d.: 11). And it is not just true of individuals; it is also true of systems: 'the system under scrutiny is likely to oscillate between activity and rest' (n.d.: 13).

People not only fall silent before they speak, they also fall asleep before they act, and in case of the academics, before they write. In the case of anthropologists, this sleeping can be really long, comparable in a minuscule way to the *ananta-shayana* (eternal sleep) of the Lord Vishnu of Hindu mythology. Now when the Lord is asleep, he is not inactive; he is preparing himself for the next creation, he is silently meditating to 'bring forth a world' (cf. Capra 1997). That a similar process takes place in anthropological practice was brought home in a conversation I had recently with a distinguished practitioner of the field in the UK: 'Anthropologists would go out to do fieldwork and then they will come back. But they will not publish for a long time.' They do not publish not because they are lazy but because they are reflecting on their universe of study. The contemporary audit culture with its bias towards quick visible productivity has no capacity to recognize such modes of engagement. But this is not specific to anthropology; it is integral to teaching and research in any discipline.

As Strathern (1997: 318) argues:

> In teaching there must be a lapse of time – the process [of learning] is not one of consumption but one of absorption and reformulation. In research, time must be set aside for all the wasteful and dead-end activities that precede the genuine findings. Both require otherwise non-productive periods. Yet there is almost no language in the audit culture in which to talk about productive non-productivity.

She draws our attention to the inability of the audit culture to recognize experimentations in creativity in writing, research and teaching. It is because any experimentation is outside the a priori standard of the system with which auditors go out. In the words of the UK anthropologist with whom I had a conversation: 'journals like the *Journal of the Anthropological Society of Oxford* and *Cambridge Anthropology* were published by graduate students which were well publicized and [they were] publishing all kinds of papers. But now for the members of the universities it is not to their advantage to publish in these informal places. You have a substantial amount of teaching and only a little time for publication. It is important to have standards, achieve quality, but if publishing in the refereed journals is the only option then you will not have the benefit of experimental creativity.'[1] Moreover, the same anthropologist goes on to tells us: 'It is not to your advantage to publish in many of the journals which are not refereed. If your publication is too autobiographical then it is not regarded as sufficiently within the field of anthropology. You have to produce publications in recognized places. But if the journals are controlled by particular ideological groups, then those who do not subscribe to it can feel excluded from the process. There is a kind of normal science way to do things.'

This interlocutor also tells us that there has been a general trend towards more accountability in universities and other parts of society, 'but this is not democratic accountability but bureaucratic accountability. . . . The way questions are asked make you to answer in a certain way. If you look at the form, the way questions are asked conforms to a natural scientific model. Therefore the expectation is that people would work in research groups. That is why anthropology departments have a problem. Anthropologists believe in individual research.' Therefore an in-built bias towards quantification and the application of an abstract standardized model, a model which is based on the natural sciences, is a cause for concern in coming to terms with the work of audited accountability in institutions of higher education. In this context, what Power (1994: 46) writes deserves our careful attention:

> We would benefit from having less abstract forms of portable knowledge and more respect for non-standard and tacit kinds of knowledge which are complex and close to their products . . . The tide of consumer enfranchisement may empower students in one sense but it may also impoverish them in the longer run by cultivating an aversion to difficulty, ambiguity and critique unless it is carefully managed. Courses will increasingly be designed primarily with student evaluations and other audits in mind such that teachers will avoid risk and therefore innovation.

Another cause for concern is the way audit culture creates an environment of inauthenticity and alienation in institutions of learning. The experience of one colleague at a prestigious university in the Netherlands is germane. A few years ago, there was a meeting in his department for drawing up an academic plan for the coming five years. He suggested to the meeting that everyone should be involved and that all members of the faculty should submit their teaching and research plans. But the head of department pointed out this was not to be done since 'we are making a plan not for ourselves but for the auditors'. The head went on: 'This is just a plan for the auditors and we write what the auditors would like to hear. If they like it, we get the money. Then we have the real autonomy to do what we have been doing or would like to do.' For this colleague, this is an instance of the vitualization of reality (Baudrillard 1993) where we are creating a reality which does not exist and we are writing what we are neither doing nor believing. In his words, 'The auditors are ghost-writing the script when we as authors are dead. This destroys authenticity.'

This colleague further states that his head of department had promised autonomy by writing a report the auditors would like. But in reality the result was quite different. By writing an inauthentic report, and on his own, the head mariginalized the members of his faculty, excluding them from the domain of planning and report-writing. 'While the head wanted to create autonomy, instead it only gave rise to a growing sense of alienation. There was estrangement on both sides. While members of the department no longer felt any meaningful relationship with the formal structures, the head himself was alienated in the same process. In the end he lost the support of his own colleagues and simply became the executor of a plan which he had written for the auditors and which they approved. It is exploitation in an indirect way.'[2]

The contemporary audit culture claims that it does not impose anything on either the system or the subject; rather, it works through self-audit. But 'forms of self-audit rely upon bureaucratic procedures which can in principle be used for independent verification. . . . Indeed, checklists and protocols for apparently internal purposes often derive their authority from their potential use for external verification' (Power 1994: 4–5). Two young members of the faculty of a UK university narrate their experience of going through self-audit exercises: 'They tell you that the whole process is confidential but it makes you feel rubbish; the whole process is awful. But Tom [pseudonym for the leader of the evaluation team in the anthropology department where they work] would tell you that it is a chance for you to reflect upon. But it is deeply humiliating. You speak for ten minutes and you feel better but then still the control lies with somebody else.' Such experiential responses can be better understood with the following comments: 'the "self" in the invitation to self-scrutiny turns out to be already a particular kind of self – to be judged by criteria that agree what the self is' (Strathern 1997: 313).

Audit certainly could not function without this foregrounding of a particular kind of self, a standardized self created in the image of the system. It is because in both the UK Teaching Quality Assessment (TQA) and Research Assessment Exercise (RAE), the institution, whether department or university, is given a distinct presence over and above the performance of individuals. This is a crucial problem, and we shall see in our dialogue with Gandhi and Kant how this diminution of the individual can sound a death-knell to any move for accountability. A dialogue with Maturana, the founder of the autopoietic way of thinking, also yields us such an insight.[3] Maturana is quite emphatic about the place of creativity in the emergence of systems. For Maturana, systems are emergent formations, rather than a priori fixations, and such a view of systems is crucial to going beyond the primacy of the systems logic which governs the contemporary audit culture (see Mengers 1996).

> It is only through interactions operationally not defined within the society that a component organization can undergo inter-actions that lead to the selection, in its ontogeny, of a path of structural change not confirmatory of the society that it integrates. This is why social creativity, as the generation of novel social relations, always entails interactions operationally outside the society, and necessarily leads to the generation, by the creative individuals, of modes of conduct that either change the defining relations of the society as a particular social system, or separate them from it. Social creativity is necessarily antisocial in the domain in which it takes place.
> (Maturana 1980: xxviii)[4]

Audited accountability not only privileges organizations over individuals, it has a very particular notion of organizations which are monological and teleological.

> [Yet] one can imagine that an institution such as a university will not only have diverse aims but may have conflicting and

competing ones. It may wish to do several things at once and in different arenas: not only instruct persons but also to help them think independently; not only to provide the back up for well-established research projects that have visible outcomes but also to tolerate hidden niches for the unexpected maverick or the genius . . . to foster both productivity and creativity, knowing that these sometimes go together and sometimes do not.

(Strathern 1997: 313)

The imperative of responsibility

In critical responses to the work of audited accountability, there is an implicit or explicit attempt to put all the blame on the audit culture for the bureaucratization of academic life and threat to the autonomy and creativity of individuals and institutions. But there seems to have been no self-examination on the part of critics as to whether academics and academic institutions were doing their work properly before the onset of the audit culture. Among the critics, Strathern is probably a little more self-critical, but she is more genealogical than self-critical. Strathern traces the genealogy of the preoccupation of audit with enhancement to the method of examination of institutions of higher education. Yet there is an element of irony which works against self-criticism in Strathern's genealogical treatment of audit culture as she writes in the Introduction: 'audit is almost impossible to criticize in principle – after all, it advances values that academics generally hold dear, such as responsibility, openness about outcomes'. But did and do academics as well as academic institutions really hold dear the values of responsibility and openness? Is it that their failure and lack of concern about upholding these values has contributed to the audit explosion in the first place?

As we explore these self-critical questions, let us begin with an interesting essay entitled 'Autonomy and accountability' by Simkins (1997); he writes: 'the dominating government concern which underlay the reforms was a concern that preexisting accountability mechanisms within the school system were too soft, and consequently new control mechanisms had to be established' (1997: 23). This increasing governmental control has been, at the same time, accompanied by the diminution of the role of the local body and governing body in the accounting of things. Though it is easy to blame the government for this diminution and the usurpation of the power of the local body, Sinkins urges us to realize that in the schools he studied none of the governing bodies played an accountable role. 'The factors which will influence the role which a governing body actually plays include the type of individuals which are elected and co-opted' (1997: 26), and these individuals are mostly those who go along the lines of management rather than hold the schools responsible and accountable to the standards they have set for themselves.

Therefore in the prevalent procedure of internal institutional accounting there was probably an element of incestuous self-gratification which was crying out for an answer for a long time. This problem was heightened by the elitist character of many of the academic institutions and their failure to realize that they have a role to play in the enrichment of life and public discourse in the wider society, the community. In countries such as the UK, with the walls of separation between what is called the town and the gown, this self-closure of educational institutions posed a problem of responsiveness to the expectations of the wider society. Academics now accuse audit of being a self-closed system, but academics also have to ask themselves whether they and the institutions they work with also worked as enclosed systems with only occasional inter-action with the wider society, treating it as an external environment. Taking cues from Habermas we can certainly blame audit for the propagation of a specialized semantics, but what about the language academics themselves use? In recent times, we might remind ourselves (Jacoby 1987), university-based professionals have killed the public intellectuals and speak and write in a language which ordinary people cannot understand. The language of critical academics today is beyond the comprehension of even educated citizens of society. Such an incomprehensible semantics is a reflection of withdrawal from a larger public discourse on the part of the academics and a narcissistic preoccupation with oneself and the clubs of mutual references to which the academics belong (see Giri 1995, 1998f; Kurien 1996). So if audit poses a threat to the autonomy of academic institutions, then it has not invented the problem in the first place. Moreover, we have to ask ourselves whether auditors have not learnt the use of a specialized semantics from the academics themselves. In this context, it is worth listening to the views of two persons on this. One, an engaged critic and educational experimenter in India, says: 'Earlier social scientists were writing clearly and one could understand what they were trying to say. But now it is difficult.' The other, a professor in an English university says: 'Now how many from the general public are buying anthropology books? Not many! It is because of the way they write. But the question is not just one of style. The question is taking anthropological commitment seriously and contributing to public enlightenment and public discourse.'

It is certainly true that autonomy is of deep value in the case of individuals and institutions. But is it an end in itself or is it a means to some transformational aspiration? Autonomy is linked to the quality of intersubjective relations that a unit embodies and seeks to practise (Giri 1998c). Autonomy is also linked to what Habermas (1995) calls the democratic discursive formation of will of a wider society and the public sphere. In order that a unit may be truly autonomous, it has to demonstrate, on its own, its sense of commitment and attitude of servanthood to the wider society (Giri 1998b). This of course does not mean subservience to the illogic of a majority but a dialogical creative engagement with the wider society. Secondly, an autonomous unit has to create a self-critical space for reflection and interrogation of its basic foundations (cf. Unger 1987). Autonomy is not just a pious word to utter but is a value to live for, and as a value it requires creative and critical preparation on the parts of individuals and institutions.

Therefore, if academics and academic institutions feel incensed about the threat to their autonomy by the audit culture, then they would have to create conditions of responsibility and critical self-reflection on their own before being asked by the government to do so. As the Indian social scientist Beteille (1990) has emphatically argued, academics cannot expect a benevolent state to give them autonomy and continue to preserve it. Academics themselves have to fight for it. And, for Beteille, academics have so far not shown sufficient determination about it. They have asked for autonomy of the institutions in which they work in addition to many other things such as a good salary, promotion and other securities of life. But, Beteille asks, if academics hold the value of their own autonomy so dear then are they prepared to sacrifice some of these other securities of life? And if sacrifice is a strong word in these days of self-gratification and consumption, then are they prepared to give these a secondary priority next only to the values of creativity and autonomy? And, we can add, are they prepared to be better exemplars of creativity and responsibility so that people around also feel inspired by them and realize that they are not misusing their autonomy, since without it their creativity would be hampered? He further comments on the impasse created when academics only attend to issues of autonomy and excellence and the government is left to itself insofar as issues of accountability and the checking of wastage are concerned. 'There is something wrong when academics think that their concern is only with excellence and it is up to the government to ensure accountability' (Beteille, pers. comm.).

A recent issue of *The Times Higher Education Supplement* announced the launching of a new institute for teaching and learning in the UK. This institute is aimed at being a professional body conceived and owned by the members (1998: 5). 'It would be separate both from the QAA (Quality Assessment Agency) and the government' and its approach to accreditation 'will not be a prescribed course but will enable universities to tailor a programme of professional development according to their own mission'. Thus there is a move to initiate accountability procedures within universities on their own, to be facilitated by the formation of a professional body. But such a move has to meet with the mistrust of the audit culture and the wider public regarding impartiality. Here again, instead of being defensive, we have to be properly self-critical about the interest and ability of professional bodies and associations or institutions to ensure accountability. If it is true that in audit even independent inspectors 'are not deemed trustworthy, because they are embedded within the profession' (Power 1994: 20), then auditors have not created this loss of trust in relation to professionals. It is professionals themselves who are responsible for this. Because of their expert knowledge, professionals occupy an unchallenged position in contemporary societies as the complexity of contemporary systems and the issues they deal with put them outside 'the effective controls by the demos' (Dahl 1989: 335). Yet the increasing systemic significance of professionals has not been accompanied by much effort, either institutional or subjective, 'to arouse moral consciousness within them not to use their expert knowledge and power for exploiting the ordinary people who do not have such power and knowledge' (Giri 1998b: 108). Moreover, they seem 'loath to give to their own influence the same severe and critical scrutiny they give to that of others' (Dahl 1989: 334). Added to this is the problem of what Pels calls professions of duplexity. More than the realization that the moral exhortation for standards is accompanied by 'its subsequent betrayal by particular interests' (1999: 102), Pels considers anthropology a profession of duplexity. Pels argues that this duplexity is due to the oscillation of professional morality between ethics and politics. A professional ethics with a conceit of impartiality 'only *masks* politics – the struggles between culturally specific and historically embedded interests' (1999: 103, original emphasis).

This brief encounter with professionals and professional ethics helps us understand two points. One, even with the articulation of professional ethics, it is politics which has mattered most rather than devotion to ethical ideals *per se*. Second, the problem with professional ethics has been that it has not able to adequately develop what Habermas (1990) calls 'moral consciousness and communicative action' on the part of individuals (also see, Giri 1998a). For this, we must now initiate dialogue and re-establish friendship with Kant and Gandhi, two of our greatest friends in the pilgrimage of life and human history, who have invited us to be ever wakeful to the imperatives of responsibilities in our lives.

Beyond the primacy of the political and the systematic, and the Calling of Swaraj

The notion that professional ethics masks politics has to be understood in the light of the fact that the Western philosophical tradition from Plato to Hobbes, even to Rawls, is characterized by a 'politicization of morality' – the attempt to 'derive moral principles from political considerations' (Edelman 1990: 9). Morality here is not an end in itself. Yet the imperatives of responsibility implicated in the contemporary discourse and practice of the accountability regime require us to treat morality as an end in itself, not simply as a means to some ulterior motives. Actors of institutions of higher education are accountable to themselves – the creative selves within themselves, the institutions they work with, the students with whom they work and teach, and the wider society. Fulfilling these obligations requires a moral commitment for which we get moving inspiration from Kant. Kant tells us of the autonomy of moral ends and from him we can learn that the moral autonomy and devotion to its categorical imperative is central to the autonomy of institutions. But the Kantian idea of autonomy also warns that nothing should be imposed on a moral subject. The human person has an autonomy, and the unique contribution of Kant lies in helping us realize that even while obeying a moral law as a categorical imperative one is not obeying an external command but a law which one has enacted oneself (see McCarthy 1993). 'But the law-making which determines all values must for this reason have a dignity – that is, an unconditional and incomparable worth – for the appreciation of which the word "reverence" is the only becoming expression' (Kant 1964: 103). So Kant certainly provides us with resources to critically interrogate the contemporary regime of audited accountability in as much as it works as an imposition and in whose work there is very little self-enactment and co-operation among different units and selves. A dialogue with Kant also makes us self-critical. Before criticizing audit systems as controlling mechanisms, it urges us to look into the quality of our moral commitment to the aims which we supposedly hold dear and relations of which we are parts.

Thus a Foucauldian critique of audit as a contemporary governmentality is not enough (cf. Shore and Wright 1997). There is need for a post-Foucauldian response in terms of subjective preparation and the development of moral commitment, and here Kant provides much needed reflections for self-criticism. While some interpretations of the audit culture are satisfied with treating audit as a cultural performance in which organization participants may construct their cultural performances in ways that make themselves visible to each other, both as members and managers who are in control (Afterword to this volume), the more important challenge here is to cultivate a post-Foucauldian mode of being which does not consider acquisition of power as the ultimate end of life. Kant's challenge that 'all politics must bend its knee before the right' (Kant 1795: 96) provides us with an alternative practice (Giri 1998g). Even proponents of audited accountability are realizing the significance of 'meta-values which will underpin the management of services which is a central issue for the future of reform' (Simkins 1997: 33) – and for this Gandhi also provides with us moral resources.

Autonomy or *Swaraj* is a meta-value we learn from Gandhi. If the work of audited accountability does away with the autonomy of individuals and institutions, a critique of the contemporary audit culture can be enriched by this Gandhian meta-value. *Swaraj* means self-rule or self-govermnent. Thus a Gandhian critique and reconstruction of contemporary audit exercises would expect these to be based on the *Swaraj* of individuals and institutions where self-rule and self-responsibility go together. For Gandhi makes it clear that before demanding self-rule one should prepare oneself for self-responsibility. Self-rule also must be accompanied by self-restraint and an unconditional ethical obligation on the part of the self to the other. Before demanding autonomy, one has to be worthy of it and whether one is worthy or not has to be decided by the actor concerned. Thus this ethical precondition for *Swaraj* cannot be used by systems to suppress the aspirations for autonomy. In Gandhi, the calling of *Swaraj* is accompanied by *satyagraha*, the desire for Truth. For Gandhi, 'Truth is the fundamental precondition of *Swaraj*. . . . Individually, it means that the individual is truthful and non-violent in thought, word and deed' (Vedaparayana 1998: 3/43).

Gandhi's *satyagraha* can teach us novel ways of resisting the contemporary regime of control of which audited accountability is a manifestation. Gandhi's first *satyagraha* in Ahmedabad 'involved a confrontation with the mill owners but a confrontation which was predicated not on a contest of sheer power or force but on the existence of "truth force" and thus on a deep-seated sense of ethical responsibility' (Dallmayr 1996: 7). And Gandhi's Truth presents us a challenge of adequate self-preparation for being a worthy seeker of it which 'exceeds the range of human management' (1996: 12).[5] Gandhi's *satyagraha* is a non-managerial form of action whose inspiring embodiment is the *Karmayogin*, the active doer of truth. In fact, as Dallmayr argues (1996: 15), 'Gandhi characterized himself as a *Karmayogin*, that is, an active "doer of truth" who yet refuses blandishments of control'. *Satyagraha* also contributes to the preservation of the world, to what is called *lokasangraha*.

Our previous encounter with the critique of audit culture has pointed to the problem of hyperaction generated as its consequence. Here, it is worth remembering the challenge presented to us by Strathern (1997: 320): 'Somehow we have to produce embedded knowledge: i.e. insights that are there for excavating later, when the context is right, but not until then.' Thus one of the important challenges in rethinking contemporary audit culture is to rediscover the value of quietude and quiet action and Gandhi's *satyagraha* helps us not only realize this but also realize the path of what Dallmayr (1996: 15) calls 'consecrated action'. The logic of enabling technology, to which Strathern also draws our attention, can be critically re-examined with the help of Gandhi's critique of technology. Gandhi objects to the technological fixation of human possibility and, like Heidegger, thinks that technology can conceal our being rather than help unfold it.[6] It is probably keeping this technological threat to our creative unfolding in mind that leads Strathern (1997: 319, emphasis omitted) to ask: 'How to reduce information flow; how to foster the conditions for tacit and implicit knowledge to grow unknown; how to avoid the computer-aided bibliographic search becoming a paradigm for research as such?' Finally, Gandhi helps us to explore alternatives to the 'representational fix' (cf. Strathern 1995: 98) generated by the technologization of the word, self and the world.

Gandhi's *satyagraha* teaches us to pay attention to the significance of experimental creativity in our lives and in the structuration of social systems. We have seen how audited accountability has very few resources for recognizing experimental creativity. Gandhi encourages us to be experimental but his experiments are different from scientific experimentations. His practical experiments with the others – going beyond the bounds of conventional behaviour – took place in 'the context of responsible and disciplined social action which presumed love of the other' (Srinivasan 1998: 76).[7] For the *Satyagrahi*, 'truth-seeking is not a mere attempt to secure [a] mirror-copy of some out-there object. The attempt is to transgress the relativity of their initial truths as well as that of their opponents and thereby move on to a post-relativist plane of truth' (Pantham 1996: 220).

One of his most challenging passages is the following, where Gandhi provides us a talisman to judge our actions, keeping in view the face of the poorest of the poor. He writes:

> I will give you a talisman. Whenever you are in doubt, or when the self becomes too much with you, apply the following test. Recall the face of the poorest and weakest man whom you have seen, and ask yourself if the step you contemplate is going to be of any use to him;[8] will he gain anything by it? Will it restore him to control over his own life and destiny? In other words will it lead to Swaraj for the hungry and the spiritually starving millions? Then you will find your doubts and self melting away.
>
> (Gandhi quoted in Chambers *et al.* 1989: 241)

With Gandhi, then, we – practitioners in higher education who complain about the controlling regime of the audited accountability – can ask ourselves whether our teaching leads to the enrichment of our students or not? Are we performing our duties to our students or not? Research brings many rewards for a practitioner which are far more than the reward one receives from teaching and this has led to dilemmas in the minds of many academics who now give more priority to the fame, money and power that comes out of research rather patiently labouring with students. Here, Gandhi's talisman would help us remember the face of our students and cultivate responsibility towards them. This moral responsibility would be an alternative to the contemporary move to ensure student empowerment through assessment procedures. If we feel uneasy about the representation of students as customers then the challenge lies before us to be examples and embodiments of an alternative model of relationship. Similarly, in the case of research, we can also remember the face of the other. This remembrance is particularly crucial for anthropology which has continued to study the poor and the marginalized others who constitute the bulk of the anthropological subjects. Apart from the Research Assesment Exercise of the contemporary audit culture in the UK, we also need to ask self-critical questions, such as whether the research we are doing brings enrichment and enlightenment to the people on whom we carry out our research. Thus the challenge in thinking about accountability today is to always remember the face of the other while preparing oneself for being a more responsive and responsible person. As Levinas (1995: 189; emphasis added) challenges us:

> The approach to the face is the most basic mode of responsibility. As such, the fact of the other is verticality and uprightness; it spells a relation of rectitude. *The face is not in front of me but above me . . . the face is the other who asks me not to let him die alone, as if to do so were to become an accomplice in his death.*

Acknowledgements

I am grateful to Dr Peter Pels, Filippo Osella, Caroline Osella and Mr D. P. Dash for their kind help with reference materials. The chapter has also benefited from comments of colleagues at the Institute of Anthropology, University of Copenhagen, and the Department of Cultural Anthropology and Non-Western Sociology, Free University, Amsterdam. I am grateful to Drs Georg Ulrich,

John Liep, Michael Whyte, Susanne Whyte and Philip Quayles von Ufford for many important insights; my thanks also to Professor C.T. Kurien for his comments on the chapter.

Notes

1 We should remember that capacity for experimentation is at the heart of any genuine self-organization. Paslack makes this point in his discussion of the relationship between self-organization and the new social movements. '[New Social Movement] groups not only organize themselves, whether it be a non-legally binding or associated form, but they also cultivate self-organization, and by so doing, aim at creating something like an alternative self-organization culture, which for its part, should prepare the way for the gradual transformation of the existing society into a type of self-organization society for which self-determining willingness for social experimentation is characteristic' (1990: 245).

2 This colleague further tells us: 'The culture of auditing is based on an emphasis on efficiency and consequentialism which does away with the notion of duty. In the academic field it institutes the idol of the marketplace and creates a culture of fear and competition. It makes universities battlefields where many are left wounded, some are killed, and some become managers. But managers do not realize that society becomes unmanageable as a result of management rather than the other way round'. (Cf. Mintzberg 1989.)

3 I was interested in carrying out a detailed dialogue with Maturana since he is considered a source of inspiration to contemporary systems thinking. But this would require special treatment.

4 In his recent writings, the anthropologist Ingold (1998a, 1998b) also presents such an emergent view of creativity, evolution and systems.

5 As Dallmayr (1996: 12) tells us about Gandhi's Truth: 'While psychologism tends to reduce truth to internal intuition (or a psychic state of mind), discursive epistemology – insisting on initial ignorance or fallibility – perceives truth as emerging through a process of interacting or communicative constitution or construction. What is missed in both accounts is the 'otherness' or demand-quality of truth – the aspect that search for truth while proceeding in ignorance is yet impelled by something which exceeds the range of human management or construction.'

6 In his Heideggerian appreciation of Gandhi's *Hind Swaraj*, Pillai (1985: 77) writes: 'Gandhi's participation in the life of his time was always (at the same time) an interior journey, an exploration of his being, and not just the working out of a preestablished strategy. It is this insistent questioning of himself which distinguishes his actions from all self-sanctifying "social service" based on representation. Every decision for Gandhi was simultaneously the laying open of himself.'

7 As Srinivasan (1998: 76) writes: 'All his experiments, whether in the realm of caste, communal, race or gender relations sought to de-

classify the Untouchable . . . harijan, muslim, white or women through a non-violent exchange of places and meanings within them.'

8 It may be noted here that Gandhi is deploying the term 'use' broadly, in the sense of responsibility, and not in any narrow utilitarian sense. Gandhi does not suggest an extreme position, for example, the view that the utility of what one does becomes ethical simply because it is useful for someone else. Applying the Gandhian talisman requires recognition that the pursuit of our ethico-moral engagement requires simultaneous work on self-knowledge and self-development and attentiveness to the other. In contemporary ethical discourse there is an impasse. There are thinkers such as Foucault (1986) who foreground the agenda of care of the self in our ethico-moral engagement, and others, such as Levinas (1995), who emphasize our unconditional responsibility to 'the other'. The Gandhian talisman suggests the mutual implication of both efforts; in fact the life and vision of Gandhi urges us to be attentive to both the calling of self knowledge and self-development and one's responsibility towards the other.

Bibliography

Beteille, A. (1990) 'A Career in a Declining Profession', *Minerva:* 1–20.

Baudrillard, J. (1993) *Symbolic Exchange and Death*, London: Sage.

Capra, F. (1997) *The Web of Life: A New Synthesis of Mind and Matter*, London: Flamingo.

Chambers, R., *et al.* (1989) *To the Hands of the Poor*, London: Intermediate Technology Publications.

Dahl, R. A. (1989) *Democracy and its Critics*, New Haven: Yale University Press.

Dallmayr, F. (1996) 'Satyagraha: Gandhi's Truth Revisited', paper presented at the International Congress of Vedanta: University of Madras.

'Dearing Committee' (1997) *Higher Education in the Learning Society*, Report of the National Committee of Enquiry into Higher Education, London: HMSO.

Drucker, P. (1993) *The Ecological Vision: Reflections on the American Condition*, New Brunswick, NJ: Transaction Publishers.

Edelman, J. T. (1990) *An Audience for Moral Philosophy?*, London: Macmillan.

Foucault, M. (1972) *The Archaeology of Knowledge and the Discourse on Language*, NY: Pantheon.

—— (1986) *The Care of the Self*, New York: Pantheon.

Giri, A. K. (1995) 'Universities and the Horizons of the Future', *Social Change* 25 (4): 35–43.

—— (1998a) 'Moral Consciousness and Communicative Action: From Discourse Ethics to Spiritual Transformations', *History of the Human Sciences*, 11 (3): 1–27.

—— (1998b) *Global Transformations: Postmodernity and Beyond*, Jaipur: Rawat Publications.

—— (1998c) 'Well-Being of Institutions: Problematic Justice and the Challenge of Transformations', *Sociological Bulletin*, 47 (1): 73–95.

—— (1998d) 'The Calling of an Ethics of Servanthood', *Journal of Indian Council of Philosophical Research*, xvi (1): 125–34.

—— (1998e) *Values, Ethics and Business: Challenges for Education and Management*, Jaipur: Rawat Publications.

—— (1998f) 'The Role of the Intellectuals in a Changing World', New Delhi: *University News*, 36 (22): 1–3.

—— (1998g) 'Moral Commitments and the Transformation of Politics: Kant, Gandhi and Beyond', Madras Institute of Development Studies: Working paper.

Habermas, J. (1990) *Moral Consciousness and Communicative Action*, Cambridge: Polity Press.

—— (1993) *Justification and Application: Remarks on Discourse Ethics*, Cambridge: Polity Press.

—— (1995) 'Reconciliation Through the Public Use of Reason: Remarks on John Rawl's Political Liberalism', *The Journal of Philosophy*, XC11 (3): 109–31.

—— (1996) *Between Facts and Norms: Contributions to a Discourse Theory of Law and Democracy*, Cambridge: Polity Press.

Ingold, T. (1998a) 'The Evolution of Society', in A. C. Fabian (ed.) *Evolution: Society, Science and the Universe*, Cambridge: Cambridge University Press.

—— (1998b) 'Culture, Nature, Environment: Steps to an Ecology of Life', in B. Cartledge (ed.) *Mind, Brain and the Environment*, Oxford: Oxford University Press.

Jacoby, R. (1987) *The Last Intellectuals: American Culture in an Age of Academe*, NY: Basic Books.

Kant, I. (1795) *Perpetual Peace*, NY: The Liberal Arts Press.

—— (1964) *Groundwork of the Metaphysics of Morals*, translated and analysed by H.J. Patton, NY: Harper Torch Books.

Kurien, C.T. (1996) *Rethinking Economics: Reflections based on the Study of Indian Economy*, New Delhi: Sage Publications.

Levinas, E. (1995) 'Ethics of the Infinite', in R. Kearney, *States of Mind: Dialogues with Contemporary Thinkers on the European Mind*, Manchester: Manchester University Press.

McCarthy, T. (1993) *Ideas and Illusions: On Reconstruction and Deconstruction in Contemporary Critical Theory*, Cambridge, MA: MIT Press.

MacIntyre, A. (1999) *Rational Dependent Animals*, London: Duckworth.

Maturana, H. R. (1980) 'Introduction', in H. R. Maturana and F. Varela, *Autopoiesis and Cognition: The Realization of Living*, Dordrecht: D. Riedel Publishing Co.

Mengers, J. (1996) 'A Comparision of Maturana's Autopoietic Social Theory and Giddens' Theory of Structuration', *Systems Research*, 13 (4): 469–82.

Mintzberg, H. (1989) *Inside Our Strange World of Organizations*, New York: Free Press.

Pantham, T. (1996) 'Post-Relativism in Emancipatory Thought: Gandhi's Swaraj and Satyagraha', in D. L. Sheth and A. Nandy (eds) *The Multiverse of Democracy*, New Delhi: Sage Publications.

Paslack, R. (1990) 'Self-Organization and New Social Movements', in W. Krohn *et al.* (eds) *Self-Organization: Portrait of a Scientific Revolution*, Dordecht: Kluwer Academic Publishers.

Pels, P. (1999) 'Professions of Duplexity: A Prehistory of Ethical Codes in Anthropology', *Current Anthropology*, 40: 101–36.

Pillai, P. V. (1994) 'Hind Swaraj in the Light of Heidegger's Critique of Modernity', in H. Swaraj, *A Fresh Look*, New Delhi: Gandhi Peace Foundation.

Power, M. (1994) *The Audit Explosion*, London: Demos.

Shore, C. and Wright S. (1997) 'Policy: A New Field of Anthropology', in C. Shore and S. Wright (eds) *Anthropology of Policy: Critical Perspectives on Power and Governance*, London: Routledge.

Simkins, T. (1997) 'Autonomy and Accountability', in B. Fidler *et al.* (eds.) *Choices for Self-Managing Schools: Autonomy and Accountability*, London: Paul Chapman Publishing Ltd.

Srinivasan, A. (1998) 'The Subject of Fieldwork: Malinowski and Gandhi', in M. Thapan (ed.) *Anthropological Journeys: Reflections on Fieldwork*, Hyderabad: Orient Longman.

Strathern, M. (1995) 'Nostalgia and the New Genetics', in D. Battaglia (ed.), *Rhetorics of Self-Making*, Berkeley: University of California Press.

—— (1997) '"Improving Ratings": Audit in the British University System', *European Review*, 5 (3): 305–21.

—— n.d. 'A Case of Self-Organization' (unpub. manuscript), University of Cambridge.

Unger, R. M. (1987) *False Necessity: Anti-Necessitarian Social Theory in the Service of Radical Democracy*, Cambridge: Cambridge University Press.

University of Durham (1998) *Continuation Audit: Analytical Account*.

Vedaparayana, G. (1998) 'Gandhi's Concept of Swaraj: A Critical Examination', paper presented at the National Seminar on 'Rethinking Swaraj', University of Hyderabad.

Chapter 7

Self-accountability, ethics and the problem of meaning

Vassos Argyrou

This chapter focuses on self-accountability and criticism.[1] Its aim is not to examine why outside agencies, such as government bureaucracies, might conceivably be concerned with 'auditing' anthropology – no doubt, an important question in its own right.[2] It is rather to explore how and, more importantly, why practitioners themselves bring their discipline to task and to draw out the implications of this long-standing practice.

Is there anything special in bringing anthropology to account, Strathern (1997b: 11) asks. This is a crucial question, one not really raised before, certainly not in relation to the anthropological practice of self-accountability. The failure to raise this question is all the more surprising, since, as I will argue, self-accountability and criticism have always been part and parcel of the discipline – always meaning from its inception as an academic discipline in the nineteenth century to, literally, the present day. This failure is not only surprising but also pregnant with implications, as anything is that goes without saying – because it comes without saying, as Bourdieu (1977) would say – and thus anything that is taken for granted and becomes a self-evident truth. There is indeed something special about self-accountability and criticism in anthropology, something fundamental that we have not as yet begun to consider.

The contributions to this volume afford a context in which to extend arguments presented elsewhere (Argyrou 1999). Indeed, I shall comment on two of them in some detail. However, to point to the differences between my discourse and theirs, I shall adopt a different term for the discipline. Rather than the Anglo-Saxon term 'anthropology', I follow my own earlier usage and from here onwards employ the term 'ethnology', in its Continental sense. I find 'anthropology' rather problematic. It retains something of the pretentious enlightenment attempt to construct an all-encompassing science of 'man'. It can of course be qualified by such epithets as 'social' and 'cultural', but they are both partisan; 'sociocultural anthropology', on the other hand, is simply too cumbersome.

Bringing the discipline to task

The other two chapters in this section aim precisely to bring the discipline to task, and it might be worthwhile to begin this discussion by making a brief reference to them. Let us first say that in both of them, ethnology, whether in its modern or postmodern versions, emerges as a discipline in need of radical modifications. Let us also say that why ethnology must be modified is because of the Other in its Otherness. For Otherness is not merely difference (for difference pure and simple is after all celebrated by the discipline as 'cultural diversity') but difference understood as cultural inferiority. In other words, if ethnology is in need of drastic change, it is for the sake of a certain unity between Self and Other, a unity-within-diversity, a Sameness at the level of cultural value (rather than the level of cultural form).

Chapter 6 finds fault with the increased bureaucratization of the university system, itself a manifestation of the wider bureaucratization of society which spills over to the various academic disciplines, including ethnology. The result of this bureaucratization in ethnology is a 'legal minimalism', a largely procedural, socially disengaged form of accountability, the kind (say) that does not go beyond what the ethnographer is expected to do, namely, to produce knowledge about others. And yet accountability, Giri argues, 'is intimately linked to the calling of responsibility' and should contribute 'to the growth of oneself and the other and thus . . . to the creation of *dignified* relationships in society' (pp. 173–4; my emphasis). Giri admits that societal modernization and postmodernization have a role to play 'in fostering a climate of accountability' as moral responsibility. Nonetheless, in ethnology these processes have led to an almost exclusive concern with politics and 'the view that political awareness is the only key to emancipating itself as a discipline and the people it works with'. Over and above politics, however, ethnology 'needs to develop a moral language to speak about accountability and the imperative of responsibility . . . a responsibility emerging out of the conversations . . . between us as interacting subjects' – 'us' being 'the ethnographer and the informants' (p. 175).

There is something fundamental lacking in ethnology, then, a large moral deficit that stems from its practitioners' failure to exhibit responsibility towards their informants – not just any kind of responsibility but, Giri (p. 175) suggests, 'an unconditional ethical obligation of the self to the other'. This absence is fundamental because what is at stake in ethnology is not, as we are accustomed to saying, only or even mainly knowledge of humanity, but rather 'dignified' human relations: human dignity itself. The task of ethnology, in other words, is not so much to say things about others as to say things conducive to human dignity or, at any rate, things that do not contradict and undermine it. Giri's argument is well taken, but is it really true that ethnology suffers from a moral deficit? I would argue otherwise. Ethnographers have always been vociferous in condemning all those Western discourses – particularly their own – that undermine 'dignified' human relations. They have even coined a special term for such discourses, by now extensively employed outside the discipline as well, namely, 'ethnocentrism'.

This brings me to Chapter 5. The quotation by Foucault with which the paper begins, and in which the celebrated philosopher expresses his misgivings about humanism, along with Pels's Foucauldian argument that ethics is 'a technology of the self', may suggest to the reader that what is to follow could well be a critique of ethnological humanism. But this possible misunderstanding is soon cleared up and, as one reads on, it becomes apparent where the emphasis of Pels's argument lies. Pels is not about to argue that humanist morality is a way in which ethnographers control themselves by themselves and become subjects, thus doing away with the need to have them subjected to outside authorities; he is not about to argue that ethnological ethics act as an impediment to the autonomy of the ethnological self; and he is certainly not going to call for a non-humanist ethnology. Far from it. Pels brings ethnology to task not for its ethics writ large, but for a specific kind of ethics. His concern is not about the autonomy of the ethnological self, but about the autonomy of the Other.

The problem with ethnology, according to Pels, is its *professional* ethics (along with its methodology and the confessional mode of ethnological discourse). For they reduce morality to a mere set of guidelines of conduct. It is *these* ethics that constitute a technology of self. By internalizing them and acting accordingly, the liberal ethnological self is kept isolated from the real world and under the illusion that it is also free of the contaminating influence of politics and power. This isolation, Pels argued at the EASA session,[3] the prophylactic function of ethics and method, is something to be decried because, in his words, it tends 'to maintain the one-way traffic of authority characteristic of modernization theory'; it maintains 'the moral or factual superiority of a certain centre of civilization by picturing historical change as a movement of ideas and institutions from this centre to the other parts . . . of the world'. It should be clear, then, that what Pels finds objectionable in ethnology is the power which ethnological discourse exercises over others – the 'one way-traffic of authority' – and the contribution of this disourse to the idea that the West – 'a certain centre of civilization' – is culturally superior to the rest of the world. In short, he objects to ethnology's ethnocentric tendencies.

Pels' position, then, is hardly Foucauldian. Rather than less humanism, he is calling for more. As stated in his conference paper, he wants to 'undo the marginalization of ethics' and its reduction 'to professional guidelines of conduct, and place morality and its politics squarely within the everyday practice of the anthropological discipline'. Much like Giri, Pels is bringing ethnology to task by suggesting that the discipline is suffering from a moral deficit. Again, I argue otherwise. Ethnographers do not need to place morality squarely within their everyday discursive practices because it has always been there from the beginning. It is the foundation on which the entire discipline rests.

Ethnology's moral principles

Ethnology has always exhibited unconditional moral responsibility towards Others. Indeed, the discipline as we know it can exist only insofar as it places beyond questioning two principles inextricably associated with moral considerations. The first is 'the psychic unity of mankind', as Tylor (1874) would have it, the tenet that human beings everywhere and at all times have the same mental constitution. Without this principle, that is, as long as others were considered to be less than human, ethnology would not become a social science, even if for a long time it was merely the science of the evolution of Western social and cultural institutions. The discipline would still be a branch of natural science, as it clearly was in the early nineteenth century.[4] Psychological Sameness, then, is historically and structurally one of ethnology's conditions of possibility.

The second principle is 'cultural relativism' broadly understood, the notion that despite or because of their differences, all societies embody the same cultural value or worth. Without this principle, ethnology would still be the study of the rise and evolution of Western civilization. Nor would fieldwork – the hallmark of all twentieth-century ethnology – make much sense. Why invest so much time and effort to study magic from close range, for example, if one is certain, as Tylor clearly was, that it is nothing more than a delusion? Why try 'to grasp the native's point of view . . . to realize *his* vision of *his* world', as Malinowski (1922: 25, original emphasis) insisted, and as every ethnographer has been trying to do since then, if that vision were not significant in its own right? Sameness at the level of cultural value or worth, then, is ethnology's second condition of possibility, that which transformed the discipline in the early twentieth century into the synchronic, comparative study of other societies and cultures.

Given these two fundamental ethnological principles, psychological Sameness and Sameness at the level of cultural value or worth, the entire history of the discipline can be read as a persistent attempt to redeem Others from the calumny of inferiority, whether racial inferiority, cultural, or both. Indeed, in their quest to demonstrate Sameness, ethnographers have been employing three distinct strategies of redemption. The first locates manifestations of the Self in the Other – social and cultural institutions, for instance, or a certain 'practical rationality'.[5] The second strategy locates manifestations of the Other in the West – the Other 'within', as the current parlance would have it.[6] And the third tackles Otherness itself. Its aim is to demonstrate that although Otherness has form, it lacks content or, another way of saying the same thing, that its content (value) is the same despite its different form.

There are innumerable examples of these three strategies of redemption in the ethnological literature, but here I will provide only one of each from the work of Tylor. I choose Tylor because he is more often than not regarded in the discipline, if not as an outright racist (cf. Stocking 1968: 110–32), certainly as ethnology's ethnocentric villain par excellence. My aim is not so much to defend Tylor as to show that this is a rather facile understanding of his work. He did nothing different, structurally at least, from what most, if not all, ethnographers have been doing ever since.

As Morris (1987) points out, the understanding among the learned in Victorian England was that natives were so primitive as to have no religion at all. Tylor was one of the first ethnographers to dispute this claim. He argued that his compatriots failed to recognize native religion because they were rather narrow-minded; they understood religion in terms of 'the organized and established theology' of their own society (1874: 419–20). Tylor made certain that religion would be easily located in native societies by anyone interested in looking for it. He thus defined religion in the widest possible terms, as belief in spiritual beings. And yet, if others had religion and were the same in this sense as Europeans, they were also known to engage in occult practices and this, one could argue, set them clearly apart. Not so, according to Tylor. This particular manifestation of Otherness was still very much part of European societies themselves. In Germany, for instance, 'Protestants get the aid of Catholic priests and monks to help them against witchcraft, to lay ghosts, consecrate herbs, and discover thieves' (1874: 115). As for magic itself, this Otherness certainly had form (it was false) but it lacked content (it was not the product of different minds). For Tylor the human mind operates, everywhere and at all times, on the basis of the three principles of associating ideas identified by Hume (1977 [1758]) in the previous century – by means of resemblance, contiguity in time and space, and cause and effect. Magic, Tylor argued, was simply the result of using associations of resemblance and contiguity as if they were associations of cause and effect. This was a mistake, no doubt, but one that nonetheless proved that in principle at least native minds operated in the same way as European minds.

To these three strategies of redemption we must add a fourth, that employed by postmodern discourse. Postmodern ethnographers strive to uphold Sameness by calling into question the means of producing and reproducing Otherness, namely, ethnological representations. The latter, according to the argument, are inevitably contaminated by our social and historical circumstances, whether circumstances that determine our perception of Others or our textualization of them, that is, the way in which we present them in our written discourses. As a result, we produce images of Others in which they emerge not as they truly are – as they exist in themselves – but as they appear to us and as they must be described in our texts. In short, such images are 'fiction', things that we 'make up' and which are not objectively present (Clifford 1986).

The postmodern strategy of redemption, then, is to be located in this negative dialectic. If we can demonstrate that Otherness is 'fiction', if we can be certain that it is nothing more than our imaginary creation, then we can also be fairly certain that its contrary, Sameness, is true.

With these brief remarks, I have tried to show that far from suffering from a moral deficit, as the previous contrubutors suggest, ethnology's very condition of possibility and rationale lies in a fundamental moral principle: humanism. Indeed, Sameness or 'common humanity' is precisely what ethnographers have been striving to demonstrate for the last one and a half centuries. It is possible, of course, to raise the objection that 'the psychic unity of mankind', if not 'cultural relativism', is not a moral but a scientific principle that comes to us from natural science. If one endorses the postulate that the laws of nature are regular, uniform and universal, one has no option but to apply the same notions to human nature as well. This argument cannot be dismissed out of hand, but nor can it be easily defended. To substantiate such a claim, one should be able to demonstrate clearly that the ethnological struggle against racism is entirely motivated by a concern with scientific truth and has nothing to do with the question of good and evil; one should be able to show, in other words, that ethnographers attack racism simply because it is scientifically groundless and not because it is also morally wrong. Does the former exclude the latter, or is it rather the case that both are inextricably intertwined?

It is true that Tylor often appeals to the natural sciences when he talks about the psychic unity of mankind. In a well-known passage, he argues that 'it is no more reasonable to suppose the laws of mind differently constituted in Australia and England, in the time of the cave-dwellers and in the time of the builders of sheet-iron houses, than to suppose that the laws of chemical combustion were of one sort in the time of the coal-measures, and are of another now' (1874: 158–9). But we would be rather short-sighted to take such appeals at face value and overlook their rhetorical intent. By postulating a homology between the laws of mind and the laws of chemical combustion, Tylor is using the natural sciences to legitimize his discourse on common humanity. Moreover, there is really nothing in this strategy to show that Tylor was exclusively concerned with upholding a purely scientific principle. Indeed, evidence suggest that the psychic unity of mankind was the point at which Tylor's faith in science and his moral convictions converged.

It is characteristic, for example, that, as Stocking (1987: 159) points out, Tylor resigned his post as foreign secretary of the Anthropological Society of London because 'the "pugnacious" racism of its president offended his humanitarian Quaker principles'.

If it is true to say that even in its most scientistic guise, ethnology does not suffer from a moral deficit, if it is committed more than any other Western discourse to the redemption of Otherness, what is one to make of the fact that Otherness is precisely what the discipline has been producing and reproducing for more than one and a half centuries now? Indeed, if the history of the discipline is anything to go by, there is no ethnological paradigm – evolutionism, functionalism, structuralism, or culturalism, to name only the major ones – that has not been found guilty of the ultimate ethnological transgression, ethnocentrism. It is perhaps because of this overwhelmingly negative historical experience that ethnologists are led to the conclusion that the discipline must make an unconditional ethical commitment to Others. Unconditional ethical obligation and ethnocentrism are mutually exclusive; hence, if the discipline has been, and is being ethnocentric, it must be because it lacks the necessary moral commitment. And yet, if what I have argued so far has any truth to it, it would seem that ethnology is both morally committed to Sameness and, somehow, capable of ethnocentrism. Indeed, this is where the paradox lies. It is here also that we must locate ethnology's unhappy predicament: a will to redeem Others that can do little more than to produce and reproduce Otherness. Because of this predicament ethnology is predisposed to bringing itself to account quite frequently – a discipline inevitably highly critical of itself.

How is the paradox to be explained? What is it that renders ethnological attempts to demonstrate Sameness and to redeem Others from the calumny of inferiority self-defeating? I have discussed this issue in detail elsewhere (Argyrou 1999), and here can only touch on the broad outlines of that argument. By way of introducing the argument, I shall first turn to a structurally similar paradox, namely, gift exchange.

When there is time, Derrida (1992) argues, the gift is impossible. This is not to deny the existence of the gift as a phenomenon. Apparently people exchange what they call 'gifts'. But a closer look reveals that these 'gifts' are not what they appear to be. The gift as such is impossible because it unfolds in time, which destroys it as gift. To begin with, time is precisely what is needed for the gift-giver to receive a return – even if this return is nothing more than the pleasure of giving. Any return, however, renders the gift an investment, that is, it destroys it as gift. Second, time is also what is needed for the gift-receiver to destroy the gift as gift. If she makes an immediate counter-gift, the initial gift is thereby refused and hence annulled. If she does not, the gift becomes a debt, that is, it no longer is a gift.

The ontological impossibility of the gift applies with equal force to the principle of Sameness. When there is time Sameness is impossible. Once again, this is not to deny Sameness as a phenomenon. Indeed, ethnographers imagine, desire and strive to demonstrate something that they call 'common humanity'. But on a closer look this Sameness turns out be nothing more than division and difference. Sameness as such is impossible because time renders the subject that posits Sameness – the ethnologist, the ethnographer – different from everyone else. By positing a world of Sameness, that is, by symbolically constituting the world as such, at that very instant, the subject places itself outside of this world. It becomes the creator of a world of Sameness and hence establishes the sort of relation that exists between creator and creations, which is a relation of difference, even if in this world everyone – as creations – maintains a relation of Sameness. There is, then, a temporal boundary or, another way of saying the same thing, a threshold of consciousness, which Sameness cannot pass without destroying itself. No doubt, constituting difference in this way is an unintended consequence. Indeed, the positing subject claims to be the same as everyone else. But this is possible only because the subject has conveniently forgotten the initial act of positing this world. Here, as in other similar cases, the subject is caught in an ontological circle, in the double bind of trying to be both the creator of the world and a creation in the world of which it is the creator or, as Foucault (1970) has it, and Pels and Giri would agree, both subject and object.

This abstract argument can be illustrated with innumerable ethnographic examples. Due to paucity of space, I can only use one, and have chosen Evans-Pritchard's classic argument that Zande witchcraft is a way of explaining unfortunate events. Evans-Pritchard's aim is to demonstrate that although this Otherness has form, it lacks content, and that the Zande are not irrational and mystical but reasonable people like us. If witchcraft is an idiom that explains unfortunate events, rather than 'an oval blackish swelling or bag' (Evans-Pritchard 1976 [1937]: 1) in the witch's body, as the Zande claim, Sameness begins to emerge. But before this Sameness has any time whatsoever to take root, it is utterly destroyed. It is destroyed instantly because a new difference is born, the difference between, on the one hand, Evans-Pritchard who knows the truth of witchcraft and every ethnographer who adopts his explanation and, on the other, the Azande who are oblivious to this truth. A world of Sameness, then, can exist only on the condition that we are completely and utterly unaware of its existence, which is another way of saying that it cannot exist for us, that it is impossible. As soon as we posit Sameness, difference enters in the world.

It may be pertinent at this point to return to the question raised at the beginning, namely, whether there is anything significant about bringing ethnology to account, and attempt to address it. To the extent that ethnologists bring their discipline to task and criticize it, as they obviously do and have been doing for a long time, it is because ethnology or better still its practitioners cannot avoid being what they detest most – ethnocentric. They are being ethnocentric not because their moral commitment to Others is partial and incomplete but, paradoxically, precisely because it is unconditional. If ethnographers divide the world between Self and Other, it is because they strive to demonstrate its unity, that is, Sameness, which is impossible. And yet this only begs the question: Why is it that we, in contrast to scholars in other disciplines and people outside academia, find ethnocentrism so disturbing? Why is it that we appear unable to deal with the prospect that the world may be by its very nature a world of division and difference? To answer these questions, it is necessary to examine the principle of Sameness more closely and raise a further question: What is the vantage point from which we all appear the same? Where does one need to go and what does one need to do to have such a vision of the world?

'The problem of meaning'

In his celebrated essay on Religion as a Cultural System, Geertz (1973), following Weber, raises what the latter calls the problem of meaning, and makes a distinction between three sub-problems: the problem of knowledge, the problem of suffering and the problem of evil. I am here concerned with the last.

The problem of evil, according to Geertz, has to do with our ability, or otherwise, to make sound ethical judgements. 'The vexation here is the gap between things as they are and things as they ought to be if our conceptions of right and wrong make sense' (1973: 106) – vexation of the kind which arises when the rain falls mostly on the just fella because the unjust has the just's umbrella.[7] If there is justice in the world, this sort of thing should not be happening. If it is happening, it may be because there is no such thing as justice. A persistent gap, then, between what ought to be and what actually is throws into question our ethical standards. Indeed, what is even more vexing is the suspicion that there may be no moral standards to live by at all, that the world is intrinsically ethically arbitrary and absurd.

What religion does, again according to Geertz, is to deny such suspicions. It denies them not by refusing to acknowledge that there is injustice in the world, but by refusing to accept that injustice is an inescapable fact of the human condition. In other words, to the world of experience and commonsense, religion juxtaposes another, really real world: 'an image of . . . a genuine order of existence' (1973: 108) which explains the former, and explains it away as a profane reality. Geertz does not discuss the conditions of possibility of this image of the 'really real' world of religious belief; he takes it for granted that it is a metaphysical world. We, however, cannot make the same assumption about the image of the 'really real' world of ethnological belief – the image of Sameness. If Sameness is itself a metaphysical notion, and if it does for the ethnographer what religion does for the believer – as I intend to argue here – this is something that cannot be assumed but must be demonstrated. We must, then, raise the question once again: What is the vantage point from which we all appear the same? Where does one need to go to have such an image of the world?

Let us first point out the obvious, namely, that in the same way in which the world of experience contradicts the conception of divine justice so does it contradict Sameness. The world is replete with glaring examples of racism, ethnocentrism, and many other kinds of division. This suggests that the world of experience is not the place to look for that position from which we all appear the same. It is necessary to search for another world that transcends it, that is, a world beyond experience. I shall try to do so with the help one ethnographic formulation (and cf. Argyrou 1999) which takes us to the island of Cyprus in the eastern Mediterranean, among its Greek Cypriot inhabitants, and has to do with local conceptions of death. I should point out that these conceptions are not unique to Greek Cypriots, but are also found among mainland Greeks and other southern Europeans.[8]

I turn to Cyrpus, however, because this is a culture that I know best. It may be said that by showing, in what follows, how Cypriots invoke Sameness, I am implictly suggesting that they are thinking along the same lines as Western ethnologists and perhaps Westerners in general. This is true enough, but a couple of qualifications are in order. As I will argue in greater detail, Sameness is a metaphysical notion closely related to the sacred. It should not be surprising therefore that it is not uniquely Western. Having said that, I think there is something distinctive about Western Sameness which makes it highly problematical, indeed impossible. Because in the West there is no outside referent to Sameness, those who strive to uphold it end up denying it. Cypriots on the other hand – or, at any rate, some Cypriots – argue that we are all the Same by referring this Sameness to an outside authority, namely, God. Thus, while Western ethnologists are caught in the trap of trying to be both Creators in a world of Sameness and creations in the world they have created, which is impossible, the Cypriots of the example that follows reserve for themselves only the status of creations. They say that there is a *plastis* (Maker) and they are *plasmata* (Creations).

On the occasion of someone's death, people in Cyprus often remark: 'We [human beings] are a lie' – a lie because lies do not last forever; sooner or later, they are bound to be discovered for what they are and disappear. When rich, powerful, or famous individuals die, people often make a sharp and poignant contrast between what such individuals have been and their present state. 'Look at such and such,' they point out. 'He was saving and saving as if he was going to live forever. What's the point! No one takes anything with him; we all end with two metres of earth.' Apparently, such comments are meant to highlight the absurdity of the struggle for wealth and power. But their goal is also to underline the essential equality of all people, rich and poor, important and unimportant. In the face of death, all of life's differences are obliterated, and what remains is the same for all, 'two metres of earth', the grave.

In this view, then, death acts as the ultimate human equalizer. But what is the position that one must occupy to have such a vision of life? At first sight it appears that it is a position in the midst of the empirical world. Cypriots speak about death as a human equalizer when someone dies, and apparently people die in the course of everyday life. Surely, there is nothing metaphysical about this. No doubt this is true as far as it goes, but it does not go far enough. We hardly ever conceptualize death as the end; we certainly think of it as the end of life, but this already suggests the beginning of something beyond life. Death, in other words, is always thought of as a passage, a passage through which, according to Cypriots, no one takes anything with him. What lies on the other side of this threshold could be anything that one cares to imagine. It could be an eternal life, nothingness, or the unknown. The point is that the 'other side' is imaginable and imagined. It is imagined, and necessarily so, because it is impossible to speak about life in this way (as an abstraction) without positing something other than life, that is, without stepping 'outside' of it. In this sense, even nothingness is something and not nothing. It is a metaphysical position that we must assume if we are to speak at all about this side of the threshold.

The ultimate human equalizer, then, is not death as such. Rather death is the occasion when the ultimate contrast can be made between the human and the non-human condition. It is the contrast between human finitude and the infinity of the beyond – be it God, Nothingness or the Great Unknown. From any of these positions beyond the world, that is, from infinity's point of view, human difference – racial, cultural, ethnic or of any other kind – are completely invisible. There is no human difference, however vast it may appear, that can withstand the comparison with the absolute difference between the finitude of the human condition and infinity. Indeed, Sameness is precisely how human differences appear from the point of view of the Infinite.

There are several points to be made at the conclusion of this discussion on death. First, Sameness is a transcendental notion, a metaphysical ontology, since it becomes possible from an imaginary position beyond the world. Second, as the ethnographic example from Cyprus suggests, from this metaphysical position, it is the world of experience which becomes unreal. Wealth and power emerge as nothing, when, as common-sense dictates, they make the world go round. Differences and divisions become nothing, when, as experience clearly suggests, they structure and constrain most people's lives, often in compelling ways. And third, this denial of the world of experience and common-sense helps to restore, symbolically no doubt, the moral equilibrium of the world. It is certainly unjust that some people are rich and powerful, but this does not mean that justice is a mirage. In the wider scheme of things, in 'reality', we are all the same. Proof of this is that no one takes anything with him. This denial, then, which does not deny the existence of injustice but rather denies that injustice is intrinsic to 'reality', helps people maintain faith in the moral coherence of the world. In short, it makes an otherwise ethically arbitrary and absurd world meaningful and bearable.

With this, we have arrived at a critical juncture, the point where what we say about Others begins to turn in on itself and haunt us with vengeance. Ethnological discourse now begins to seek a kind of revenge because of our presumption that it is applicable only to Others, the hubris of assuming that it cannot be possibly used to explain our own beliefs and practices. We must, then, complete this discussion by carrying out the same sort of operation that we reserve for Others on ourselves.

Let us first say that taking up an imaginary position beyond the world predisposes ethnologists to view certain aspects of human reality as unreal. For us, the unrealities par excellence in the world are racism and ethnocentrism. This, of course, is not to say that ethnologists deny the existence of such profanities. What they deny rather is that racism and ethnocentrism are intrinsic to human reality, an inescapable fact of the world. Indeed, as far as ethnographers are concerned, the 'really real' world is a world of human unity. Let us also say that by means of this denial, ethnographers, much like ordinary Cypriots, maintain faith in the moral order of the world. The world as it is may be racist and ethnocentric, but this is only because people are ignorant or insensitive; in reality, the world is not like this at all. In short, by means of these denials, ethnographers transform an ethically arbitrary and absurd world into a meaningful and bearable one.

In this context, the question regarding the significance of bringing ethnology to task acquires a different import. Ethnology must be criticized whenever – which is always – it reproduces, inadvertently but inevitably, what it strives to deny. It must because, as its practitioners know only too well, the existence of unaccountable injustice 'sets ordinary human experience in a permanent context of metaphysical concern and raises the dim, back-of-the-mind suspicions that one may be adrift in an absurd world' (Geertz 1973: 102). Self-accountability and criticism is the road that ethnology has travelled for many years, a long winding road that leads from Victorian anthropology to the present day. It is the mechanism by which ethnographers struggle to maintain a vision of a symbolically unified, that is, ethically meaningful world.

I close by highlighting a paradox. One of the things I have tried to do in this chapter is to disenchant and demystify Sameness. To the perceptive reader, however, it should be apparent that, paradoxically, I have tried to do so for sake of Sameness itself. In effect, my argument has been that Western ethnologists, and ethnographers, are as susceptible to the problem of meaning as any of the people whose magico-religious systems they study and disenchant. I say this as a corrective to the possible misunderstanding of this chapter as an attack on ethnology. If, as I have argued here, ethnology is fundamentally about upholding Sameness in a racist and ethnocentric world, then this is a thoroughly ethnological paper.

Notes

1 An earlier version of this paper appears in *Current Anthropology*, 40: S29–S41.
2 On government audit in the British university system see Strathern (1997a).
3 I draw here on his conference paper (Pels 1998, revised for this volume and not otherwise published in this form).
4 Kuklick (1991: 6) points out that the British Association for the Advancement of Science classified anthropology under Natural History, a category that also included botany and zoology.
5 To quote only one example: 'I take the position that practical rationality . . . must exist in most, if not all, societies' (Obeyesekere 1992: 205, n. 48). For an earlier version of this argument see Evans-Pritchard 1965.
6 For recent examples, see Carrier (1995) on gift exchange and Lindstrom (1995) on Western cargo cults.
7 I am following Geertz's own anecdote (1973: 106).
8 A colleague who attended the workshop on accountability informed me that the Portuguese entertain similar ideas.

References

Argyrou, V. (1999) 'Sameness and the Ethnological Will to Meaning', *Current Anthropology* 40: S29–S41.
Bourdieu, P. (1977) *Outline of a Theory of Practice*, Cambridge: Cambridge University Press.

Carrier, J. (1995) 'Maussian Occidentalism: Gift and Commodity Systems', in J. Carrier (ed.) *Occidentalism: Images of the West*, Oxford: Clarendon Press.

Clifford, J. (1986) 'Partial Truths', Introduction to J. Clifford and G. Marcus (eds) *Writing Culture: The Poetics and Politics of Ethnography*, Berkeley: University of California Press.

Derrida, J. (1992) *Given Time: I. Counterfeit Money*, Chicago: University of Chicago Press.

Evans-Pritchard, E. E. (1965) *Theories of Primitive Religion*, Oxford: Clarendon Press.

—— (1976) [1937] *Witchcraft, Oracles and Magic among the Azande*, abridged and introduced by E. Gillies, Oxford: Clarendon Press.

Foucault, M. (1970) *The Order of Things*, New York: Vintage.

Geertz, C. (1973) 'Religion as a Cultural System', in *The Interpretation of Cultures*, New York: Basic Books.

Hume, D. (1977) [1748–1758] *An Enquiry Concerning Human Understanding*, Indianapolis: Hackett.

Kuklick, H. (1991) *The Savage Within: The Social History of British Anthropology*, Cambridge: Cambridge University Press.

Lindstrom, L. (1995) 'Cargoism and Occidentalism', in J. Carrier (ed.) *Occidentalism: Images of the West*, Oxford: Clarendon Press.

Malinowski, B. (1922) *The Argonauts of the Western Pacific*, Prospect Heights, Il: Waveland Press.

Morris, B. (1987) *Anthropological Studies of Religion*, Cambridge: Cambridge University Press.

Obeyesekere, G. (1992) *The Apotheosis of Captain Cook: European Mythmaking in the Pacific*, Princeton: Princeton University Press.

Pels, P. (1998) 'Beyond the Liberal Technologies of Self, or Anthropological Morality after Professionalism'. (Paper given at 1998 EASA conference.)

Stocking, G. (1968) 'The Dark-skinned Savage', in *Race, Culture, and Evolution*, Chicago: University of Chicago Press.

Strathern, M. (1997a) 'Improving Ratings: Audit in the British University System', *European Review* 5(3): 305–21.

—— (1997b) 'Auditing Anthropology: The New Accountabilities', *EASA Newsletter* 21: 11.

Tylor, E. B. (1874) *Primitive Culture*, New York: Henry Holt.

Part IV

Chapter 8

The university as panopticon

Moral claims and attacks on academic freedom

Vered Amit

On Monday, August 24, 1992, Dr Valery Fabrikant walked into the Hall Building of Concordia University in Montreal, Quebec and shot five people. One, a secretary, recovered from her wounds. Four others were either killed immediately or died later. Those murdered had been Fabrikant's faculty colleagues: three had taught in the same faculty of engineering where Fabrikant held an appointment and another had served as the head of the faculty association which had represented Fabrikant in several grievances. During Fabrikant's nine years at Concordia University, he had been successively promoted from a research assistant to a tenure stream associate professorship but he had also alarmed an increasing number of staff, administrators and faculty members with his episodes of bizarre behaviour, accusations, email campaigns, threats, confrontations and acrimony which had escalated in the year or two just prior to the events of August 24. In the immediate aftermath of the killings, attention, both within and outside Concordia University, focused on the choices made by its senior administrators who had apparently been aware of and concerned about the danger posed by Fabrikant's increasingly threatening conduct but had not taken sufficient measures to protect the institution's personnel. The Board of Governors almost immediately terminated the contract of the top administrator; it also commissioned a number of formal reviews. In the course of these inquiries, attention shifted away from the administration to the academic faculty with the insinuation that while administrative deficiencies had undoubtedly occurred, they rested most of all in a failure to hold academic faculty generally, rather than just Fabrikant, properly accountable for their intellectual authorship, financial dealings and civility.

A line of reasoning which appeared in one of these reports exemplifies the premise of this shift. One external reviewer was very critical of decisions made by a number of administrators but argued that, beyond the incompetence of particular managers, Fabrikant's Concordia employment history reflected more general problems in university culture, the most prominent of which was a 'recent and disturbing mutation of what academic freedom means to some within the university community in Canada' (Cowan 1994: 6). According to this reviewer, in Canada there was no longer much danger to university professors of discrimination based on political ideology. Issues of academic freedom had moved on to other more personal terrain.

> Academic freedom issues continue to converge with ordinary anti-discrimination issues, to the point now where they are often indistinguishable. Given the tradition of toleration of personal eccentricity in the universities . . . it is not surprising to hear faculty fall back on academic freedom to defend practices which have little connection to academic issues . . . Nonetheless, one extension of the concept I have yet to come to terms with is the 'academic freedom' to be brutish and miserable to colleagues and students, so that little work is assigned, and so that students consult one infrequently. When academic freedom is extended without caveat from the contents of discourse to the conduct of that discourse, it opens up the prospect of a range of 'protected' behaviors which interferes mightily with the well-being of others.
>
> (1994: 7)

He did not, however, provide any instances of the occurrences of this brutish behaviour in any other university or even in Concordia, apart from Fabrikant's own extreme conduct. So, how did the actions of a madman who killed four people and whose behaviour, even before this last horrific act, was so extreme that a number of his colleagues had feared for their physical safety, become identified with a much more general misbehaviour of academics hiding behind the cover of academic freedom? In the period following this and other similar reports, the flow of administrative memorandums extolling the crucial importance of maintaining a civil atmosphere, the increased rigour of auditing controls applied to the administration of research grants, the installation of a new code of rights and responsibilities which stressed again the importance of a 'safe and civil environment', the replacement of the sexual harassment office with an office mandated to explore a wider range of harassment and discrimination complaints, would appear to suggest that the reviewer's line of reasoning was shared within at least some quarters of the Concordia administration. But his argument that this behavioural problem extends well beyond Concordia University also appears to be echoed by the adoption of similar control mechanisms in most other Canadian and also many American universities.

How did university professors come to be viewed as being so irresponsible, even abusive or dangerous? However preposterous we may regard this characterization, few professors have been able to avoid the institutional practices which have accompanied its entrenchment in much of the North American post-secondary educational sector. Ethics reviews, codes of conduct, sexual harassment policies, increasing limits on the way in which researchers use and administer their own research grants combine with a host of frequent auditing exercises (work load assessments, grant reports, performance reviews, annual departmental reports, student course evaluations) to ensure that professors must constantly and frequently provide an account of how they spend their time and the 'value' of these activities. Yet this increasingly elaborate system of accounting crucially depends on the general co-operation of university faculty. The university is being remade into a panopticon in which university professors censor, police, audit and market themselves while institutional administrations strive ever harder to limit their own liability.

I agree with the reviewer that this transformation is inextricably related to issues of academic freedom, but whereas he sees academic freedom being used as a cover for abuses of power, I see the continued invocation of academic freedom by the agencies and through the vehicles exercising surveillance as a painfully ironic cover for the implementation of an increasingly repressive system of political control. This appraisal of the remaking of universities begs two crucial questions: Why now? And why have academic faculty, by and large, co-operated with these measures? I think that at least some of the answers to these questions can be attributed to a convergent clamour for intellectual accountability and moral obligation from sources both within and outside academia. Implicit in this discourse is the presumption that in one respect or another, academics have been examined, found seriously wanting and can therefore only be redeemed through the medium of new requirements and controls.

The search for funds

To set the scene for the panopticization of the university it is first necessary to briefly consider some of the public policy agendas which have been shaping the context of Canadian academia over the past decade.[1] During the 1990s, Canadian academics have been seriously affected by spending cuts at both provincial and federal government levels with direct impacts on a wholly public university sector overwhelmingly dependent on state support. In Quebec, as in most provinces, universities were hit by substantial and repeated cuts to their operating budgets. For several years, federal research granting agencies such as the Social Sciences and Humanities Research Council also experienced reductions in their budgets affecting access to research monies for academic researchers across the country. Universities scrambled to meet the new financial exigencies by using buyouts, early retirement packages and even new redundancy clauses to reduce their faculty and staff complements, introducing salary constraints, larger faculty/student ratios, depleting library resources, merging or eliminating academic programmes and searching out new sources of funding. Hence at a time when traditional sources of research funding were especially constrained, faculty members came under increased pressure to secure grants as a necessary supplement to the incomes of their cash-starved institutions.

In the midst of these fiscal constraints, another pressure became increasingly manifest and influential: the drive for a market driven university scholarship which can provide immediate economic, social or commercial 'value' for money. The disbursement of research funding has increasingly been incorporated into programmes requiring collaboration between university researchers and 'partners' in the public and private sectors, a partnership which in turn sets the agenda for inquiry. Thus over the last ten years, the federal government has established and enhanced its Networks of Centres of Excellence (NCEs). The NCEs consist of research consortiums bringing together hundreds of agencies including business companies, hospitals, universities, provincial and federal departments and a variety of other organizations. NCEs have their own administrative infrastructure; grants are disbursed by the NCE directorate which consists of staff from the three major federal research funding councils, individual networks have a Board of Directors, researchers are bound by the Network Agreement signed by member organizations. In short, while dependent on university expertise and research capacity, NCEs incorporate academicians as members of parallel organizational infrastructures with their own objectives and mandates. Specifically, these parallel and potentially competing structures are officially 'designed to develop the economy and improve our quality of life'[2] and as such are oriented towards innovation that provides for the transfer of technology and knowledge, the creation of jobs and the development of commercializable products and services.

But the NCEs are hardly alone; they simply form a pivot for an increasing proliferation of market-driven research. Apart from its contributions to the administration of the NCEs, the Social Sciences and Humanities Research Council of Canada (SSHRC) also sponsors programmes for strategic research that are policy driven, and involve 'an active partnership with the potential users of the research results, who, ideally, can help researchers transfer this knowledge to others who will benefit from it' (SSHRC Grants Guide 1999). It has also recently sponsored a new initiative for 'innovation centres' which yet again are supposed to respond to community demand and involve community partners who, according to the president of SSHRC,

> will help the researchers decide what are the priorities in terms of research projects in the future. The idea is that there is a *buy-in* in the questioning. There is a *buy-in* in the process of research. There is a *buy-in* in the results dissemination.
> (Renaud cited in Kondro 1998; my emphasis)

The SSHRC continues to direct the largest segment of its direct funding towards basic research, but its sponsorship or involvement in a growing proportion of tied, product-driven research is quite deliberate. In a recent speech, Renaud claimed that universities are now 'moving from the ivory tower to the market place, [and] granting agencies such as SSHRC have to provide the right tools and incentives to do it properly' (1999). Nor is the SSHRC a pioneer in this regard. As he noted, it has hopped rather late onto the bandwagon of 'market realities and commercialization', more rapidly 'adapted to' in the biomedical, natural sciences and engineering fields.

Furthermore, if the recommendations contained in a report of an expert panel on the commercialization of university research convened by the Prime Minister's Advisory Council of Science and Technology are adopted, then 'innovation', defined as 'the process of bringing new goods and services to market, or the result of that process' will be adopted as the fourth mission of universities in addition to their teaching, research and community service functions (1999: 4). In addition, universities will be required to 'provide incentives to encourage their faculty, staff and students engaged in research to create IP',[3] including recognition of such work in tenure and promotion policies.

The recommendations of the expert panel have elicited condemnation and anxiety from such sources as the Canadian Association of University Teachers (CAUT) as well as among individual faculty members, although, given the processes sketched above and the ubiquitous commercialization offices and policies already entrenched in many Canadian universities, this response resembles – more than a little – locking the barn door after the horse has bolted. The galloping corporatization of the university, transfer of knowledge from the publicly funded university sector to the private commercial sector and continued encroachments on academic independence, especially on the capacity of researchers to set their own inquiry agendas, are only some of the most obvious and serious outcomes of a shift in the status of commercialization as a possible outcome to a key objective of academic research. It is also not difficult to understand why post-secondary institutions facing severe fiscal constraints and scholars competing for scarce but ever more strategic (as a performance measure) research monies would be attracted by the funding possibilities afforded by these new market-driven initiatives. If Canadian governments did not deliberately underfund the post-secondary sector in order to render university administrators and faculty members alike more receptive to commercialization, they have not been averse to capitalizing on the 'persuasive' effects of their cuts. So we appear to have here a quite cynical but apparently rather straightforward scenario of manipulation and compulsion in which one political hand reduces state support for more traditional forms of university activities while the other hand tantalizes with new funding possibilities intended to remodel some fundamental elements of the academic mission.

But perhaps this scenario is a little too simple. For there are various points of leverage implicit in recent developments, not all necessarily favouring the political and commercial patrons of academe. Running throughout most of the speeches, reports or programmes extolling the virtues of a more utilitarian university are two strands revealing in their contradiction. The first strand promotes the presumption that, if universities do not shift their educational and research priorities to meet the training and development needs of businesses in a new globalized information economy, they will be marginalized or, as the Science Council of Canada claimed in a 1988 report, 'these needs will be satisfied elsewhere and universities will diminish in importance' (Graham: 1998: 20).

Yet, as producers and stewards of the paramount resource in post-industrial economies, knowledge, universities also tend to be represented as fundamental economic resources.

> Universities have always played a key role in discovering the new ideas that lead to social and economic progress. But, in the knowledge-based economy we now live in, universities are now literally the idea factories that will shape our future prosperity.
>
> (Crane 1999, cited in Report of the Expert Panel on the Commercialization of University Research 1999: 10)

Viewed thus, however, it would seem universities and academicians should be in a much stronger, not a weaker position, to call the shots, as it were, in their relationship with both private and public patrons. It is therefore not difficult to understand why a subtext of compulsion and social obligation so often enters into demands that universities supply more research with commercial application. 'Unfortunately, Canadian universities are not achieving their full potential in generating innovations from research results. Canadian taxpayers have a right to expect a greater return on their investment' (Crane 1999: 34).

It is not difficult to understand why an expert panel largely comprised of industry representatives should invoke a rhetoric of *rights* in its insistence on an augmentation of commercialization activity which, by its own admission, would primarily benefit private sector businesses while providing universities only a very minor augmentation of their revenues (1999: 2). It is not difficult to understand why these corporate executives and the neo-liberal government which commissioned their advice would be concerned to extend their managerial control over the kind of valuable, economically strategic information resources so much associated with universities. But why would academicians and universities buy this bluff? Why at a time when their investigative and pedagogical work appears more sought after than ever before would they be ceding any part of their capacity to define their own agendas for inquiry? Yet if the growing numbers of academics participating in the 'collaborative' research programmes are any indication, they are indeed increasingly ceding this capacity for self-direction. Nor is this the only field where university faculty members appear to be willing to accommodate an increasing margin of constraint, direction and monitoring of their professional activities. Why?

Intellectual accommodations and militancies

Given the very limited record of reports, public policy statements and personal observations from which I am working, my attempt to answer this question is admittedly speculative. I am, quite frankly, still baffled by this question but think that at least part of the answer lies in the degree to which many Western academics, Canadian scholars included, have accepted as unexceptional a populist devaluation of the intellectual enterprise, that is, the pursuit of knowledge and inquiry as valuable in its own right rather than just as a means to an end. In its most common form, this acceptance manifests itself in somewhat apologetic efforts by scholars to justify basic research as *eventually* if not immediately leading to socially useful or commercially applicable products. So, the difference between basic and product-driven research of the kind increasingly promoted by Canadian governments and research councils becomes just a matter of timeline rather than of ontology. Such a justification, however, may succeed in wresting a bit of space and time for researcher-led inquiry but in accepting the underlying premise – that it is an eventual practical outcome from which such inquiry derives its merit – it implicitly underwrites a utilitarian model of research.

But explicit validations of a socially redemptive scholarship hardly come from outside academia alone. There has always been a significant stream of applied academic research, whether social policy or invention driven, and tension between promoters of this and more abstract forms of inquiry is not uncommon. This familiar tension is imparted a new and more militant twist by calls for what D'Andrade has called a moral model of scholarship. D'Andrade (1995) is concerned with a particular version of critical anthropology but his analysis of an intellectual paradigm that combines attacks on science and objectivity with a measure of moral righteousness is by no means unique to our discipline. While sometimes critical of the extreme relativism and textual focus of postmodernism (Scheper-Hughes, 1995; Harrison, 1991), critical anthropologists have tended nonetheless to be influenced by the postmodernist focus on the situated nature of discourse and knowledge and its associated call for intellectual accountability, demands that scholars account not only for the content but also for the political, cultural and social location of the ideas they are attempting to promulgate. When this focus on the social location of the analyst is combined with more general denunciations of a 'Eurocentric canon' (Harrison, 1991: 6), invocations of the taint of previous colonial associations (Scheper-Hughes 1995: 418) and a general critique of scientific generalization as a language of power and social detachment (1995: 414; Abu-Lughod 1991: 150–1, cited in D'Andrade 1995: 405), the scene is set for moral prescriptions that demand a decolonized anthropology 'oriented towards social transformation and human liberation' (Harrison 1991: 8), a cadre of grounded, committed shock trooper 'barefoot anthropologists' (Scheper-Hughes 1995: 417–20). The anthropologist that refuses this role risks being identified as lacking in political responsibility, a collaborationist, a supplier of 'intelligence' information used for political control (Scheper-Hughes 1995: 419; Harrison 1991: 10).

While their rhetoric and interests situate these critical anthropologists and neo-liberals at opposite ends of the political spectrum, the structural implications of their stance vis-à-vis the academic mission are not dissimilar. Their demands, respectively, for a radical, politically committed or, conversely, a market-driven scholarship use similar invocations of moral obligation, human liberation in the former instance, or wealth creation in the latter. In both perspectives, without being harnessed to these particular moral obligations, the cultivation of intellectual curiosity and the pursuit of research inquiry are rendered merely frivolous and irresponsible dilettantism. By now there is a growing literature documenting the excesses, in Canadian as well as American academic establishments (Dominiguez 1994; D'Souza, 1991; Bernstein 1994; Fekete 1995; Loney 1998) of the kind of identity politics promoted by Harrison (1991: 6–7) and bearing witness to the danger that these kind of moral claims, even in the hands of well-meaning people, can 'turn fascist and bit[e] us all' (O'Meara 1995: 427). Neo-liberal demands for commercially applicable research as a necessary return on public investments are by no means the only source of attacks on academic independence. In the name of 'distributive justice' (Tri-council Policy Statement: 1998) or ethical primacy, university scholars are also quite capable of bowdlerizing complex debates concerning issues of representation and critical reflexivity into institutional mechanisms for quite crude doctrinaire surveillance and enforcement.

Ethical orthodoxies and controls

In 1994, the three major Canadian federal research granting agencies (Medical, Natural Sciences and Engineering, and Social Sciences and Humanities Research Councils), the same three research councils which administer the NCEs described earlier and which have been promoting commercialization policies, formed a Tri-Council Working Group to develop a unified set of ethical guidelines for research with human subjects. These guidelines provoked a good deal of controversy but none more so than the first draft of the proposed code of conduct which was published in 1996. The 1996 code was nearly 100 pages long but some of the sections elicited particularly strong reaction. In particular, the code had special provisions for research involving collectivities. Collectivities were defined as 'population groups with social structures, common customs and an acknowledged leadership' including nations, cultural groups, small indigenous communities, neighbourhood groups and families (1996: 13–2). Where research involved any groups of this kind, the code prescribed that informed consent be obtained not only from individuals but also the 'appropriate authorities' for that collectivity. It was also incumbent upon the researcher to protect the collectivity as well as its individual members from harm, to ensure that the collectivity has an opportunity to participate in designing the project, to subsequently submit his/her findings, reports and publications arising from the research to the collectivity *and* incorporate their reactions into these published materials, thereby to ensure a relationship of partnership between the researcher and the collectivity (1996: Section 13).

Many of these dictums will have a familiar ring. They reflect debates about representational authority, authorship, multivocality, dialogical ethnography, orientalism and the power relations implicated in the fieldwork enterprise that have occupied anthropologists over the last decade, as they have scholars in other social sciences and humanities. Indeed, the essays by D'Andrade, Scheper-Hughes and O'Meara cited above are a case in point. D'Andrade and Scheper-Hughes' contrasting stances were featured as essays in the same issue of *Current Anthropology* and O'Meara's was one of a number of commentaries which were solicited as responses to these articles.

This particular issue of *Current Anthropology* illustrates some obvious points about the nature of scholarly discourse and the importance of engaging in debate, but also that these discussions, especially over issues that really matter, are highly contested and unresolved. The D'Andrade/Scheper-Hughes debate, for example, while thought-provoking certainly did not result in consensus, nor was it expected or meant to. Yet the first draft of the Tri-Council code in effect took from the public domain a complex, constantly changing debate[4] and attempted to close it off, reduced it to a set of unequivocal 'principles' and then re-issued these as a priori prescriptions. It was a set of pronouncements that allowed neither for the legitimacy of different research epistemologies nor for the possibility of dissidence among the collectivities it was so desirous of protecting. In that latter sense, as in much identity politics intruding into universities (see Amit-Talai, 1996a, b; 1999), it ironically combined a postmodernist concern with voice and positioning with a Boasian version of collectivities as discretely bounded and clearly articulated owners of a shared culture. That the political effects of this vision were conservative, imparting legitimacy to anointed 'leaders', potentially providing even repressive leaderships or bureaucracies the possibility of shaping or vetoing critical research, was noted by the Canadian Association of University Teachers (CAUT Bulletin, October 1997: 8). That this self-righteous but also fairly flippant dismissal of the importance of the independent intellectual voice had come from fellow academics, acting on behalf of key educational institutions, made the assault on independence that much more breath-stopping.

Anthropology as a discipline has been somewhat more than incidentally implicated in these developments. The CAUT response to the section on collectivities which also appeared in modified form in a subsequent 1997 draft of the Tri-Council code, pointed out that 'the difficulty has arisen because the authors tried to generalize particular concerns about research on aboriginal peoples into a general code for all collectivities' (1997: 8) and anthropologists have been key players in Canadian research on aboriginal peoples. The Tri-Council Working Group on Ethics, which drafted both the 1996 and 1997 versions of the code of conduct for research involving humans, included an anthropologist. By the time the Tri-Council issued its much amended policy statement on ethical conduct, the section on collectivities had been reduced to a statement on research involving aboriginal peoples which was presented as an starting point for discussion rather than a enunciation of policy. Interestingly, this final version cited the American Anthropological Association (AAA)'s 1971 code of ethics as well as an AAA statement on ethics as support for its positions. The claim therefore by the AAA that in recently amending its Code of Ethics it was abandoning its previous regulatory role and restricting itself to ethics education (Flueher-Lobban 1998: 179) is more than a little naïve. Concordia University's protocol for ethics approval requires that the researcher making the application indicate whether s/he is 'familiar with and complies with the following agency/association ethical guidelines'. The AAA is one of only seven such associations explicitly listed. Thus whether or not the AAA directly assumes a regulatory role, it cannot ignore the ways in which its ethical guidelines can be used by other institutions to approve or sanction anthropological research. The AAA code is still being used as a sanctioning mechanism whatever the explicit intention and actions of the association that drafted it.

The quite drastic reduction of the sections on collectivities between the first two reports and the final Tri-Council policy statement provides both cause for hope as well as some ironic notes. There is little reason to doubt that the revision was influenced by the representations and objections voiced by various disciplinary associations as well as more general lobbying groups such as the CAUT, suggesting the potential capacity of academics to successfully contest restrictive policies. But the Tri-Council appears to have been especially impressed by opinions it solicited from the Federal Justice Ministry, which urged an abandonment of the collectivities section not because it infringed on academic freedom but because the Tri-Council itself had not consulted with the affected groups

(Kondro 1998). Indeed, this is the nature of the justification which was produced in the final policy statement to explain why the section on research involving aboriginal peoples was to serve only as a starting point for discussion rather than policy (Tri-Council Policy Statement 1998: 6.1). But there were other equally significant modifications contained in the final Tri-Council policy statement. The 1996 requirement (reminiscent of the moral model of scholarship invoked in the D'Andrade/Scheper-Hughes debate) that university ethics review boards (REBs) assess not only whether research has the potential to harm human research subjects but whether it provides them with social benefits has been rendered somewhat less prescriptive. However, it is retained as a principle of 'beneficence', as well as incorporated into 'inclusion' requirements for a fair social distribution of the benefits and burdens of research (1998: i.6, 5.1). The requirement that peer reviews of 'scientific validity' be incorporated as a matter of course into ethics reviews now appears to be restricted to research posing more than minimal risk (1998: 1.6). Perhaps most significant has been the recognition that research in the social sciences and humanities can legitimately be critical of public figures and organizations.

These are not minor changes. However, what remains even when these revisions are taken into account is an elaborate system of monitoring and surveillance which leaves much to the interpretative discretion of ethics review boards. Research must now be monitored not only at the beginning of a project but throughout. Most tellingly, the federal research granting agencies have in effect been able to use the imposition of a unified ethics code as a means to extend their jurisdiction far beyond the projects they fund to all research involving human subjects conducted by university employees and students, whether funded or not, whether intended for publication or not, whether intended for teaching, training, or for the acquisition of knowledge, whether conducted inside or outside Canada. All Canadian universities must develop and seek approval for ethics review protocols which comply with the Tri-Council policy or they and their employees and students will no longer be eligible for funding from the granting agencies administering this policy.

The potential for censorship and prescription is alarming. I have already personally become aware of at least one case in which an experienced anthropologist with a long record of research attentive to ethical concerns and the protection of informant confidentiality has had to substantially change his proposed research methodology, even to some extent his research orientation, in order to meet the terms required by his university's revamped ethics review procedures. And this danger of censorship appears to be recognized by the Tri-Council policy-makers since sprinkled throughout their statement are reminders that REBs should not reject research proposals because they are controversial or challenge mainstream thought or offend the powerful. So from where does the onus for developing such an intrusive and risky policy derive? One might have expected a catalogue of past abuses as justification. Instead we get only this vague statement: 'Unfortunately the history of research involving human subjects contains chapters on the misuse or serious abuse of research subjects' (1998: 5.1) No examples or substantiating citations are offered. Thus with this vague offhand statement, we come full circle to similar notes of unsubstantiated moral claims which also appeared in the Cowan report with which we started and which charged that academic freedom was being used as the cover for 'brutish and miserable' behaviour without offering any substantiation. Along the way we can take note of D'Andrade's observation that attacks on objective models by such anthropologists as Abu-Lughod

> do not present any evidence of the damage done by objectivity. In the same vein, evidence about the good done by science is ignored. A major reason for the unimportance of evidence, I believe, is what is being asserted is not a set of empirical facts but whether one's first allegiance is to morality or truth.
>
> (1995: 405)

In the name of civility, wealth creation, human liberation or ethics, it seems easier to get away with calls for a crass commercialization of academic research, with the institution of a risky and elaborate system of research surveillance, with an assertion in Cowan's words that a 'mutation of academic freedom' contributed to the 'uncivil' atmosphere in which four professors were killed. It is easier to get away with attacks on the independence and integrity of academic inquiry which have frightening implications and potential because they are being linked with principles of morality and citizenship espoused by many, probably most academicians themselves. Hence the suspension of critical judgement and tendency to accommodate where one might otherwise have expected vociferous objections.

Knowledge, fear and contestation

Noting the persuasive power of moral invocations should, however, not be taken to mean that Canadian academics are complacent about the state of the institutional contexts in which they operate. To the contrary, although my evidence is anecdotal and is derived from my own limited observations, I think there are indications of a growing fearfulness among university professors, and here I am talking of the Canadian situation at large. The fearfulnesss shows in various forms of risk assessment, stated as advice, expectation or explanation – advice such as that of the senior female professor who counselled me to ensure that I never met with a student behind closed doors even if the subject at hand required private consult-ations; expectations held by competent, experienced and productive junior faculty who were sure that they would face difficulty in acquiring tenure in spite of their accomplishments. There is the trepidation of department chairs or individual faculty members when a complaint is made to the ombuds office, even where this is a strictly advisory role without powers of sanction or even much evidence of political influence. There is the unwillingness of faculty members to challenge defamatory accusations made by students or staff or to go on record with their experiences of various granting agencies or institutional adjudication tribunals for fear of punitive retaliation. And then there is the conviction, promulgated by some faculty members, that we have no choice but to explore means of effecting fiscal cuts or tailoring our research projects to strategic political priorities because if we do not figure out how to do it ourselves, it will be done to us.

Yet, in spite of the proliferation of these claims of risk and the apparent sincerity of the fears they incite, what is almost always missing from these accounts is a detailed or informed analysis of the institutional mechanisms, procedures and policies by which tenure can be denied, unfounded harassment charges successfully prose-cuted, retaliation imposed and of course the claim that self-imposed contraction and accommodation will forestall even worse impos-itions is by its very nature self fulfilling and therefore unverifiable. In a recent survey of the experiences of members of the Canadian Anthropology Society in applications for research funding, there was general uncertainty about how grants were evaluated and allocated by the Canadian Social Sciences and Humanities Research Council, the principal and in some provinces the only source of funding for anthropology. Fully two-thirds of the respondents were unaware, for example, which procedures were used to select referees to judge their proposal (Dyck 1998: 3), yet many were clearly very anxious about their future funding prospects through this agency. The fervour, therefore, with which risks are assessed by faculty members appears to have an almost inverse relationship to the degree of knowledge they actually possess about the structure of the bureaucracy to which they are trying to respond tactically.

Given both the internal and external pressures for accountability which I have just outlined, it is surely not difficult to understand the general sense of embattlement felt by many North American university scholars generally and Canadian academics more specifically. Nor, given the institutional emphasis on confidentiality and the hypocritical willingness of some administrators to duck their own obligations for accountability while seeking it of others, is it surprising that faculty are not especially well informed even about the structure and practices of their own institutions. That this has not prevented academics from speculating about very specific sources and enactments of risk is surely an instance of what Herzfeld has termed 'secular theodicy', pragmatic explanatory mythologies for coping with the regular disappointments of ongoing engagement with a bewildering bureaucracy (1992). In so doing, like institutional clients elsewhere, scholars have helped to reproduce the bureaucracies they fear.

Canadian university academics have, for some time, been subject to far stricter oversight and limits on their powers of investigation than journalists. The danger is that they may become more limited in their right to consult, to investigate and to speak than the average citizen. For example, while I was writing this chapter I sought out the views of several fellow academics. I did not seek ethics clearance for these consultations/interviews even though if the Tri-Council guidelines had already been in effect I would have had to get ethics clearance or at least consulted with the Concordia ethics review board to ascertain whether in their view this constituted research requiring ethics review. By the same definitions, the survey conducted by the Canadian Anthropology Society of its members (Dyck 1998) would also be in violation of the Tri-Council guidelines since its authors did not seek ethics clearance from any of the institutions with which they are affiliated. In this context of moral claims, anxiety and limited information, retaining an illusion of academia as a privileged nexus for critical reflection may become increasingly implausible, however much university mission statements trumpet the continuing protection of academic freedom or expert panel reports on commercialization and speeches by research council presidents extol the virtues of basic research.

Yet I do think there is potential for university scholars to call two important bluffs in these institutional attacks on academic independence. The first bluff, which tries to treat the commercialization of the university as an implacable outcome of a globalizing information economy, I have already discussed. The second bluff is entailed in the presumption that the institutions of the educational sector, whether universities, granting agencies or academic associations, would be willing to enforce the regime of accountability they are attempting to adopt even if they did not receive the full co-operation of the scholars they are trying to regulate. To the contrary, in Canada at least, there are some telling indications of their unwillingness to assume the full panoply of surveillance and enforcement mechanisms as well as legal and political liabilities entailed in attempting to police and control a population of hostile scholars. To return to the Tri-Council ethics committee, one of the rare instances of a concerted collective campaign organized by the Canadian Association of University Teachers protesting against the disastrous 1996 draft succeeded at the very least in forcing substantial redrafts and a shift to introduce the code as a 'policy' rather than the more prescriptive regulations that had first been intended. In effect, the Tri-Council downloaded responsibility for policing their ethics code to the universities on which it has been imposed. There is, however, evidence the universities are just as reluctant to assume legal liability in the area of ethics. A graduate student in criminology at Simon Fraser University, Russell Ogden, subpoenaed in 1994 by the Vancouver Coroner's Court, was charged with contempt of court when, in keeping with the confidentiality guarantees he had made in the course of the SFU ethics review, he refused to divulge confidential information acquired in the course of his research on assisted suicide and euthanasia. The refusal of the Simon Fraser administration to support the student and their attempt to introduce requirements for limited confidentiality provisions elicited so much public attention and condemnation that the university was forced to institute several reviews of its ethics policies. Ogden was eventually reimbursed for his legal expenses and a recent redrafting of the SFU policy and practices for ethics reviews of research involving human subjects includes an explicit acknowledgement of the university's responsibilities in future cases.

There is, therefore, at least some indication that the stridency of institutional demands for accountability is not necesarily matched by a similar depth of willingness to shoulder the consequences of maintaining the regulatory regime. As the Ogden case also suggests, this form of institutional hypocrisy can be effectively resisted and exposed but, like the emperor's new clothes, if university scholars are too frightened to systematically challenge such administrative sleights of hand, the parade of one-sided accountability will go on.

Ethnography and political will

Given the political contestations entailed in the rhetorics and institutional practices of accountability, the fearfulness, secular theodicy and fallacies that are implicated in this struggle, what can university professors generally and anthropologists particularly do? At the EASA meetings held in Barcelona (1996), I noted that as an outcome of an earlier round of these struggles in my university, I and several colleagues had agreed to serve on committees which we had worked hard to avoid for most of our academic careers (Amit-Talai: n.d). Some years on, I have concluded that attempting to use the academic sector's own institutional structures as vehicles for opposing its prevailing policies is unlikely to be effective. There is nothing more frustrating and fruitless than watching your co-optation unfold in the slow motion of endless minutiae that university committees appear to have perfected. Nonetheless, knowing and understanding these structures and practices are crucial to framing any kind of informed stance. So, when I started writing this chapter, I had planned to conclude by arguing that ethnography had the potential to make an important contribution to an understanding of the bureaucracy in which anthropologists and their fellow scholars are implicated. I planned to cite Herzfeld who had suggested 'that anthropological sensitivity to immediate context – ethnography – helps shift the focus away from perspectives that are already, to some extent, determined by the institutional structures they were set up to examine' (1992: 15) and I still agree with that recommendation. I had planned to argue that a discipline which has made so much of giving voice to those who have not had the means to be heard should surely now be capable and desirous of finding some way to bridge the fearful silences of many scholars including its own practitioners.

However, just as education is necessary but not sufficient to correct the determined biases of racism, so too information about these bureaucracies will not be enough, in and of itself, to counterweigh the political pressures of accountability. If all that we produce are carefully nuanced ethnographies which avoid clear statements of our political stance, then we will do little to advance a struggle for academic freedom however much information we gather. Our challenge will be to combine ethnographic insight with political courage, the courage to challenge institutional controls cloaked in self-serving invocations of ethical care, to resist bureaucratic accommodations that demand intellectual subjugation to the most conservative and instrumental of political and economic interests, the courage to speak out if even if our colleagues remain fearful and silent, the courage to insist that the true measure of the intellectual project must be the curiosity of a critical and independent mind.

Notes

1 It is worth noting that several of the public reports cited in this chapter refer to American and other international sources to back up their contention that, in following these prescriptions, Canada would simply be following international precedent. Indeed, the language of legitimation for these measures is increasingly vested in the rhetoric of globalization as requiring a particular kind of institutional framework.
2 Information taken from the NCE web site: http://www.nce.gc.ca/facteng.htm
3 IP stands for Intellectual Property which the expert panel defines as 'an invention, discovery or new idea that the legal entity responsible for commercialization has decided to protect for possible commercial gain, based on the disclosure of the creator' (1999: 1).
4 Indeed, although for rather different reasons, I suspect that neither D'Andrade with his calls for a separation between moral and objective models of anthropology nor Scheper-Hughes with her call for the anthropologist as companheira would be happy with the Tri-Council's initial demand for collective informed consent.

References

Amit-Talai, V. (n.d.) 'The insidiousness of bureaucratic banalities: some implications for anthropological fieldwork', unpublished paper presented at the 1996 EASA meetings, Barcelona.

—— (1996a) 'Anthropology, Multiculturalism and the Concept of Culture', *Folk* 38: 125–33.

—— (1996b) 'The Minority Circuit: Identity Politics and the Professionalization of Ethnic Activism' in V. Amit-Talai and C. Knowles (eds) *Resituating Identities: The Politics of Race, Ethnicity and Culture*, Peterborough, Ont: Broadview Press.

—— (1999) 'Revolutionary Claims and Political Stalemates: A Review of the Relationship between Multiculturalism and Postmodernism' in C. Levitt, S. Davies and N. McLaughlin (eds) *Mistaken Identities: The Challenge of Cultural Radicalism at the End of the Millennium*, New York: Peter Lang Publishers.

Bernstein, R. (1994) *Dictatorship of Virtue: Multiculturalism and the Battle for America's Future*, New York: Alfred A. Knopf.

CAUT (1997) 'CAUT Responds to Tri-Council Code', *CAUT Bulletin*, vol. 44, no. 8, October, 1997, pp. 1, 8.

Cowan, J. S. (1994) *Lessons from the Fabrikant File: A Report to the Board of Governors of Concordia University.*

D'Andrade, R. (1995) 'Objectivity and Militancy: A Debate, I: Moral Models in Anthropology', *Current Anthropology* 36 (3): 399–408.

Dominiguez, V. R. (1994) 'A Taste for "the Other": Intellectual Complicity in Racializing Practices', *Current Anthropology* 35 (4): 333–48.

D'Souza, D. (1991) *Illiberal Education: The Politics of Race and Sex on Campus*, New York: Random House.

Dyck, N. (1998) *Funding Canadian Anthropological Research: The Experiences, Views and Concerns of Members of the Canadian Anthropology Society (CASCA)*, report presented to CASCA, May 1998.

Expert Panel on the Commercialization of University Research (1999) *Public Investments in University Research: Reaping the Benefits*, presented to: The Prime Minister's Advisory Council on Science and Technology, 4 May 1999. Available online at: http://acst-ccst.gc.ca

Fekete, J. (1995) *Moral Panic: Biopolitics rising*, Montreal and Toronto: Robert Davies Publishing.

Fluehr-Lobban, C. (1998) 'Ethics', in H.R. Bernard (ed.) *Handbook of Methods in Cultural Anthropology*, Walnut Creek, London, New Delhi: Altamira Press.

Graham, B. (1998) 'What's Wrong with Dialogue on Education?' *CAUT Bulletin*, June 1998: 20.

Harrison, F. V. (1991) 'Anthropology as an Agent of Transformation: Introductory Comments and Queries' in F. V. Harrison (ed.) *Decolonizing Anthropology: Moving Further toward an Anthropology for Liberation*, Washington DC: Association of Black Anthropologists, American Anthropological Association.

Herzfeld, M. (1992) *The Social Production of Indifference: Exploring the Symbolic Roots of Western Bureaucracy*, New York and Oxford: Berg Books.

Kondro, W. (1998) *Perspectives*, vol. 2, no. 4, Pilot Project of the Humanities and Social Science Federation of Canada. Available online at: http://www.hssfc.ca/Pub/PublicationsEng.html (15 June 1998).

Loney, M. (1998) *The Pursuit of Division: Race, Gender and Preferential Hiring in Canada*, Montreal and Kingston, London, Buffalo: McGill-Queen's University Press.

O'Meara, T. (1995) 'Comment on Objectivity and Militancy: A Debate', *Current Anthropology* 36 (3): 427–8.

Renaud, M. (1999) Notes for a Speech Presented by Dr M. Renaud, President of SSHRC, at the 30th Annual Sorokin Lecture, Department of Sociology, University of Saskatchewan, Saskatoon, February 4. Available online at: http://www.sshrc.ca/english/resnews/speeches/sorokin.html (26 July 1999).

Scheper-Hughes, N. (1995) 'Objectivity and Militancy: A Debate, 2: The Primacy of the Ethical: Propositions for a Militant Anthropology', *Current Anthropology* 36 (2): 409–20.

SSHRC (Social Sciences and Humanities Research Council) (1999) Grants Guide: Strategic Themes, Challenges and Opportunities of a Knowledge-Based Economy. Available online at: http://www.sshrc.ca/english/programinfo/grantsguide/theme-kbe.html (last updated 9 March 1999).

Tri-Council Working Group (1996) *Code of Conduct for Research Involving Humans*, The Medical Research Council of Canada; The Natural Sciences and Engineering Research Council of Canada; The Social Sciences and Humanities Research Council of Canada, Ottawa: Minister of Supply and Services.

—— (1997) *Code of Ethical Conduct for Research Involving Humans*. June, 1997.

Tri-council Policy Statement (1998) *Ethical Conduct for Research Involving Humans*, Catalogue No.: MR21–18/1998 E. Public Works and Government Services Canada. Online. Available: http://www.nserc.ca

Chapter 9

Academia

Same pressures, same conditions of work?

Thomas Fillitz

The following contribution deals with events that occurred in Austria in 1996. At that time, Austrian academia was in a phase of transition into an audit culture. But at that moment it was afflicted by government measures which at first sight had nothing to do with the Austrian system of higher education, but rather conformed to the new standards of the European Union. However, the outcome was an experience of an audit 'regime', in which scholars, teachers and students felt they were marionettes in the iron grip of political and economic powers. Much of what had made one feel at unease with the introduction of auditing suddenly had become reality. The contribution is thus a reflection on (active participant) observations from the specific Austrian case and its relationship to transnationally negotiated standards.

Since the 1970s, Austrian academia could be characterized by certain democratic structures, conveying a right of co-determination in studying matters to assistant professors and students via chair-holding professors. Furthermore, no major pressures were imposed regarding research, publication and teaching performances, and once a job in academia was gained it could be easily transformed into a lifelong position. Students, on the other hand, had free access to any scientific discipline with no fees to pay; there were no rules regarding the duration of one's studies, and social support by the state was assured within certain limits. In short, academia in Austria constituted an overall liberal system with the three pillars of freedom of research, freedom of teaching and freedom of studying.

The major problems within Austrian academia concerned the scarcity of human resources in teaching and administration, and financial and material means. Other serious problems included the too lengthy studying times of students, high drop-out rates, and the high number of students who several times changed their scientific discipline. From within academia, the responsibility for these problems was assigned either to the government which did not provide the needed infrastructures, or to the students, who would not accomplish their moral obligation as students. Then, in the early 1990s, Austrian academia had to face the reproach that it had not undertaken enough research upon itself (Brünner 1993: 5), and that it had not reflected upon the seriousness of the problems within the academic system. A new University Act (UOG 93) was passed by the National Assembly in 1993. The importance of teaching was acknowledged and would have to be totally restructured; evaluation of research and teaching had to be introduced, and monocratic power hierarchies were re-installed, although free access to academia was maintained. Criticism was articulated in different respects by the three curiae, of the professors, the assistant professors and the students.[1] But the overall mood was a kind of resignation, with people hoping to go on with their daily agenda within their own, small 'golden cage'.

But a few years later, quite suddenly, Austria's academia was in movement, its problems becoming for the first time a major topic in public debate.

Abandoning teaching in Austria's universities

During the non-teaching period of February 1996, when most scholars used their privilege to pursue research outside their working place (the university), the Austrian government decided an overall Economizing Package in order to fulfill requirements for the introduction of the common European currency. It heavily affected academia, as budget cuts of one milliard Austrian schillings (about fifty million pounds) were imposed and were supposed to be realized almost there and then.

These financial cuts concerned teaching and administrative employees, and were to be achieved by stopping appointments to vacancies, reducing the adminstrative realm in the first instance, and then in the teaching-staff domain. Second, salaries of the assistant professors (the middle curia) were to be cut down while their teaching was increased. Third, salaries of freelance lecturers[2] were also cut and their number had to be decisively reduced. And, finally, high pressure was put on the students' conditions of work, as many of their social support measures were simply erased, and their right to finish their studies in the minimum time required by law was declared a social obligation.[3]

Academia was in an uproar. The government wanted these measures to be implemented as soon as the coming semester (March to June 1996), with teaching reductions of 30 per cent, but the Austrian universities decided to abandon teaching and took to the streets. However, the strike was not total. At the peak of society's sympathy for the strike,[4] the conservative-intellectual newspaper *Die Presse* reported that there was partial-teaching at the Technical University, and full teaching by professors at the Soil Culture University of Vienna. Full teaching was assured at the Technical University of Graz, at the Coal, Iron and Steel University of Leoben in Styria (Montanuniversität), at the medical and law faculties of the University of Innsbruck, and at the veterinary university in Vienna (*Die Presse*, 18 March 1996).[5] At Vienna University, however, few were those who dared to teach, committees of the Austrian students' union aiming at hindering them in doing so.

By the third week, academic pressure forced Austria's Union (professor dominated) to revoke the previous agreement upon the University Economizing Package (*Der Standard*, 20 March 1996).[6] Nevertheless, one day later, newspapers started reporting the dismantling of the front, with the dean of the Technical University of Vienna declaring publicly the need to take up teaching again (*Der Standard*, 22 March 1996). Conservative and populist newspapers filled their headlines with comments on the strange coalition of assistant professors with chaotist, anarchist and communist students (*Neue Kronen Zeitung*, 23March 1996: 2–3; *Die Presse*, 23 March 1996: 2).[7]

> On the side of the students, more and more student groups refrain from an unconditional strike as well as from any violent actions. Even the often quoted 'silent majority' articulates itself and demands possibilities to continue their studies. What remains is a basically incredible coalition between two totally different groups: here the action groups which are supported by the anarchos[8] in the student scene, there the academic middle curia – assistant professors and senior lecturers – who want to inforce their own interests. Truly a strange coalition.
>
> (Witzmann 1996: 2)

Public opinion in support of the movement crumbled to 13 per cent (*Die Presse*, 27 March 1996: 1, 6). To understand that shift, several events seem important. At that time, Austria's Students Union had widened its argument in wanting to bring down the whole Economizing Package. Furthermore, the political parties forced their young-generation factions to align at last with their decisions. And the government put pressure on freelance lecturers and students, by asserting a firm decision not to pay the salaries for the abandoned courses, and to consider the semester as an irregular one by stopping financial support for students. Hence, academics had to return to the lecture-halls by the end of March.

Little had been achieved in the negotiations about finances. Concerning the situation of the students, three years on (1998) the result of the measures is obvious: a three-class student system with 20 per cent living in 'economic emergency', 35 per cent experiencing a 'heavy burden', and 40–45 per cent having no subsistence problems (*Kurier*, 16 July 1998: 3).[9] Confronted with these data, the Austrian government rapidly allocated funds for the students in need.

However, although economic questions instigated the movement, longer existing problems in relation to the mass higher education system and the new University Act[10] quickly became a topic of concern.[11] Large debates were launched in newspapers, inside universities, and in university negotiations with the Ministry of Science and Transport.[12] Whereas such topics had been badly neglected in previous public discussion, perhaps because universities had not taken the offensive,[13] by the second week of the movement, the opinion of newspapers such as *Kurier* and *Der Standard* (liberal-intellectual) had openly shifted towards sympathy with the universities. Therefore, and besides their daily comments, *Kurier* opened a series under the rubric of 'University in uproar', while *Der Standard* continuously reserved a full page for articles by those involved. Drop-out rates, the question of the free access to academic education, the mockery of the university system by the government, and debates on research at Austrian universities, were some of the topics lengthily discussed.

On the other hand, the conservative-intellectual *Die Presse* chose a commentary style characterized by disapprobation of the events, accusations of the inflexibility of the universities towards reform, and sympathy towards a government opening up debate on the real problems, with typical statements such as 'problems have to be solved, by acting not waiting' (*Die Presse*, 23 March 1996: 2),[14] or 'the minister of science and the minister of finances knew about the urgency of reordering teaching, in order to avoid the untenable situation that teaching assignment had become a supplementary occupation for assistant professors' (*Die Presse*, 2 April 1996: 2),[15] while actually, with the new regulations, they were having to teach more, with stricter control by the head of the institute and especially by the newly created 'dean of studies' of the respective faculties.

The topics raised by newspapers can be classified into three overall domains: structural changes, free access to universities,[16] and tutelage of state bureaucracy.[17] These topics are of interest.

Structural changes

- Reordering of education – new offers required (e.g. *Die Presse*, 25 March 1996)
- Opposition to mass-university education (e.g. *Der Standard*, 18 March 1996)
- Crisis of the education system (e.g. *Der Standard*, 18 March 1996)
- Education intersections: school – university – vocational training (e.g. *Der Standard*, 18 March 1996)
- Scarcity of scholar-teachers (e.g. *Kurier*, 18 March 1996)
- Inefficiency of research and teaching (e.g. *Kurier*, 18 March 1996)
- Scarcity of financial means for research (e.g. *Der Standard*, 26 March 1996)
- Salaries of teachers and costs for students (e.g. *Kurier*, 25 March 1996)

Free access to university

- Failure of the political dimension of free access to education for Austrian citizens (e.g. *Kurier*, 18 March 1996)
- Normative time and real studying time (e.g. *Kurier*, 18 March 1996)
- Knock out exams (e.g. *Kurier*, 18 March 1996)
- Scarcity of seminar and laboratory places, of technical equipment (e.g. *Kurier*, 18 March 1996)
- Drop-out rates (e.g. *Kurier*, 21 March 1996)

• Unemployed scholars (e.g. *Die Pesse*, 20 March 1996)

Tutelage of state bureaucracy

• State bureaucracy holding a university in tutelage (e.g. *Kurier*, 24 March 1996)
• State bureaucracy vs scholars' opinions (e.g. *Der Standard*, 23 March 1996)

Ulrike Felt, the spokeswoman for assistant professors and for a long time for freelance lecturers (they are not constituted as curia on their own), considered the following topics essential for a university's inner debate during the movement:

• Teaching and research – duties of teachers and expectations towards them.
• The university as a research institution.
• The new monocratic structures (UOG 93): the relationship between university and freelance lecturers/researchers; the freedom of teaching for assistant professors and freelance lecturers; the omnipotence of the president-manager; the power of the dean of studies; the evaluation of teaching and research – the notion of 'efficiency'.
• The university as a place for channelling students through instead of a place to stay.
• Teaching as feeding in a short time small bites of knowledge – the loss of reflection.

The question concerns not only each of the topics which are being dealt with, but how they are dealt with. If one takes the example of mass-university education and free access, it is noteworthy how different authors in different newspapers emphasize certain arguments. The following quotations from three newspapers (*Die Presse, Der Standard, Kurier*) and from a (political) resolution by the academic staff of the University of Vienna are chosen as examples of the structure of the debates. Dealing with the same topic, free access to Austrian universities (mass higher education), the arguments are chosen in conformity with the interest of political factions or interest groups (e.g. public opinion vs academic community or Austrian Union vs Association of Austrian Industrialists). It was not possible to discuss problems in an analytical way. Rather, the debates became power discourses of exclusion, each negating the other's arguments.

> Austria's universities will still be stuck in a deep crisis if teaching is [fully, properly] taken up at all the institutes. And this crisis urgently needs an overall societal debate. It may be formulated in a principal sentence: There isn't enough money to let anybody study as long as he wants, and as many scientific disciplines as he wishes to, without any fees but with as much social support as possible. And with such premises it is not possible to maintain a high scholarly level in the higher education system. . . . Our universities have been destroyed by mass assault and by the absence of any evidence of performance of the teachers. In future, the Republic will have to formulate clear handicaps for them. On the financial side it will also have to choose, as do most other countries, between two quite unpopular solutions: between the introduction of fees . . . or a numerus clausus.
>
> (Unterberger 1996: 2)

> Only if one proceeds to a fundamental and common reform of school and university education, as well as of a vocational preparation, may one get control of the problem . . . and then one may also be able to propose to children of poor parents the financing of a vocational education according to their aptitude. If the government refrains from such a reform because of cowardice or laziness, protests will go on, protests will remain useless. . . . And quietly, we will end up with non-egalitarian principles. The clever and fast ones will not succeed, but those having the means to flee an idiosyncratic educational system will.
>
> (Maier 1996)

What is at stake is the political failure of free access to academic education. Education policy did acknowledge mass-university in the 70s, but it did not solve the cost of it: a lot more students have only few more teachers and a few more premises at their disposition. For more than twenty years, politics avoided worrying about this problem. It made professors keep quiet by paying them exam taxes, and by supporting and relieving them of teaching with assignments to assistant professors. Now that even the financing of these measures is no longer possible, because of pure state budget urgency, the whole misery of the badly financed mass-university becomes incalculable. As, in the mean time, the vocational facilities of the graduates become dramatically deteriorated . . . [and] the situation gets explosive.

(Rabl 1996: 2)

The assembly of the academic staff of the University of Vienna declares its solidarity with the students and asserts: the Economizing Package of the government is an attack against quantity and quality of teaching; it functions as a punishment for the actual upholding of teaching under precarious conditions; it undermines the current quantity and quality of research; the government introduces with these measures a numerus clausus for students and therefore produces new social problems. . . . The assembly of the academic staff of the University of Vienna therefore calls upon the government and National Assembly to: secure at least the conditions of current teaching; to recognize and make use of the will to meaningful reform of the universities and its employees.

(Dienststellenausschuss 1996)

In all these debates, the government has remained mostly deaf and cynical. Small changes were accorded in the case of salaries and the teaching duties of assistant professors, and for the first time in years, the necessity and importance of freelance lecturers was recognized in order to maintain teaching and the curricula, especially in the social sciences, humanities and business, although severe reductions are still being effected. It is a continued cynicism on the part of the Minister for Science and Transport to declare in TV interviews, without any foundation or argument, that the Austrian university system is backward.[18] It is cynical of the government to cut down budgets and jobs in universities while asserting free access as a pillar of its politics and to call on teachers to abolish exams in the first year or to adopt other measures hindering young people from studying.[19]

Goodbye to the academy as an ideal community?

In their debate on the 'postmodern' university, Smith and Webster

(1997: 1) speak of the 'University as Imagined Community', a community of scholars, 'a model of rational and disinterested discourse' that existed once. Of course, the notions 'rational' and 'disinterested' refer to Kant, who developed the idea of the university as an institution of intellectual activity and which ended in the constitution of the German modern university as installed by Humboldt in Berlin. And one does not feel at ease in dropping that idea of community which has existed beyond the diversity and the postulated competition between universities. Is not the community of scholars and, I would also add, students, an ideal, which we all constitute and recreate, by basing our work on values 'of education, of moral and intellectual standards of the highest possible' (Gewirth 1990: 8), on 'rules for critical inquiry' (Simon 1990: 250–1)? Are we not a community of people in the search of knowledge on the basis of responsibility?

Relating the idea of the university as an imagined community to the events of early 1996 in Austria, one is tempted to say that the university really is no more than an 'imagined' community, a mirage, the general view being of a widely incoherent group of linked institutions, which lacks even collective solidarity – neither mechanical nor organic in Durkheimian terms. The differences seem deep when the Dean of the Technical University of Vienna opts for the return to teaching at the same moment as the president of the University of Vienna interrupts negotiations with the Ministry, declares solidarity with the students and takes the lead in student demonstrations involving over fifty thousand university members in the streets of Vienna. And when, a few days later, the president of the Coal, Iron and Steel University in Styria goes even further and rejects in an interview any idea of protest, appreciates all government measures, proposes 'performance ethics' for his university, and accuses his Viennese colleague of being childish and not keeping up with events (*Die Presse*, 2 April 1996).[20]

A similar impression can be achieved by analysing the press articles on the problems of higher education. They partly aim at explaining actual problems to a wider public, but are often too generalizing. The differences between types of universities, whether technical, economic, and so forth, are not reflected. Overall solutions are sought according to slogans of 'efficiency' and the 'practical [market] orientation' of education. They speak of 'the' research situation at Austrian universities, and demand that the 'supply' of scientific disciplines should be clarified. However, they also express an unease with this huge diversity which they can hardly incorporate within one framework. How to compare in actuality or to suggest similar conditions for such a 'monster' as the University of Vienna with over 6,000 employees, eight diverse faculties,[21] over 130 institutes, and 94,000 students (in 1996) with the small universities[22] of Salzburg, Innsbruck or Graz? How to treat homogeneously the teaching assignment of assistant professors of the Vienna University, if professors of the Faculty of Law tend to monopolize teaching, whereas in other faculties the teaching of professors and assistant professors has to be supplemented by a high proportion (up to 80 per cent in some disciplines) of freelance lecturers.

Some authors speak of this as a goodbye to the academy as a community of all scientific disciplines, and of the fiction of equality between universities (Müller-Böling 1995: 39). Theirs is the vision of highly specialized universities competing with one another for students and research funds. Others claim the same in the name of the American concept of 'excellence' (e.g. Readings 1997). Both refer to systems of audit, evaluation and competition. In such perspectives, the dissolution of market-inefficient departments (and research) does not seem to represent a major concern. A somewhat different line of argument is taken by some of the contributors to *The Postmodern University?* (Smith and Webster 1997), as the shift to difference among universities is argued through a postmodern terminology as 'the plurality and multi-vocality of the present-day [collectivity] . . . that offer the universities . . . the chance of emerging successfully from the present challenge' (Bauman 1997: 25).

The university system has never been that homogeneous, not even in Humboldt's ideal. And the proposition of a former equality between (all) universities belongs to the realm of historical idealization – we did and do compare research and researchers (Mussnug 1993: 54). Without postulating the end of academia as community, Strathern (1997: 313) emphasizes the transformation of the university as an institution, its characteristic of having diverse, possibly even conflicting and competing aims, 'becomes judged by acts that presume unity'. Then, one might argue, it is a new unitarian profile for each university which is replacing the former uniting grand principle of the 'imagined community'.

However, my argument is based upon another element. Dichotomies in the Austrian protest have to be related to deeply different conditions of work for students, researchers, and teachers, as well as to the requirement of enhanced vocational training.[23] The University Studying Act (UniStG 97) is explicit about the latter, as curricula have to be submitted for hearing and evaluation to non-academic institutions, e.g. to the Austrian Union, to the Association of Austrian Industry and to specific professional group associations (Österreichisches Hochschulrecht 1997: 24, ¶24 (3), (4), and (6)). Also, the topics mentioned by Felt (see above) show that there is a growing uncertainty about the duty of and expectation in research and teaching, about the kind of knowledge to be produced and taught, and about the places of the various groups of teachers within this new framing of the university. Moreover, this uncertainty was augmented in relation to the Ministry's discourse, which was stolidly about clarification and the reduction of the complexity of work conditions, and which refused to accept fundamental institutional diversity. In its overall claim for vocational orientation, it did not consider differences between schools of law or medicine, the humanities or the social sciences – which had the effect of producing great anxiety on the side of the humanities and social sciences (both students and teachers).

From such a viewpoint, the university as an 'ideal community' is a fiction, a piece of rhetoric but, as Felt states, a fiction that is important even though one has to appreciate the level of fiction involved. In respect to Austria's situation, this is striking in relation to the difference between universities as well as within the institution of the University of Vienna. Considering the level of fiction, Felt (1998) places it between the poles of our ethics as scholars and teachers – our striving for knowledge by the disinterested, rational debate of problems – and the exercise of power – interest in hierarchy, allocation of financial means, and state tutelage. The concept of the ideal community fails, as these latter aspects become emphasized, and as they structure our internal discourse to the disadvantage of discourses on the substance of our research and teaching under these new conditions. Neither before nor after the events of February–March 1996 in Austria, did we achieve any transformation of our discourse, based on our ethics as scholars and teachers, in order to launch a debate about using the spaces of diverse, possibly conflicting aims for qualitative improvement.[24]

The mass-university and changing necessities

For years, if not for decades, Austrian universities were afflicted by high student attendance without concomitant improvement of the infrastructure, of financial means or the number of scientific staff.[25] It is obvious that these problems constituted major topics of complaint. Today, with the new University Act, the question of free access is put into the foreground by the media and other forces in society which now see the chance of erasing it. Interestingly, it is a topic for the Technical and Business universities, while the University of Vienna, the most heavily affected, generally refuses fees or places them in the realm of symbolic amounts. For its president, the government measures have already destroyed the financial capacities of students.

Another topic is, of course, the required market orientation of teaching and research. Stuck between the pressures of the mass higher education system on one hand and the market orientation on the other one, the community of scholars and teachers cannot but fear for the preservation and improvement of its ideal of cultural knowledge. Moreover, the state conveys clear signs of wanting to rid itself of its former cultural mission; it wishes to be seen in the monocratic university structures on the side of the executive, with the president having enhanced high managerial qualities, being backed by an advisory board from industry, government (the state re-entering the scene here) and alumni (Bast 1994: 155–6). Actually, similar trends at a different speed of realization can be observed in respect to the restructuring of the organization of Austria's national theatres and national museums.

Concerning universities, the state's argument deals with the long studying times,[26] the high drop-out rates, the growing potential and importance of people without university degrees who have nonetheless received a level of higher education from society, and the future need to improve lifelong learning. Such arguments conform with publications of the European Commission, which even promote the slogan of the 'cognitive society' (Europäische Kommission 1995). Obviously, today's societies are deeply grounded on scientific disciplines whatever the domain (Müller-Böling 1995: 28; Gibbons et al. 1994; Böhme 1991), be it in daily life or in any government decision. Nevertheless, our internal discourses express the feeling of the state's hostility towards science, and we experience the new measures as being dictated from the government. In a recent article, one of the highest officials of the Ministry of Science and Transport was quite explicit in stating that the foundation of an audit agency, the implementation and routinization of evaluation, would be the only way for an autonomous, qualitative university to survive. Implicitly, those opposing or problematizing this were turned by his rhetoric into being backward, lazy or of low quality.

> 'Evaluation' is new in our country. It is definitely wanted by the many successful university teachers and researchers, because they expect an improvement of their situation and an enhancement of the performance of the universities. Others demand it, because there is no other way than to surrender to the new fashion of universities which have traditionally valued high performance. The introduction of an 'evaluation culture', of a national central agency, is being requested. This agency should be in charge of all data, and [develop] highly developed methods which should enable comparison with Europe and the whole world. An evaluation agency which as a neutral institution chooses evaluators and advises universities and the Ministry in methodological matters should be installed soon. On the contrary, [the kind of] evaluation agency which is being requested, which knows all about performances and about performance shortcomings, would be harmful. It would be a centralistic authority, which the Ministry never was, at a time . . . where the Ministry is withdrawing from all operative matters and is concentrating on strategy development and controlling.
>
> (Höllinger 1998: 39)

One could analyse the supposedly logical juxtaposition of state withdrawal and university autonomy for flexibility, which his rhetoric would not allow as a contradiction and which led straight to the need for evaluation in order to improve the quality of the university and enable the state to develop new strategies – the so-called requests and claims for a 'centralistic evaluation agency'. However, it may be of more interest to reflect on debate within the universities. Felt complained about the omission of discourses which would address the kind of knowledge we teach and research within the University of Vienna. According to her, we are still producing that Humboldtian ideal which separated science from the state and economy. We do not reflect on what higher education without free access would mean; we do not discuss what kind of knowledge we are producing or what other possibilities there are. We do discuss how to teach (with all the hi-tech facilities) but not what to teach (Felt 1998). Why, one may add in this respect, do we need the Austrian Studying Act to remind us that the organization of courses should be established in conformity to the specific situation of working students (Österreichisches Hochschulgesetz 1997: 17, ¶.7(2)). In other words, the university appears to us as a separate institution, but not as an institution which is constituted as such by our acting and interacting. Hence we also feel ourselves overrun in matters of restructuration.

The problem is not the production, reproduction and improvement of our ideal. And the Austrian case outlined here is in certain ways a regional phenomenon. It is specific in the way and in the speed with which new measures have been enforced by the state. Some of the restructurations directly affected aspects of the Austrian higher education system yet without submitting the free access to universities to discussion. Free access is a social achievement and, as such, a pillar of the system. The Austrian case is not specific, as the main intentions were conformity to the guidelines of the European Commission and the installation of a system of selectivity, basically adapted from other countries (e.g. the USA). In an overall perspective, mass higher education has changed the function of universities in social life. We not only observe but also experience the changing character of universities, as elite teaching and research (the realization of the ideal) becomes more and more difficult, even though we put more time into teaching, supervision and research work. And there are nowadays concepts about the highly specialized universities as globally competing corporations. Nevertheless, governments expect us to act according to our old ideal, even in administrative tasks.

It can be acknowledged that the universities' structural forms have to be newly conceived (Filmer 1997: 48). It seems that the changing order of knowledge (Spinner 1994), the commercialization of knowledge, the combination of ideal and interest, and the change in the relationship between science, state and economy, as well as both quantitative and qualitative aspects of students' lives – working students, shift in the gender of students, students as consumers (is learning equivalent to consumerism?)[27] – are factors which have not been thought through in their full dimensions by the members of universities. We should wonder and be concerned about how much these factors are affecting the questions we raise in our work and how this may affect research project designs.

Acknowledging that universities have to be restructured is one side of the problem. Dissolving highly specialized departments because there is no direct market interest is another one. The problem therefore is a relational one, between our own high standards and assumptions and the necessities of transformation in working conditions. Too much do we keep to our own side, the government being free to design and dictate on the other side, even defining the intersection between higher education and vocation.[28] In that sense, if we were once accustomed to make up our own mind about quality in relation to the community of scholars, now government and economy define it from outside and therefore influence (control) the adaptation of our scientific questions to the purported quality.

To be a community within a discourse of power

At this point one may take up again the reproach Austrian academia faced, that it did not undertake enough research upon itself (Brünner 1993: 5), and pose the question to our discipline and to us as social anthropologists. Why is it that so little work has been done on academia, on the changing conditions for research, for teaching and learning anthropology?[29] And why is it that we may wonder whether reflecting upon and working on such issues – one of the projects of this volume – is or is not anthropological? The question is how the changing political, economic and institutional conditions would or could affect us academically and therefore affect the discipline of social anthropology, and whether these changing conditions imply the development of new practices, which are obviously differently articulated according to places and social spheres.

Social anthropology has always aimed at refining the methodology of field research, has problematized the question of writing, has raised new issues to be pursued. In all the works on the various societies, on social and cultural phenomena, the 'ethnographic eye' was in the meantime, sometimes more sometimes less, scrutinizing the process of data-gathering and data presentation. From this viewpoint it seems that it would take just a step further to analyse the social reality of these new practices and their effects on education and research. In this respect, research based upon an ethnographic methodology is anthropological. If the 'ethnographic eye' is an aspect which constitutes a pride of our discipline, we

should be seriously concerned about how these new practices lead
to qualitatively new relationships between research and teaching on
the one hand, and interests (economic, etc.) on the other.

It is somehow unsatisfactory to connect the end of the university
as an 'ideal community' to postmodern 'plurality' and 'multi-
vocality' and to postulate the disappearance of any grand principle
for the academy. Each university institution has always been specific
in its structure; nevertheless there has always been one grand
principle: the search for knowledge. The recent demands requiring
clarity of profile, to be specified alike by each university, is based
upon state and economy discourse. The vastly different requirements of institutes, faculties, and universities, as they have been
unmasked for instance by the 1996 events in Austria, dispute such a
dubious solution. It is hard to imagine such a design for the
University of Vienna, where it is more than questionable whether
any centralized, monocratic executive power structure could get
control of the fundamental un-lucidity ('Unübersichtlichkeit') of
the institution. Moreover, the problem has to be placed within the
framework of a mass higher education system and vocational
orientation (what are we to teach and research; how do we consider
the intersections of school–university and university–vocation?). A
major factor for reflection is the ongoing leap in students numbers
(in 1997/98 more than 300 beginners in Vienna took social
anthropology), their changing characteristic as working students
(increasing with the time of studying, reaching 80 per cent in the
seventh or eighth semester), and the state definition of studying
being consumption.

The position of the Austrian state to these problems is evident.
It withdraws from its former overall cultural mission (protecting
the freedom of teaching and research, conveying the means for the
disinterested search for knowledge). It is ready, however, to support
projects with a European dimension, EU programmes such as
Socrates where students are accorded generous supplementary
grants. It nevertheless redefines – also in accordance with a
European dimension – the grand principles of the academy as now
being education for vocation, for the 'development of society' and
for the 'preservation of environment'. Therefore, priorities are
given to teaching and administration (in Austria, administration
activities have to cover 30 per cent of full working time), with
research coming only in third place. Cognitive, in the notion of
'cognitive society' used by the European Commission, obviously

means continuous re-education for the marketplace. However, the state leaves us a chance. In the broad definition of the framework of universities' profiles and of the goals of higher education, it relies on our ethics of the former 'ideal community'. If the state relies, then, on the old system of evaluation among scholars and teachers, one has to wonder what the function of instituting a national audit agency and introducing research and teaching evaluation can be. In the form in which they are being introduced, it seems an attempt to enhance the state's (and the economy's) control over university autonomy. The fiction of the ideal, which we constantly reproduce ourselves, is still there, but it is no longer sufficient. Inside universities, we ought to connect it to recent conditions, and to shift the debate towards questions regarding the content of research and teaching.

Notes

1 Professors are 'chair holders', that is, formerly all decisions depended upon them. Today they are still 'chair holders', but in order to get democracy into Austrian universities, the University Act 1975 recognized three interest groups (curia) in academia: professors, assistant professors and students. Any university commission therefore has to be constituted by members of all three (usually in the ratio of two professors: one assistant professor: one student).
2 The 'Lehrbeautragte' were installed in some faculties in the 1970s. They get their teaching appointment at the faculty for only one semester and for a specific topic. In the humanities and social sciences, their part in teaching varies between 50 per cent and 80 per cent; in law on the other hand, it is almost nil.
3 In social anthropology, the minimum time is eight semesters, the average being twelve to thirteen.
4 Sixty-three per cent. 'Zustimmung für Uni-Protest – 63% der Bevölkerung hinter Studenten'. *Kurier*, 18 March 1996: front page.
5 'Es wird gestreikt, diskutiert, manchmal unterrichtet, *Die Presse*, 18 March 1996.
6 'Gewerkschaft kündigt Scholten das Abkommen über Unis auf', *Der Standard*, 20 March 1996.
7 'Studentenzorn auf ÖH-Politfunktionäre!', *Neue Kronen Zeitung*, 23 March 1996: 2–3. 'Die letzte Chance', *Die Presse*, 23 March 1996: 2.
8 In German 'anarcho' refers to those one could characterize as 'autonomists' – extremely ready to start street fights, who occupy houses – while 'anarchists' are rather those who share the distinctive anarchist ideology.
9 A report of a study by the 'Institut für Angewandte Soziologie'. Other official statistics show that 65 per cent are working students (18 per cent full-time, the rest part-time). The longer the studies, the more

students have actually to work, and drift from part-time into full-time working (*Kurier*, 10 June 1996: 3).

10 It is in process of implementation.

11 Ulrike Felt, spokeswoman of the 'middle curia', leader in the negotiations with the Ministry. Interview, Vienna 2 July 1998.

12 In February 1996, these two domains were united under the responsibility of one minister. Note the omission of the notion 'research', which had been skipped at that time.

13 One commentator of the new law deplores that the opinion by scholars is largely missing from the reform debate on the Austrian higher education system (Brünner 1993: 4–5). Also articulated by Ulrike Felt (Felt 1998).

14 Erich Witzmann: Die letzte Chance, *Die Presse*, 23 March 1996: 2.

15 Erich Witzmann: Nach dem Streik, *Die Presse*, 2 March 1996: 2.

16 Austrian school graduates and non-graduates with an aptitude exam have free access without any fees. Non-Austrians have low fees and are free to choose their discipline if they have the corresponding access-right in their home country. This regulation is discriminating according to EU law and will have to be changed in coming years (personal information from a representative of the Ministry of Science and Transport, Vienna, 22 June 1998).

17 Within one month, the compilation of press articles has reached a height of more than 5 cm.

18 See also the interview of one of his highest officials in the Dutch newspaper *NCR Handelsblad*, cited after *Kurier*, 10 June 1998: 3. The Dutch article was published more than two months earlier.

19 For instance, by the suggestion of establishing in the curriculum the requirement of a longer study abroad, without assuring financial support from the state's side (a representative of the Ministry, Vienna, 22 June 1998).

20 '"Leistungsethik" statt Protestaktion', *Die Presse*, 2 April 1996.

21 Two faculties of Theology, one of Law, of Social and Business Sciences, of Medicine, of Fundamental and Integrative Sciences (to which Social Anthropology belongs), of Humanities, and of Formal and Natural Sciences.

22 Sometimes smaller than a single faculty in the University of Vienna.

23 Curricula for the MA have to be oriented towards vocational training and preparation for scholarship, the PhD only for academic work.

24 There is an attempt in our faculty with the installation of the GRUWI-forum (GRUWI–Grund-und Integrativwissenschaftliche Faculty). Unfortunately, even there power and hierarchy discourses block those about quality.

25 Our faculty, GRUWI, counted 27,000 students in 1996, and is the largest in Austria. The Institute for Social and Cultural Anthropology in Vienna, for instance, the only one in Austria, has today approximatively 2,000 students, but only two professors (since 1980) and six assistant professors (since 1990/91) as full-staff members, and between the 1960s and 1999 the room-capacity had not improved.

26 The norm is four years, the average being six to seven years.

27 Strathern (1997: 318) argues that it is not (see p. 179, this volume). Also, as Austrian students do not have any fees, the official argument for their status as consumers is that they have today (after the Economizing Package) to contribute more towards the costs of their studies. Their right for qualitative assistance and teaching is derived from that economic factor, and not from scholarly, ethical ones. 'Value for money' is the slogan of universities in The Netherlands, where students also have to contribute to the costs of their studies (see Mertens 1995: 329).

28 According to Felt, the intersections between school–university, and university–vocation have not until now been topics in the discussion within the University of Vienna (Felt 1998).

29 There was a workshop at the EASA Conference in Barcelona on Teaching Anthropology (1996), after which an EASA Network (working group) was founded on the same topic.

References

Newspapers: *Der Standard*
              Die Presse
              Kurier
              Neue Kronen Zeitung

Bast, G. (ed.) (1994) UOG 93 (Universitätsorganisationsgesetz), Vienna: Manz.

Bauman, Z. (1997) 'Universities: Old, New, and Different', in A. Smith and F. Webster (eds) *The Postmodern University? Contested Visions of Higher Education in Society*, Buckingham and Bristol (USA): Society for Research into Higher Education and Open University Press.

Böhme, G. (1991) 'Am Ende des Baconschen Zeitalters', in G. Gramm und G. Kimmerle (eds) *Wissenschaft und Gesellschaft*, Tübinger Beiträge zur Philosophie und Gesellschaftskritik, Bd 3, Tübingen: Edition Diskord.

Brünner, Ch. (1993) 'Die Unterscheidung zwischen strategischen und operativen Organen – Ein Grundgedanke der Reform', in R. Strasser (ed.) *Untersuchungen zum UOG 93*, Vienna: Manz.

Dienststellenausschuss der Hochschullehrer der Universität Wien (1996) Resolution, 14 March.

Europäische Kommission (1995) Lehren und Lernen. Auf dem Weg zur kognitiven Gesellschaft. Weiflbuch zur allgemeinen und beruflichen Bildung, Brussels-Luxemburg.

Felt, U. (1998) Interview, Vienna, 2 July.

Filmer, P. (1997) 'Distinterestedness and the Modern University', in A. Smith and F. Webster (eds) *The Postmodern University? Contested*

Visions of Higher Education in Society, Buckingham and Bristol (USA): Society for Research into Higher Education and Open University Press.

Gewirth, A. (1990) 'Human Rights and Academic Freedom', in St M. Cahn (ed.) *Morality, Responsibility, and the University: Studies in Academic Ethics,* Philadelphia: Temple University Press.

Gibbons, M. *et al.* (1994) *The New Production of Knowledge: The Dynamics of Science and Research in Contemporary Societies,* London: Thousand Oaks, New Delhi: Sage.

Höllinger, S. (1998) 'Es führt kein Weg zurück: In die Autonomie mit der Evaluierung', *Der Standard,* 18–19 July: 39.

Maier, M. (1996) 'Sackgasse Uni.', *Der Standard* 18 March.

Mertens, F.J. (1995) 'Hintergünde des neuen Qualitätssicherungssystems in den Niederlanden', in D. Müller-Böling (ed.) *Qualitätssicherung in Hochschulen. Forschung – Lehre – Management,* Gütersloh: Verlag Bertelsmann Stiftung.

Müller-Böling, D. (1995) 'Qualitätssicherung in Hochschulen. Grundlagen einer wissenschaftlichen Gemeinschaft', in D. Müller-Böling (ed.) *Qualitätssicherung in Hochschulen. Forschung – Lehre – Management,* Gütersloh: Verlag Bertelsmann Stiftung.

Mussnug, R. (1993) 'Evaluierung von Universitätsleistungen – Grundlegende Probleme aus der Sicht eines deutschen Staatsrechtlers', in R. Strasser (ed.) *Untersuchungen zum UOG 93,* Vienna: Manz.

Österreichisches Hochschulrecht (1997) Universitätsstudiengesetz, Vienna: Bundesministerium für Wissenschaft und Verkehr.

Rabl, P. (1996) 'Kommentar', *Kurier* 17 March.

Readings, B. (1997) *The University in Ruins,* Cambridge, Mass. and London: Harvard University Press.

Simon, R. L. (1990) 'A Defense of the Neutral University', in St M. Cahn (ed.) *Morality, Responsibility, and the University: Studies in Academic Ethics,* Philadelphia: Temple University Press.

Smith, A. and Webster, F. (1997) 'Changing Ideas of the University', in A. Smith and F. Webster (eds) *The Postmodern University? Contested Visions of Higher Education in Society,* Buckingham and Bristol (USA): Society for Research into Higher Education and Open University Press.

Spinner, H. (1994) *Die Wissensordnung – Ein Leitkonzept für die dritte Grundordnung des Informationszeitalter,* Opladen: Leske & Budrich.

Strathern, M. (1997) '"Improving Ratings": Audit in the British University System', *European Review* 5 (3): 305–21.

Unterberger, A. (1996) 'Zurück in die Hörsäle', *Die Presse* 30–31 March.

Witzmann, E. (1996) 'Die letzte Chance', *Die Presse* 23 March.

Chapter 10

Disciples, discipline and reflection

Anthropological encounters and trajectories

Dimitra Gefou-Madianou

Greece offers a pertinent case-study for reflection on current conditions of European intellectual production. This may sound ironic, in that Greece does not really have a centuries old academic tradition like the rest of Western Europe. As it is, social anthropology and other social science departments were established in Greek universities only in the early 1980s. That period was characterized by two main features: first, a democratization process following the end of a seven-year dictatorship in 1974; second, the country's increasingly prevailing European orientation. The introduction of the Reformative Law for Higher Education Institutions in 1982 sought to update and modernize the state-controlled system of higher education in line with the best intellectual traditions of the West.[1] Young foreign-trained academics, among others, now saw their political activities against the junta – often conducted from host countries in the West – bearing fruit. With the European civil social structures and their universities as prototypes, the prevailing intellectual, political climate in Greece was one of critical thinking and reflection.

At the same time, in the 1980s, Greece inherited from Europe another newer feature of the modernization process, that of an economistic bureaucracy: the audit culture of accountability and cost-efficiency (cf. Herzfeld 1992:149). This adversely influenced the reflective mood of academia and made successive governments rethink the nature and scope of higher education. The same Europe that had provided intellectual possibilities to a post-dictatorial Greece was now scurrying along in an attempt to muzzle them.

What this chapter intends to show is the advent and development of social anthropology in Greece within a wider historical framework covering the period between the mid-1970s and the present. Interestingly, too, and in contrast with other European cases, the emergence of anthropology coincided with that of the accountability culture in the universities and in society at large. For Greece, this has been a period of social, political and economic transformation from an underdeveloped southeastern European country under military dictatorship into a fast developing EU economy-based society that aspires monetary union in 2001. Three preliminary observations are in order.

First, it should be noted that Greece has traditionally been a fieldwork terrain for foreign anthropologists. By the 1980s, Greek anthropologists who had been trained abroad also began to work and do research at home. Only since the mid-1990s, however, have some of the anthropologists studying Greece been trained in Greek universities. The second point concerns the trajectory of educational backgrounds and professional loyalties, which may be best posed as a question: what does home mean to those Greek anthropologists – like myself – who have been trained abroad but have come to teach and do research in Greece? What does home mean to those locally trained younger anthropologists whose past, present and perhaps futures are determined by more confined geographical co-ordinates. Whom are both groups working for and whom do they identify with? Lastly, one should also consider the wider political and economic framework within which these developments have been taking place. Two points are stressed: first, the constraints which EU directives from Brussels are laying upon national policies concerning education, both in terms of general direction as well as planning of specific post-graduate programmes; second, the attitudes towards newly introduced disciplines (such as anthropology) by older positivistic disciplines which until recently dominated social sciences in Greece.

The dawning of the new future: Greece in Europe

The old Greek university system was hierarchical, inward looking, ossified. For decades it had ceased to be open to society and its current trends. Some disciplines, especially those of folklore, history and archaeology were closely allied with the government nationalist project, aimed to create a Greek national identity rooted in an ancient classical past (Herzfeld 1982: 8–10; 1987: 44; Gefou-Madianou 1993: 164). This classical past was considered by nineteenth- and early twentieth-century Europeans to be the cradle of their civilization, the most and indeed, in the view of some, the only praiseworthy element of Greek national identity (cf. Herzfeld 1997: 46). And Greeks concerned with the establishment and recognition of their national borders and their acceptance of national identity came to hold this particular past as their only viable one. The strong chairs of folklore studies established in the National University of Athens (School of Classics) as early as 1890, and then in 1926 in the University of Thessaloniki (School of Archaeology and History) were harnessed to support this national project (Gefou-Madianou 1993: 164). To a large extent, academic knowledge had to be useful, objective and ethnically correct in the service of the nation-building process. It was believed that Greece would fulfil the Europeanist visions of being the cradle of Western civilization and Greece would be an accepted member of Europe.

With the exception of the interwar period when sociology was introduced as a university course, folklore dominated the academic scene until the 1970s.[2] With the 1982 Reformatory Law for Higher Education Institutions this scene changed radically not only at the level of ideology, as it introduced a new way of approaching issues in the social sciences, but also institutionally through the introduction of new academic disciplines. These disciplines were social history, sociology, geography and social anthropology, which now would no longer be taught as courses within the old schools, but as established disciplines in their own separate sections and departments. For anthropology this meant that Greece could for the first time produce indigenous-trained anthropologists.[3]

The 1982 Reformatory Law had above all a European orient-ation. It aimed at 'making Greek universities competitive and able to co-operate closely with other European ones' (Kladis and Panoussis 1992: 17). It also was aimed at renewing academic teaching staff, often by inviting Greek scientists of the Diaspora working in Western universities to repatriate and work in Greece, and by improving the quality of the curriculum offered to students. The most important changes that this law introduced were the abolition of the all-powerful chair and the nineteenth-century concept of school assemblies, that is, of individual chairs. In their place, it introduced a more democratic structure, so that the teach-ing staff of the department were responsible for administrative and curriculum decisions. This was implemented by instituting depart-ments and sections, which corresponded to separate disciplines.

Another major change was the organization of graduate and post-graduate studies and the support of university-sponsored research. In order for all these changes to succeed, new universities with new departments and sections were established in many regions of the country and not just Athens and Thessaloniki as had been the case for many years in the past (Gefou-Madianou 1993: 165; Petralias and Theotokas 1999: 18–19).[4]

Alongside the reformative measures taken by the government was Greece's entry into the then European Economic Community in 1981. Despite its essentially economic nature, this development also assured Greece that it would be protected from the re-establishment of a dictatorship and that the democratization of the state would continue. Many intellectuals hoped that these democratic processes would affect positively the intellectual climate and research agendas within the university system to a degree which would push the Reformative Law beyond its stated aims (cf. Grimshaw and Hart 1993). Younger Greek academics, looking towards the university systems of Europe and the United States, where many of them had studied and often had taught, were optimistic that similar standards of excellence and academic freedom would eventually prevail. Reflecting on academia and science and on their own past experiences as graduate students and teachers in the West, they hoped to construct a 1960s European academic and intellectual environment in the 1980s Greece.

Unfortunately, things did not work out that way. In the period when Greek universities were opening their doors to Western-trained intellectuals and to a more reflective and critical orientation of thought, Western European universities were beginning to come under the influence of the audit explosion of the 1980s (Power 1997). Research grants, especially in the humanities and social sciences, were scarce and there was an increased emphasis placed on academic production and cost-effectiveness within the university system. This meant that the old European prototypes which inspired the Greek intellectual reformers of the 1980s were in direct conflict with the economic ideals and targets propagated by the European Union bureaucracy. The climate within which Greek academics were called upon to work was geared towards the production of informed, politically enlightened, action-oriented public servants. In turn, since European Union bureaucracy directly influenced Greek government policies and finances concerning higher education, all plans for university reform that deviated from accepted budgetary ceilings and policy pronunciations had to be shelved.

As has become increasingly clear, the policies of the European Union aim at standardizing university degrees throughout Europe with little attention being paid to the social particularities of individual countries or universities. For the state-run universities of Greece this means that decisions concerning the number of years needed to obtain a first degree; the number of new students which any one department may accept each year; the financing for the establishment of new graduate and undergraduate departments, and even the hiring of new staff, are directly controlled by the Ministry of National Education and Religion as well as by the Ministry of Economics, and thus indirectly by Brussels.

Moreover, this audit ideology and practice, introduced by the European Union through the Community Support Framework II – and particularly through the programme for education and training – and imposed by the Greek Ministry of National Education and Religion, has channelled Greek universities towards a more applied approach to both research and curriculum development ultimately aimed at meeting the market's needs. Thus new departments supported by the CSF II (see below) have to be operative within limited periods of time – in many cases, only six months – so as to absorb within the prescribed timetable the money allocated to them. The whole process is being monitored by the Greek Ministry of Education and evaluated by local and EU experts. The EU is much more interested in the flow of funds through the goverment than in the content and structure of the departments or programmes.

The reason was that the Greek government, after negotiating with Brussels, succeeded in obtaining approval for the Operational Programme for Education and Initial Professional Training, a generously funded programme which was part of the Community Support Framework II (CSF II).[5] As its title suggests, this programme was aimed at the initial professional training of unemployed young Europeans, thus creating the preconditions for their re-integration into the work market. The Greek government, however, in agreement with Brussels, decided to finance all the higher education system reforms, which were initiated by the 1982 Reformatory Law through using Operational Programme funds, thereby giving higher education reforms a more applied and technical character and consequently linking educational policy with economic development policy.[6]

The Operational Programme has been used to finance all the measures taken for implementing higher education programmes, such as the reform of existing undergraduate programmes, the development of graduate and post-graduate studies, the organizing of part-time free elective study programmes, and the establishment of new departments. Areas of top priority have been those of development, technology, environment and primary education (pedagogy and teacher-training), all applied fields associated with the country's economic development. Very few programmes which concern the area of social sciences have been approved. The applied nature that this programme assumed was supported by the Greek Minister of Education, who, in one of his official speeches concerning the programmes of professional education and training, has stated that the orientation of the current Greek educational system should aim at reducing unemployment rates and linking Greek universities to the market economy. He also maintained that the 'high unemployment rates observed in many European countries are due to badly organized educational systems which fail to provide links between educational programmes and the real needs of life and production' (*Ependytis* 1998).[7]

In this manner, Brussels has indirectly intervened in the local Greek educational system reforms despite the fact that educational and training programmes constitute a field of action belonging to individual Member States. Officially the EU can only intervene indirectly in support of or in a complementary manner to the implementation of these programmes, as clearly stated in the European legislation (Velissariou 1998: 14).

It has to be noted that this Operational Programme is scheduled to support all the above projects only in their initial phase ranging from three to five years. After this phase, each programme must look for its own financial resources. It is often suggested that these resources are to be found either in the market economy (business), or that students should pay fees. Moreover, all higher educational reforms planned by the Greek Ministry of Education have a highly technical and applied orientation. Money for education from the state budget has been reduced to a minimum. The total funding for the higher education institutions amounts to 0.7 per cent of the Gross National Product while the average funding in the OECD countries amounts to 1.5 per cent. In short, the Operational Programme for Education and Initial Professional Training has been considered by some to be responsible for the current disorganization of the Greek university system (Petralias and Theotokas 1999: 21). These developments have challenged and undermined the public character of the Greek educational system. The very recent changes both in the secondary and tertiary educational systems have resulted in greater, social and financial insecurity for the students, teachers and professors.

These changes have also meant even more examinations for students in secondary education. It should be added that although the entrance exams for universities have been modified recently, allowing more students to enter (an 8 per cent increase), they still remain extremely difficult, with a high rate of failure. As a result, increasing numbers of young Greeks are forced to study abroad.[8] The difficulty in entering the university, coupled with the exorbitant cost of supporting studies abroad, has opened the way for the establishment of private universities which find legal provison in the European Union legislation. These private institutions are all branches of foreign universities, and occasionally of well-known ones. However, the Greek constitution forbids Greek citizens from opening private universities and the degrees granted by the private universities are not recognized in the Greek public sector.

Minor modifications also have been made in the 1982 Reformative Law for Higher Education Institutions, changing in essence once again the power relations within the universities.[9] Those high-ranking academics, trained in the positivistic values which had permeated the universities until recently, found that they could relate to the audit culture sponsored by Europe. Their voices, still strong within government circles, were in part responsible for the changes once again visited upon the university system. Tenure has become again more difficult to obtain, the autonomy of lecturers in teaching and research has been limited, and reading material for taught courses has to be evaluated and accepted by the department and in some respects by the Ministry. With the recent modifications, administrative and curriculum decisions now come under the control of tenured professors, who run the governing bodies of the department. In short, the hierarchical structure of the university that had been curtailed has been momentarily revitalized once again.

It is clear, then, that the hopes of the younger researchers and scholars in the early 1980s for 'real' reforms in the educational system have been frustrated. The expectations that European influences would change the relatively introverted character of

Greek society to a more dynamic and cosmopolitan one, wherein a reflective and critical academia would blossom, were exaggerated. The old nineteenth-century positivistic values and outlooks proved to be more entrenched within Greek society than expected.[10]

To summarize, with the new auditing culture of the 1980s and 1990s, a new sense of 'objective', 'useful' knowledge is demanded by the Greek university system. Belief that the European Union would assist the development of critical thinking and institutional independence have been dashed. Instead young scholars have *again* to be accountable, *again* to produce 'objective, useful' knowledge, this time, though, in a different capacity. If in the past academic knowledge had to be objective and useful for promoting the project of nation-building, this time it has to be so in order to be accountable to the new ideology of a market-oriented EU. In the European dominant discourse, modernization is a cost-efficient project which does not allow fields such as the newly introduced one of anthropology to freely promote their theoretical inclinations without being restricted by practical and positivistic consider-ations.[11] Not that this has ever been so *in the purest sense* in Western European countries with long academic traditions, but certainly the degree of intellectual freedom ingrained in research had been considerable, at least until the mid-1970s.

Disciples, discipline and reflection: internal and external processes

At the beginning of the 1980s the first Western-trained anthropologists returned from abroad. Since cultural and social anthropology was not well-known in Greece at that time, these first Western-trained Greek indigenous anthropologists had to work in related fields.[12] Of course, this does not mean that Greece was not known to anthropology. On the contrary, a number of Western – European mostly – anthropologists had already visited Greece from the 1950s onwards and had conducted fieldwork in rural areas which, with the eyes of the 1950s and 1960s, could be described as 'exotic': Campbell, Friedl (the only American), du Boulay, Herzfeld, Hirschon are the best known names.[13] It was through the ethno-graphic lens of such researchers that native anthropologists came to observe their own culture (see Gefou-Madianou 1993).

With the Reformative Law of 1982, as already indicated, things changed perceptibly. Some of the existing departments, such as the

Sociology and Political Science departments at Panteion University and the departments of History and Archaeology at the Universities of Thessaloniki and Ioannina, introduced anthropological courses into their curriculum. The National Centre of Social Research also began to employ anthropologists and opened up a new vista of possibilities for future anthropological research. The Centre is of some importance because, as early as the 1960s, it had been one of the very few places which supported anthropological research in Greece. This took place under the aegis of the late Professor Peristiany who remained at its stewardship until the dictatorship of 1967 when the Centre dramatically changed its orientation.[14] But perhaps the most crucial developments were the establishment in 1982 of the section of Social Morphology and Social Anthropology, and a few years later (in 1989) the department of Social Policy and Social Anthropology at Panteion University (Athens), and the establishment in 1987 of a post-graduate programme-cum-department of Anthropology in Mytilene, on Lesbos. The two departments came to play an important role not only in the development of anthropological research in Greece, but also in the production of locally trained anthropologists.

Within the ameliorating atmosphere that the newly introduced Reformative Law had inculcated, young anthropologists turned academics felt that social anthropology could indeed offer much to the educational system and the country in general. In a sense, Greek anthropologists became the disciples of a newly flourishing discipline with the self-knowledge and deep understanding of their own society and its political climate, which demanded that they converse with the other older and perhaps more traditional social science disciplines. The dilemma that Greek anthropologists faced, and still do, was how to maintain a dialogue with anthropological theory as it had been and is formulated abroad while interacting and conversing with other established disciplines. This meant that the anthropology developed in Greece must bridge the divide between Western theory, and locally produced knowledge and disciplinary practice. Greek academic anthropology would of necessity develop along different lines from those anthropologies that have developed elsewhere. And though it must maintain its independent and critical nature it also must be a locally defined and locally created anthropology, consciously rooted in the particular, historically-based academic milieu. And because anthropology in Greece knows itself as a young discipline, there is a constant looking-forward as to what can be done. Indeed, this is a running concern of Greek anthropologists. As Strathern maintains, 'anthropological habits of thought may be as continuous with the folk models of the society to which they belong as they are discontinuous from models anthropologists encounter elsewhere' (1992: 185).

This process could be accomplished only through reflection, a state which anthropology by definition induces in its practitioners. Important here is the fact that anthropologists were generally trained to see anthropology as a 'pure science', in the sense that it is not intrinsically related to applied and, most importantly, government-sponsored projects. Simplistic as the proposition is, this is clearly how many perceived the subject, especially as compared to sociology. But there are more substantial points to be made.

First, as Firth (1981) has maintained, anthropology is an 'uncomfortable discipline', and for Greek anthropologists of the 1980s and 1990s this has been particularly apt as the critical view taken by anthropological theory of positivistic history and the nation-building project has meant Greek anthropologists having to walk a fine line within the established academic community.[15] However, this reflexive stance has also been liberating because it offered the opportunity to think about Greek culture within the wider context of the Balkans with a degree of 'enlightened objectivity' and scientific meditation. Ethnographic studies on ethnicity, especially in the Macedonian region, may be seen as part of this trend.[16] This opened the way towards dialogue and co-operation in contrast to the more customary feelings of distrust and aversion that have been the products of nation-building in the late nineteenth and early twentieth centuries. An anthropological heritage of critical observation and cosmopolitan perspective was instilled in all of the new disciplines.[17]

Second, as more distant locations for fieldwork, such as Africa, became increasingly closed off and with the critique of anthropology's relationship to colonialism, southern Europe came to hold an increasingly more 'exotic' appeal, particularly for those living and working in cities such as New York or London. Greece became a privileged field site, and who better suited to study Greece than indigenous Greek anthropologists? Thus, fresh Greek graduate students were sent 'to Greece' equipped with the shining armour of a Western intellectual tradition: natives to study the natives. And this suited Greek students because funding for fieldwork was scarce and demands to study something 'useful' to Greece were coming to prevail. This self-confidence was shattered with the more systematic questioning of what exactly anthropology at home might be. However, it did not make fieldwork any less appealing to indigenous graduate students; possibly, it made it more challenging.

Questions arose when these graduate students 'came home' to teach in the newly established departments. How was the newly created anthropological knowledge about Greece to be introduced into the intellectual corpus of other disciplines such as sociology and history? In particular, how was anthropology to converse with folklore studies which were criticized as ossified and conservative? Folklore imaginings of Greece did not really coincide with those of a critical reflexive imagining, though it had to be acknowledged that folklore studies had amassed a vast amount of 'ethnographic' data that anthropologists could somehow use. Reflection and meditation were believed to be the basic tools for building the bridge between the realities of local and Western anthropology that would enable anthropology in Greece to flourish in ways similar to those experienced in the Western institutions where Greeks had been initially trained.

Third, reflection can also acquire a rather more mundane face than all this may allow. To be an anthropologist is one thing; to be a professional anthropologist and a teaching anthropologist is another one. The task to be accomplished was the organization of anthropology at an institutional level. Being at the lower echelons of the university hierarchy, anthropologists had to combine their vision of the discipline with the stark realities of a university bureaucratic institution with no independent funding, but rather one wholly dependent on the state and with demands by students that upon graduation jobs should be at hand.

Ironically, the European intellectual tradition which the young anthropologists brought with them turned against itself at the very moment they tried to disseminate their new discipline through dialogue with other older disciplines and the educational establishment as a whole.

As I have already argued, two interconnected but contradictory tendencies informed the admission of Greece into the European Union. On the one hand, it had naturally boosted the expectations of many among the intelligentsia for modernization in accordance with Western European standards. Only in such a climate, it was held, could the social sciences flourish – especially true of anthropology. I maintain this for a very particular reason. A modernization process coming from Europe could assure the security of Greece, as a state as well as a civic society, and lessen the perception of immediate and irrevocable danger from outside its Balkan borders. Anthropology then, which by definition questions the viability and even the existence of unifying and homogenous discourses, might perhaps be allowed to exist without being seen as a national threat or a radical project against the established order of things now that order was politically and economically assured.

On the other hand, the European orientation of Greece and, to an extent, its position as a fund-receiving country of the South, made the newly acquired reflexive gaze of the social sciences more vulnerable to the shift in emphasis towards a more economistic approach to social services and public institutions. The turn towards 'audit culture' reintroduced a certain version of positivism which this time was not so much political but economic and bureaucratic. The cry heard from Whitehall and the other European parliaments was 'what is the use of it and how much will it cost?' The mechanism of European Union followed that trend in due time. The financial situation of European societies and of the Union itself ceased to be a model of healthy growth. Unemployment and huge public deficits brought in armies of consultants and auditors.

This turn of events and of ideological principles has transformed the universities from knowledge-creating institutions into organizations which function as offshoots of the market world and business conglomerates (Power 1997). In a sense, this connection between business and universities has always existed for hard-core science departments and medical schools. But it now has come to engulf the social sciences too. The question is no longer 'how well does your product fit the market?', but rather 'do your products fit into the market at all?'

Audit has to be an object of new critique. Let me raise some insider's views. And here I should not want to be misunderstood. I am not against accountability as such. I am against that sort of accountability that assumes in an authoritative and self-serving manner that everything can be counted as if it were an entry to some 'Ledger of the State'. Rather, we should observe that there are conflicting views of accountability. A government is accountable to the people. Because of this, the government is accountable to the universities in that it must provide them with what they need in order to fulfil their ends. However, accountability also implies a notion of 'better value for money' achieved by the public sector. A knowledge-creation model would lead one to ask how this can be interpreted. Is it that universities should be left to produce knowledge for knowledge's sake with no reference to any sense of usefulness in market terms (cf. Tsaoussis 1993)?[18] If so, the best way to profit from universities and research would have been to allow researchers a relatively free hand to pursue their interests (Firth 1992).[19] An audit model, on the other hand, implies that those who deliver services – universities included – should be 'answerable' to those who finance them and to those who use them and their products.

If the latter is true, as I am afraid it is, universities must produce 'knowledge' which is answerable to at least four masters. First, the Greek state which, despite the steps forward taken by the Reformatory Law, still cherishes the idea of a state-controlled and state-run university which produces 'ethnically correct' knowledge stuffed into people who will eventually end up in the civil service. Second, a rather contradictory European Union agenda that, on the one hand, cherishes the protection of ethnic minorities while, on the other, does not really bemoan the dissolution or weakening of nation-state borders and the boundedness of their integrity. Third, the auditing officers of the European Union financial departments who demand a more positivistic approach in research and a narrowing of research intentions so that they fit with the notion of 'usefulness' and with the commoditization of knowledge. Fourth, the general public of Greece who still expect, contra to the downsizing realities of modernization, that their children upon entering the university will eventually manage to obtain lifelong jobs in the public sector together with the already more than 50 per cent of the country's working force.[20]

If serving one master is difficult enough, serving four seems to be impossible. Or is it?

Inside the Greek academia, these considerations have been taken to heart by some. A considerable number of professors and other high-standing administrators of the old guard who conventionally followed the tradition of the previous decades have retained positions of power within the state bureaucracy and, more rarely, the Greek delegation to the European Community in Brussels. From there they have become the interpreters, arbitrators and disseminators of the European Union Directives and have managed to argue that there is just one master after all, accountability, with four faces (cf. Day and Klein 1987: 28–9 and 157). Among other slogans put forward, the most emotionally loaded is that 'a small country like Greece with limited resources must not simply be carried along wherever the spendthrift goddess of knowledge wants to take it.'

Encounters and trajectories

All this has consequences for how anthropology is to develop within the Greek university system. Anthropology at home, a peripheral trend in anthropology in the West, is in Greece the core discourse. Lacking funds for graduates to conduct research abroad, and having at our doorstep a 'field' defined by classic anthropology, the trend is to study 'at home'. Most of the established academics, after all, had conducted their fieldwork in Greece. So what was an obvious field-site choice for those first few Greek students studying in the West has now become an institutionalized given. Moreover, in attempts to establish a dialogue with other sister disciplines, anthropology finds itself criticized when it refers to other cultures, particularly those considered 'exotic and remote', that is, non-Greek, non-Western. As for actual research, the view most generally held is that one should concentrate on problems at home or close to it (e.g. Europe) and leave researchers of other nations to do their own work. Even in the classroom, material concerning the African, Melanesian, South American ethnography is criticized by many non-anthropologists as irrelevant. In this manner, the anthropology developing in Greece is under pressure to turn forever inward; to become truly a 'home-based anthropology'. This may become especially problematic for the generations to follow who have been raised in Greece, who will be locally trained and who will conduct their research in Greece. Theoretically, and in practice, anthropology in Greece is in danger of losing its comparative and cosmopolitan character (Gefou-Madianou 1993: 176).

What kind of solutions have presented themselves? One obvious solution to these constraints is the study of 'our neighbours', for example the Balkan societies to the north, Turkey to the east, and even the Middle East and North Africa. This has the advantage of 'fitting' into the positivistic discourse in relation to national integrity, economic expansion, and a historic relationship with these societies through the Byzantine and later Ottoman Empire, particularly as these refer to Greek heritage and continuity. For anthropologists it provides a means of studying the 'other' abroad, while encouraging a particular kind of critical and reflexive outlook. I am not implying that anthropology at home cannot be critical and reflexive; only that anthropologists who refuse to look outside their national borders may forgo an important critical perspective.

Another way of accommodating the national agenda within the study of anthropology in Greece is for Greek anthropologists to conduct research with the Greeks of the Diaspora, numbering over five million people, from a motherland population of ten million. This would mean fieldwork conducted in faraway places such as Australia, the United States, Canada, Africa: a perfect chance for a dip in the anthropology of colonialism.

And even if Greeks are to remain within their national boundaries, there is increasing scope to study people other than Greek nationals. Over the last decade Greece has itself become a multicultural society. Traditionally, Greeks migrated to other countries in search of a better life. Now there are over one and a half million immigrants living and working in Greece from many parts of the world. Despite the fact that many of the older generation of society at large do not recognize the multicultural character of Greek society, politicians and government administrators are now beginning to see that research in these fields may be utilized to confront the problems of acculturation of economic migrants and the rise of criminality and drug abuse, to the extent that these can be related to the migrants, as many state functionaries are fond of thinking. Aside from the opening of the northern borders of the country, which resulted in the entry of half a million illegal Albanians and a considerable number of Bulgarians, there are large numbers of Filipinos working predominantly as domestic helpers; Pakistanis and Indians as agricultural manual labourers, and others. Many of the immigrants have married and established families, schools and communities here in Greece. This means that Greeks studying these communities not only are exposed to the problem of 'others' within Greece, but can and will come into contact with the immigrant's respective cultures in their homelands.[21]

In short, anthropologists in Greece are caught in an ambivalent position. On the one hand, they must seek to maintain the interplay between national and international agendas, that is, to maintain a balance between the inward-looking, nationalistic discourse and European Union demands for the opening of national borders and recognition of ethnic and cultural minorities. On the other hand, they are obliged to meet the demands of the new 'audit culture' which supports in an odd fashion the traditional positivistic perspective of the established and dominant disciplines, and to maintain the reflexive stance which they learned in the West and which is for anthropologists in Greece vital for their continued creativity.[22]

Not having a centuries old academic tradition of critical thought, and being on the periphery of where anthropological knowledge and theory are produced, has its drawbacks. But this may also allow anthropologists who live and work in Greece to regard the theory produced in the West with greater freedom, distant from the ideological constraints and practical considerations that may worry our fellow academics in the West. Similarly, throughout the relatively short history of the Greek nation-state, Greek intellectuals have had to cope with the confining demands of a national agenda and a positivist, utility-oriented perspective. Yet this delicate balancing act must include the constant reflection upon and questioning of both Western and Greek anthropologists in a highly complex and interrelated global community. This will avert the danger of both glorifying the Western tradition with its all-embracing (asphyxiating?) glamorous appeal and of vilifying local tradition as being hopelessly positivistic and quaint.

If social anthropology is to have a future as a reflexive and critical discipline in Greece, then Greek anthropologists must establish a tradition of fieldwork abroad *as well as* at home, and must maintain an open and constant dialogue with the centres of anthropology in the West. They must also maintain their dialogue conversing with the older, more established disciplines. All this can only be done by treading carefully on a difficult terrain of constant questions and ancient uncertainties. What does it mean to do fieldwork at home for those who have been taught anthropology in the West? What are their motives? To whom are they (really) accountable? What sort of feedback could or would they receive from colleagues outside Greece? After all, as has already been argued above, Western anthropological tradition is itself in battle with the audit culture of European and American politics (Strathern 1997; also Shore and Wright 1997; Shore 1997; Martin 1997).

Greek intellectuals have always tried to create a balance between giving account to government administrators and ideologues and following their desire to think creatively. In short, they have been forced to constantly bridge the gap between evaluation and reflection. For anthropologists now, this balancing act appears to be increasingly more difficult since they must respond to seemingly irreconcilable demands: as Western-trained anthropologists; as Greek anthropologists working at home; as members of the local academic establishment with all the included constraints of an audit culture promoted by Brussels. Strathern (1997: 305) has recently observed of auditing in the British university system: 'While the metaphor of financial auditing points to the important values of accountability, audit does more than monitor – it has a life of its own that jeopardises the life it audits.' If British academics with their long academic tradition feel the constraints of the audit culture as threatening, for Greek anthropologists newly arrived on the scene of Greek academia the situation would seem to be far worse. And from one point of view it is. However, as I have noted throughout, Greek intellectuals have had to deal with auditing and evaluation, with constraints imposed by government programmes and administrative and national ideologies for a very long time.

Thus, ironically again, Greek anthropologists may already be well equipped to deal with the constraints they face from Europe and within, while still maintaining their academic integrity. However, this can only be done with the support from and interaction with their Western colleagues. And in the end these constraints may constitute a challenge bringing with it opportunities for the creation of new trajectories of thought and practice which may in turn provide the disciples of anthropology in Greece with a truly open discipline.

Acknowledgements

The chapter was commented upon by Jean-Claude Galey and I thank him for an insightful and helpful discussion during the plenary session at the EASA conference. My thanks also extend to the participants of the conference, and especially to my colleagues Marina Iossifides, Makis Makris and Sibylla Dimitriou-Kotsoni for comments and feedback.

Notes

1 The older system which this law came to replace, established in the nineteenth century with the creation of the Greek nation-state, had

itself been modelled on the French and German prototypes of that time (Kyrtsis 1996: 131). Greek universities are state financed and run, and degrees from private universities within Greece are not recognized by the state.

2 Kyrtsis (1996) offers a thorough analysis of the meaning of the term 'sociology' in Greek academia during the interwar period.

3 However, the Reformatory Law did not envisage the opening up of the higher educational system through the establishment of new, fully independent universities. Higher education was to remain, as it still does, in the hands of the government. For example, the senate members of these new universities were appointed by the government. Similarly, during the Spring 1998 General Assembly of Rectors from all Greek higher educational institutions, an official proposal to rename the University of Aegean as 'Andreas Papandreou University' was discussed. These examples highlight the close link between universities and government and are associated with an ideology of 'free education', which means that students do not have to pay fees and that textbooks are offered to them by the state free of charge. Moreover, their future employment was, up until very recently, inadvertently 'state-controlled' through Graduates Lists which assured work in the public sector to post-graduates.

4 These were the changes introduced by the first 1982 law under a PASOK (Greek Socialist Party) government during the academic years 1982/83 until 1988/89.

5 The Operational Programme for Education and Initial Professional Training was known to Greece as EPEAEK (Epichirisiako Programma Ekpaideysis ke Archikis Epagelmatikis Katartisis). It provided a fund of 500 billion drachmas from which 170 billion drachmas were used for higher education programmes (Ministry of National Education and Religion 1996). Programmes for education and training were funded by the CSF II in other European countries (Germany, Italy, Spain, Portugal). Each programme, however, has its own internal structure since its organization was planned by Brussels in conjunction with the individual governments of each Member State in order to meet their own particular needs. The allocation of funds was thus the product of long negotiations between Brussels and the Greek government. The two parties have reached an agreement – though each for different reasons – according to which CSFII funds could be used for major higher education reforms: on the one hand, the Greek government would be able to reduce the national budget funds for higher education reforms; on the other, Brussels was pushing Greece to absorb the CSFII funds.

6 For discussion of the concept of 'development' and its association with applied anthropology programmes, see Lewis 1995: 99.

7 This is part of the Minister of National Education and Religion's speech entitled 'Reforms, a needed Policy', addressed to a Symposium on Professional Education and Training in 1998.

8 Until recently, the majority of university degrees secured the graduate a position or the promise of a position in the future within the Greek

civil service. This created the expectation that in obtaining a university degree the young person's economic survival was ensured. For this and other socio-cultural reasons (status, advancement of the whole family), the prestige associated with a university degree was and remains great (Tsoucalas 1986: 119, 128; and Tsoucalas 1996: 31).

9 The 'New Democracy' government, a conservative – centre/right-wing – political party, during the period from 1989/90 to 1993/94, introduced changes which reactivated the authority of the tenured professors. These changes were accepted by the later PASOK government of 1994/95 onwards.

10 The European Union almost by definition weakens the role of the individual Member States. The opening of borders that it advocates further undermines national integration and ethnic homogeneity. In Greece, the reaction to these European Union changes by some conservative politicians and state functionaries has been one of 'closure' and the rejection of cosmopolitanism, thus accentuating, emphasizing and promoting Greek national identity. For example, the proposal that the new European Union identification cards should not include religious affiliation has been vigorously protested by the Greek Church and state officials.

11 Donnan and McFarlane, in reviewing recent examples of policy-oriented anthropological research in Northern Ireland point out the risk suggested by these studies: that anthropology's academic and theoretical orientation may be 'dissolved' (1997: 274–78). See also Shore and Wright for a discussion of the concept of 'anthropology of policy' drawn from the British academic experience (1997: 1–10, 35); and Martin for an analysis of the concept of 'policy' and its association with social order in the USA (1997: 239).

12 For an analysis of anthropology's delayed introduction to Greek academia, see Gefou-Madianou 1993.

13 Campbell, an Oxford trained anthropologist, was perhaps the most influential of this generation of anthropologists working in Greece. His book on the Sarakatsani (1964), drawing heavily on the work of his teacher Evans-Pritchard, brought an African perspective to Greek ethnography (cf. Bakalaki 1993: 54).

14 Indeed, many social science researchers were arrested and exiled during the military junta.

15 The new trend in anthropology is globalization. Historically, anthropological theory has sought to weaken the notion of ethnic and cultural boundendness, of closure, of ethnic purity, of uniqueness. Its comparative programme has always kept cultural and social anthropology from extreme forms of relativism, and indeed the very nature of its methodology has prevented the adoption of such a position.

16 See, for example, Lafazani 1994, 1997; Danforth 1995; Agelopoulos 1997a and 1997b; Cowan 1997, 1998; Karakasidou 1997; Mackridge and Yannakakis 1997; Van Boeschoten 1997; Yannissopoulou 1998; Gefou-Madianou 1999. For a critical perspective, Herzfeld 1997.

17 Yet, anthropology could be considered by some as a dangerous discipline. For an example, see the discussions about Karakasidou's ethno-

graphic work on Macedonia (*Oikonomikos Tahydromos* 1993: 33–4).

18 As Tsaoussis has pointed out, the dilemma that the universities have to face is both how to meet the short-term needs of society, and its economy, and how to maintain their independent and utility-free nature (1993: 30).

19 For a discussion about the long-term investment of any society on theoretical research and not only on policy-oriented investigations, see Firth 1992. He maintains that in any sophisticated, 'intellectually aware society facilities should always be available for so-called "pure" theoretical research, in social fields as in the humanities and natural sciences' (1992: 212).

20 Greece has been characterized in the European Union as a Member State with a very high percentage of its work force being employed in the public sector.

21 See, for example, Petronoti 1998. A number of former anthropology undergraduate students of Panteion University are now studying in Bulgaria, Albania, Egypt, Russia and Indonesia.

22 For example, anthropologists in Greece must 'translate' the anthropological theory which was first produced in the West and adapt it to the categories of Greek society. The concepts of culture and identity as defined in Europe and North America have a different historical and philosophical background from those in Greece – in part due to the differences between Eastern and Western Christianity and their respective relations to political power and control throughout the centuries (Bowman 1995: 37, 47).

References

Agelopoulos, G. (1997a) 'Γαμήλιες ανταλλαγές σε πολιτισμικά μεικτές αγροτικές κοινότητες της Μακεδονίας' (Marriage Exchanges among Multicultural Rural Communities of Macedonia), in V. Gounaris, I. Michaelidis and G. Agelopoulos (eds) *Ταυτότητες στη Μακεδονία* (Identities in Macedonia), Athens: Papazisis.

—— (1997b) 'From Bulgarievo to Nea Krasia, from "Two Settlements" to "One Village": Community Formation, Collective Identities and the Role of the Individual', in P. Mackridge and E. Yannakakis (eds) *Ourselves and Others: The Development of Greek Macedonian Cultural Identity Since 1912*, Oxford and New York: Berg.

Bakalaki, A. (1993) 'Ανθρωπολογικές προσεγγίσεις της σύγχρονης ελληνικής κοινωνίας' (Anthropological approaches of modern Greek society), *Διαβάζω* 323: 52–8 (special issue on Social Anthropology, ed. E. Papataxiarchis).

—— (1997) 'Students, Natives, Colleagues: Encounters in Academia and in the Field', *Cultural Anthropology* 12 (4): 502–26.

Bowman, G. (1995) 'Identifying Versus Identifying with "the Other": Reflections on the Siting of the Subject in Anthropological Discourse', in A. James, J. Hockey and A. Dawson (eds) *After Writing Culture: Epistemology and Praxis in Contemporary Anthropology*, London and New York: Routledge.

Campbell, J. (1964) *Honour, Family and Patronage: A Study of Institutions and Moral Values in a Greek Mountain Community*, Oxford: Clarendon Press.

Cowan, J. (1997) 'Idioms of Belonging: Polyglot Articulations of Local Identity in a Greek Macedonian Town', in P. Mackridge and E. Yannakakis (eds) *Ourselves and Others: The Development of Greek Macedonian Cultural Identity Since 1912*, Oxford and New York: Berg. A modified edition of this article was also published in Greek (1998) in D. Gefou-Madianou (ed.) *Ανθρωπολογική Θεωρία και Εθνογραφία: Σύγχρονες Τάσεις* (Trends in Anthropological Theory and Ethnography), Athens: Ellinika Grammata.

Danforth, L. M. (1995) *The Macedonian Conflict: Ethnic Nationalism in a Transnational World*, Princeton: Princeton University Press.

Day, P. and Klein, R. (1987) *Accountabilities: Five Public Services*, London and New York: Tavistock Publications.

Donnan, H. and McFarlane, G. (1997) 'Anthropology and Policy Research: The View from Northern Ireland', in C. Shore and S. Wright (eds) *Anthropology of Policy: Critical Perspectives on Governance and Power*, London and New York: Routledge.

Ependytis (a weekly newspaper – Επενδυτής) 'Η μεταρρύθμιση αναγκαία πολιτική'(Reforms, a needed policy), 7 and 8 November 1998.

Firth, R. (1981) 'Engagement and Detachment: Reflections on Applying Social Anthropology to Social Affairs', *Human Organization* 40: 193–201.

—— (1992) 'A Future for Social Anthropology?', in S. Wallman (ed.) *Contemporary Futures: Perspectives from Social Anthropology*, London and New York: Routledge.

Gefou-Madianou, D. (1993) 'Mirroring Ourselves through Western Texts: The Limits of an Indigenous Anthropology', in H. Driessen (ed.) *The Politics of Ethnographic Reading and Writing: Confrontations of Western and Indigenous Views*, Saarbrucken – Fort Lauderdale: Verlag Breitenbach Publishers.

—— (1999) 'Cultural Polyphony and Identity Formation: Negotiating Tradition in Attica', *American Ethnologist*, 26 (2): 412–39.

Grimshaw, A. and Hart, K. (1993) 'Anthropology and the Crisis of the Intellectuals', Cambridge: Prickly Pear Press pamphlet no. 1.

Herzfeld, M. (1982) *Ours Once More: Folklore, Ideology and the Making of Modern Greece*, Austin: University of Texas Press.

—— (1987) *Anthropology Through the Looking Glass: Critical Ethnography in the Margins of Europe*, Cambridge: Cambridge University Press.

—— (1992) *The Social Production of Indifference: Exploring the Symbolic*

Roots of Western Bureaucracy, New York and Oxford: Berg.

—— (1997) *Cultural Intimacy: Social Poetics in the Nation-State*, New York and London: Routledge.

Karakasidou, A. (1997) *Fields of Wheat, Hills of Blood: Passages to Nationhood in Greek Macedonia 1870–1990*, Chicago and London: The University of Chicago Press.

Kladis, D. and Panoussis, Y. (1992) *Ο Νόμος Πλαίσιο: Για τη Δομή και Λειτουργία των Α.Ε.Ι. – όπως τροποποιήθηκε με τον ν. 2083/92* (The Reformatory Law for the Structure and Function of Higher Education Institutions as was reformed by the 2083/92 law), Athens – Komotini: Sakoulas.

Kyrtsis, A.-A. (1996) *Κοινωνιολογική σκέψη και εκσυγχρονιστικές ιδεολογίες στον ελληνικό μεσοπόλεμο* (Sociological thought and modernizing ideologies in the Greek interwar period), Athens: Nissos.

Lafazani, D. E. (1994) 'Appartenance Culturelle et Différenciation Sociale dans le Bassin du bas-Strymon: Étude d'Intégration Nationale d'une Région Macédonienne', *C.E.M.O.T.I. – Cahiers de Études sur la Méditerrannée Orientale et le Monde Turco-Iranien* 17: 123–31.

—— (1997) '*Μικτά χωριά του κάτω Στρυμώνα: Εθνότητα, Κοινότητα και Εντοπιότητα*' (Mixed villages in lower Strymon: Ethnicity, Community and Locality), *Εύγχρονα Θέματα* 63: 96–107.

Lewis, I. M. (1995) 'Anthropologists for Sale?', in A. Ahmed and C. Shore (eds) *The Future of Anthropology: Its Relevance to the Contemporary World*, London and Atlantic Highlands, NJ: Athlone.

Mackridge, P. and Yannakakis, E., (eds) *Ourselves and Others: The Development of Greek Macedonian Cultural Identity Since 1912*, Oxford and New York: Berg.

Martin, E. (1997) 'Managing Americans: Policy and changes in the meanings of work and the self', in C. Shore and S. Wright (eds) *Anthropology of Policy: Critical Perspectives on Governance and Power*, London and New York: Routledge.

Ministry of National Education and Religion (1996) 'Operational Programme for Education and Initial Professional Training – Sub-programme 3: Tertiary Education' (Επιχειρησιακό Πρόγραμμα Εκπαίδευσης και Αρχικής Επαγγελματικής Κατάρτισης – Υποπρόγραμμα 3: Τριτοβάθμια Εκπαίδευση, Τεχνικά Δελτία Ενέργειας Μέτρων), Athens: Ministry of National Education and Religion.

Oikonomikos Tachydromos (Οικονομικός Ταχυδρόμος) (1993) 'Τι σημαίνει η υπέρ Καρακασίδου συνηγορία;' (What does the Karakasidou's advocacy mean?), 39: 33–4.

Petralias, N. and Theotokas, N. (1999) 'Η Απορύθμιση του Δημοσίου Πανεπιστημίου' (The disorganization of the Greek university), *Ο Πολίτης* (O Politis) 60: 18–25.

Petronoti, M. (1998) *Το Πορτραίτο μιας Διαπολιτισμικής Σχέσης* (The

Portrait of a Cross-cultural Relationship), Athens: Plethron.

Power, M. (1997) *The Audit Society: Rituals of Verification*, Oxford: Oxford University Press.

Shore, C. (1997) 'Governing Europe: European Union Audio-visual Policy and the Politics of Identity', in C. Shore and S. Wright (eds) *Anthropology of Policy: Critical Perspectives on Governance and Power*, London and New York: Routledge.

Shore, C. and Wright, S. (1997) 'Policy: A New Field of Anthropology', in C. Shore and S. Wright (eds) *Anthropology of Policy: Critical Perspectives on Governance and Power*, London and New York: Routledge.

Strathern, M. (1992) 'Reproducing Anthropology', in S. Wallman (ed.) *Contemporary Futures: Perspectives from Social Anthropology*, London and New York: Routledge.

—— (1997) '"Improving Ratings": Audit in the British University System', *European Review* 5 (3): 305–21.

Tsaoussis, D. G. (1993) *Το Ελληνικό Πανεπιστήμιο στο Κατώφλι του 21ου Αιώνα: Ζητήματα Κοινωνικής Πολιτικής* (Greek University on the Threshold of the 21st Century: Social Policy Issues), Athens: Gutenberg.

Tsoucalas, C. (1986) *Κράτος, Κοινωνία, Εργασία στη Μεταπολεμική Ελλάδα* (State, Society, Employment in Post-war Greece), Athens: Themelio.

—— (1996) 'Ανώτατη Εκπαίδευση και Αναπαραγωγή: Δομές και Στρατηγικές της «Μορφωσιολατρίας»' (Higher Education and Reproduction: Structures and Strategies of Education-Worship'), in C. Tsoucalas, *Ταξίδι στο Λόγο και την Ιστορία: Κείμενα 1969–1996, τ 2* (Journey to Discourse and History: Texts 1969–1996, vol. 2), Athens: Plethron.

Van Boeschoten, R. (1997) *Ανάποδα Χρόνια: Συλλογική Μνήμη και Ιστορία στο Ζιάκα Γρεβενών – 1900–1950* (Awkward Years: Collective Memory and History in Ziaka, Grevena 1900–1950), Athens: Plethron.

Velissariou, S. (1998) '*Γνώση και Ευρωπαϊκή Ταυτότητα*' (Scholarship and European Identity), *Ο Πολίτης* (O Politis) 58: 12–16.

Yannissopoulou, M. (1998) 'Η Ανθρωπολογική Προσέγγιση. Αλμωπία Παρελθόν, Παρόν και Μέλλον' (The anthropological perspective. Almopia: past, present and future) in A. Michalopoulou *et al.* (eds), *Μακεδονία και Βαλκάνια: Ξενοφοβία και Ανάπτυξη* (Macedonia and Balkans: Xenophobia and Development), Athens: Alexandria.

Accountability . . . and ethnography

Marilyn Strathern

While the principal focus of these essays remains with anthropologists, or ethnologists as Chapter 7 would have it, they raise
issues which concern academics at large, and especially academics in
the social sciences whose subject is enquiry into the nature of social
and cultural life. What is the social scientist's, or anthropologist's,
task but to describe society, social organization, culture? For
anthropologists the means to this end include the practice of
writing ethnography, and its twin, the kind of (field) research which
anticipates that holistic enterprise. Indeed, ethnography is at once
claimed as anthropology's chief medium for conceptualizing the
task of description and has wide popularity as a method of empirical
enquiry which these days is pursued across a range of disciplines
within – and sometimes beyond – the social sciences. Clearly, however, this has not been a book 'about' ethnography, even though
ethnography is a background presence in many of these contributions; so why my addendum?

On the face of it, pursuing the kind of ethnography which relies
on open-ended immersement in diverse social situations seems far
removed from many of the professional concerns of academic
production. In the context of higher education, the rituals of
verification associated with audit might bear a resemblance to the
scholarly apparatus which is the focus of its scrutiny, but their
concern with quality is not carried into the content and analytical
rigour of an academic product. Rather their concern is with the
'external' mechanisms by which such products are valued – the
reputation of researchers through the journals in which they
publish or the success of teaching as it has an impact on students.
Here audit patently impinges upon conditions of work and
academic career trajectories. By the same token, it is seemingly far

removed from what many anthropologists would regard as at the heart of their 'real work'. In addition to other pursuits of scholarship, theoretical enterprise, analysis and the like, the anthropologist's investment in emprical enquiry and specifically in ethnographic research is prime.[1] One might imagine that this is hardly touched by the ramifications of audit. Not so.

Here I do no more than offer a few notes. They are organized in a way I could not have anticipated at the outset, or have invented, for that matter, had I restricted myself to this location (audit) alone. Questions about the future of ethnography are raised in not one but three locations. When laid out they intersect, form a crossroads of a kind, in a network that otherwise appears to consist of separate concerns. More than that, each location is at once a 'context' for the others and contains the others within – in the same way as audit does not just impinge upon the academic's conditions of work but also interpenetrates it, and in the same way as the 'external' mechanisms by which products are valued are also internalized. We should not perhaps be surprised after all to find ethnography folded within these embraces.

These are empirical observations. I briefly establish the interest of the three locations; I then ask for each what might be the implications for ethnography and its associated styles of research.

An emergent triad?

Elsewhere, Pels makes a startling claim. Anthropologists, he says, need to study ethics as it is becoming part of postmodern culture. He then adds: 'They have to research to what extent ethics has become a word to talk about things *that anthropologists were used to calling culture and society'* (1996: 18, my emphasis). He refers to anthropological expertise that was always built up around 'emergent [negotiable] forms of social and cultural organisation in situation[s] of cross-cultural contact'; these have now become 'situations of emergent sociability that need ethical guidelines', and he means guidelines beyond professional codes which tend to emanate from only one of the parties concerned. He even goes so far as to discern an 'emergent ethical consciousness' at large. In other words, where anthropological models of society and culture once provided a cue to the conduct of encounters, now such encounters are to be governed by professional protocols which create altogether different kinds of interacting subjects. For example, in Chapter 5, Pels suggests that one cost of this shift is (attrition of) the kind of moral responsibility already built into the qualitative negotiations of ethnography. (The suggestion is made in order, I may add, the better to critique ethnography's own illusions.)

Now this large claim for ethics is striking in its similarity to what has also been claimed for audit. Observe the phrasing. Power asserts that accountability practices have become a central part of the re-invention of government, indeed that in Britain they have reached an extreme form: 'Audit is *an emerging [coming into being] principle of social organization* [which] . . . constitutes a major shift of power: from the public to the professional, and from teachers, engineers and managers to overseers' (1994: 47, my emphasis). There is more here than the fact that new subjects for study grow under one's gaze. One could, for example, put beside Tsoukas's (1997: 831) observation about the 'recent proliferation of audits and league tables', Rose's (1999: 191) comment that the 'language of ethics is proliferating'.[2] But these two describers of social and cultural worlds (Pels and Power) are indeed claiming more, namely that audit and ethics are structuring social expectations in such a way as to create new principles of organization.[3] This striking conjunction was an impetus for bringing these papers together.

The striking was made startling for me (that is, in retrospect, Pels's observation came to seem startling) by a third character who has appeared in the wings under a similar designation, this time from an international agenda. Shore and Wright (1997: 4, my emphasis) refer to the expanding frontiers of policy: 'policy is an increasingly central concept and instrument *in the organization of contemporary societies'*. 'It has become a major institution of Western governance, on a par with other key organizing concepts such as "family" and "society"' (1997: 6). Hence its significance for the creation of subjects. Shore and Wright (1999) have pointed to new subjectivities, at least as they are conceived by neo-liberal governance even if the evidence suggests that the measures put in train very often fail to create them. This resonates with Pels' (1999) argument that professionalizing ethics has brought about a major shift in anthropologists' self-understanding of themselves in society, as well as with Power's (1994: 4) comment that more and more individuals and organizations are coming to think of themselves as subjects of audit.

In short, here is a bevy of social observers who are all claiming that practices emanating from these arenas of concern – ethics, audit, policy – are the places to be looking these days if one is looking for *society*. These locations have appeared similar from the brief descriptions I have appended here. But describing them as similar does not simply come from a position outside them, a position which hints of an external and artificial set of analytics. Here I borrow again from Riles (2000) to observe that the way in which (so to speak) ethics, audit and policy describe – and thereby reflect upon – themselves points to their implication in one another.

By way of example, policy and audit sound on the face of it like opposite ends of a process. The one deals with the inception of plans and aims (policy) while the other institutes checks on good practice in their execution (audit). Yet the distance between the poles is illusory. For the one is also inside the other: policy-makers may build auditing practices into their schema, and auditing will replay to policy the grounds of its own effectiveness. Practitioners involved in both will take account of ethics, and their own good practices will become 'ethical' for the enterprise. In this sense ethical practice may enhance a firm's or a bureaucracy's public account of itself while at the same time assisting its policy formulations. The mutual reference points here are as much within each phenomenon as without. Hence perhaps the sense that protocols to do with ethics, audit and policy have displaced other objects (autonomous institutions, responsible citizens, the rule of law, professional duty – the list is endless) which pointed to themselves as endorsing a relationship with 'society'.

Audit/policy/ethics: if this really is a triad of emergent practices, a set of related trajectories, then audit, accountability in a widely acceptable and mobile cultural form, is just one among many changing features of social life. (Another candidate in the neo-liberal world would be contract and contractualism [cf. Davis, Sullivan and Yeatman 1997], a field which has obvious intersections with both policy and the efficiency/acccountability axis which also leads to audit.) At any rate, although the principal starting point of this book lay in those cultural forms of accountability which have found their way into higher education, 'audit' has not been the only focus. As we have seen, the promotion of audit is a 'policy' matter, and particular policies are referred to throughout the chapters. However, rather than having accountability absorbed by a study of policy and policies, it seemed important to let 'ethics' offer a further point of departure.[4] Hence its character was given, so to speak, deliberate breathing space in Part III. Taken together, these essays hold the triad of trajectories as distinct yet interrelated starting points for enquiries into the conditions under which the new acountabilities create their effects.

What I now wish to do is take each location in turn, and reflect on what there might be to learn about ethnographic practice. Perhaps part of the answer, as to whether audit/policy/ethics really forms a convergent triad, will depend on how divergent the responses are. It may also depend on the demarcations which separate inside from outside, and thus on degrees of openness and closure.

Audit: verification and knowledge production

Audit's rituals of verification complicate the description of what it is that ethnography does. Among other things, that is because of its (ethnography's) relational nature (Woolgar 1997). Helping/ monitoring people to help/monitor themselves demands a kind of reflexivity – people come to see themselves both through and beyond the eyes of the auditor. Yet it is not just how they see which is interesting, but how they *describe* themselves. How, in turn, does this affect what ethographers, as describers of social and cultural life, produce? Effect is not going to be felt directly – no monitoring protocols overtly target ethnographic or similar research practices; the question is that of indirect influence. Let me briefly take this in stages.

First, academic work in general, and the knowledge to which it leads, becomes caught up in meta-descriptions (accounts) of what that work purports to be. A prime example lies in being required to state how efforts or outcomes relate to original aims and objectives. Simple as the request might seem, making the connections explicit, through the very activity of having to state them in this way, alters their role in the work.[5]

> The Open University [in the UK] . . . is filled with good social democrats. Everybody there believes in the redistribution of educational opportunities and seeks to remedy the exclusiveness of British education. And yet, in these last ten years, these good social-democratic souls . . . have learned to speak a brand of metallic new entrepreneurialism, a new managerialism of a

horrendously closed nature. They believe what they have always believed, but what they do, how they write their *mission statements*, how they do *appraisal forms* . . . that's what they are interested in now. The result is that the institution has been transformed.

(Hall, *New Statesman and Society*,
26 November 1993, quoted by
Tsoukas and Papoulias 1996: 859, my emphasis)

Second, the social sciences in particular have long had dealings with political regimes which regard the gathering of social knowledge as the gathering of knowledge for social use (cf. Moore 1996). Unlike much of applied science and technology, their tangible products are not things which work but descriptions (models) which work (as descriptions). Tailoring descriptions for others is thus taken for granted as an adjunct of social science enquiry. Here there are two apparent points of reflexivity.[6] On the one hand, meta-descriptions of what this or that work purports to be, and thus what the worker/author intended by it, presses knowledge into the service of a kind of authorial 'self'-knowledge. At the same time, on the other hand, this knowledge potentially serves what Weber (1948: 233–5, 243) saw as one of the objectives of modern bureaucracy, a crucial aid for government and commerce alike,[7] namely expert knowledge. 'Expert knowledge' is knowledge produced in a form not just available for bureaucratic use but assimilatable as the facts and opinions of experts. We might call this bureaucratic reflexivity. No wonder, then, that what is creatively generated from 'within' (Chapter 6) can seem a kind of unwelcome complicity when it is is elicited from 'without' (Chapter 8).

Finally, and thirdly, what about the anthropologist's 'ethnography'? Its symbolic importance to the way in which anthropologists think about their discipline is not to be underestimated. This also has two sides. On the one hand, ethnography stands for the idea of a self-driven, multi-stranded and open-ended mode of free enquiry likely to be damaged by too much bureaucratic control. On the other, it stands for a crucial question about how to react to auditing and its associated regimes: is not ethnography principal among the methods available for a social science response? But while, as icons, this pair of suppositions powerfully point to important elements of academic enquiry, they are not (complete) descriptions of it. Ethnographic practice was never 'free'; there have been more than two decades of reflection both on its colonial past and on the ethics of responsibility and mutuality. And nobody is actually asking anthropology for a response.[8] So the issue has to be what action this imaginary can or may mobilize.

As far as the matter of responding is concerned, anthropologists had better imagine they are being asked for a response – because they 'respond' whatever they do and, unless they imagine the dialogue, will doubtless have it imagined for them. Nevertheless, it is the first icon, ethnography as open-ended enquiry, on which I wish to dwell; I take the anthropologist's particular concept of ethnography as my model.

The kinds of audit practices which have become widely institutionalized endorse a quite particular approach to knowledge. Alsop (1999), Deputy Director of Research in the UK's Economic and Social Research Council but writing in a personal capacity, has offered a scathing critique of the essentially 'traditional' and hierarchical model of knowledge production with which, for example, research assessment in the UK is conducted. He follows here the distinction between two modes of knowledge production, Mode 1 and Mode 2, proposed by Gibbons and colleagues (1994).

Under Mode 1, Alsop describes the hierarchy of knowledges implied in distinguishing basic from strategic and applied research, and the producers from the consumers ('users') of it. By implication, Mode 1 knowledge is generated from types of universities which are themselves hierarchically organized and old-fashioned bastions of higher learning. The generation of knowledge through Mode 2, on the other hand, where such distinctions disappear, along with disciplines, is purportedley related in a direct way to its emergence via new institutional forms, such as the now numerous research centres found both within and outside the university system, commercially sponsored learning and research units, non-university institutes and no doubt the new business-based corporate universties too. It is arguable, however, that some of its important features echo those which flourished in older institutional settings, such as networks of communications among scholars and, I would add, ethnographic research.

Let me expand on the point. By contrast with the linear aims of Mode I knowledge, with its clearly targeted outputs, Mode 2 is interactive and non-linear, with 'peer and user input', and may knowingly merge the investigator with the subjects of investigation.[9] Moreover Mode 2 knowledge sits well alongside a whole stable of management techniques stressing the virtues of flexibility in time management, small-scale teamwork, trust among colleagues, risk-taking and so forth.[10] Whether or not anyone recognizes the old-fashioned university department in this, many of these techniques present no novelty to the social scientist, nor would they, one suspects, to the laboratory scientist either. What is novel is the role they are given in the (self-)description and internal organization of knowledge-producing organizations. For anthropology I want to press the point that, beyond no novelty, there is a profound sense in which there is simply no other way of doing ethnographic research. For there is – and has been – no other way (than adopting similar techniques) of grasping what the ethnographic method grasps, namely how to make room for the unpredictable.

Anthropology should not underestimate the power of its ethographic practice to produce narrational and interpretive understanding. This last phrase comes from Tsoukas (1994: 10–11), an academic professional in public and business administration.[11] It is because of the open-ended and context-dependent character of social systems that, as he says, there 'will always be an ineradicable *indeterminacy* in what the action of (or in) a social system is about and where it leads' (his emphasis).

> If the meaning of aspects of organizational life depends on the context in which they are located it follows that, placed in different contexts, the 'same' aspects acquire different meanings. Put differently, events, processes and experiences in organizations are rarely transparent, self-evident or completely fixed, but are intrinsically ambiguous and *therefore open-ended in the interpretations that can be attached to them* [my emphasis].

These are words a social anthropologist could have written.[12] To the extent that people's interpretations of one another's actions are central to social life, the practice of ethnographic interpretation, description, holds a very particular place in social science. Narrative and interpretation both imply some kind of interaction or dialogue between persons, imagined or not, a crucial source of social indeterminacy. The unpredictable (and cf. Strathern 1999) may be a matter of past as well as forward referencing, as Battaglia (1999) implies in the use of the term 'contingency'. Indeed, Battaglia's writing on the ethics of the open subject is highly relevant here.

Keeping open a place for the unpredictable or contingent can be taken as one of the *achievements* of anthropological-style ethnography. 'Ethnographic dialogues stand as model moments of social exchange' (Battaglia 1999: 120). The model does not conceal the social and cultural realities of human interchange, and thus does not conceal ambiguity; ambiguity signals the way in which claims elicit counter-claims, open themselves up to explanation by third parties, and so forth.

The anthropologist's kind of ethnography grasps not just the contingency and unpredictability of social life, then, but how description and self-description contribute to it. And in a world saturated with 'information', including expert knowledge distilled as information, maintaining a diversity of descriptive forms begins to seem important for its own sake.

Referring to the recent proliferation of audits and league tables as evidence of a managerial rationality centred on the notion that institutional behaviour can be shaped if the right kind of reinforcement is combined with the right information, Tsoukas (1997: 831) comments: 'At any rate, the assumption is that if those in charge know what is going on, they can manage a social system better. "To know" in this context means having information on the variation of certain indicators that are thought to capture the essence of the phenomenon at hand.' Like a ritual, audit tries to persuade participants of the way the world is without acknowledging its own particular perspective. Power himself uses the word 'ritual' advisedly. He does not just mean ritual in the common English sense of an empty or opaque show of form (though audit can appear as both those); he intends it also in an anthropological sense. As Chapter 1 describes at the level of a national economy, audit procedures have a certain transformative effect, bringing about the ends they anticipate, notably that it is possible to demonstrate quality and value for money across a whole range of institutions and services. In higher education they endorse a particular reading of what 'producing' knowledge is all about. Where Mode 2 encourages an open-ended approach to open-ended phenomena, and is positively interested in the uncertainties of which it is a part (Gibbons *et al.* 1994: 66–7), Mode 1 knowledge production can offer indicators. Since indicators have purportedly got to the essence of what is important already, their measurements push the unpredictable back onto what 'individuals' produce, that is, onto variablity in individual performance. (This may be individual persons within an institution or an institution regarded as a collective individual.) It goes without saying that the point or source of knowledge production is then seen to lie neither in narrative nor interpretation as essentially social practices but in the efforts of identifiable knowledge-producers. This has a political dimension; I turn to policy, stimulated by the suggestion in Chapter 2 (and the focus of Shore and Wright 1999) as to how anthropologists might adopt a political stance.

Policy: the case of the UK

As we have seen between the several essays, there are diverse governmental backgrounds to the way in which audit, in its expanded sense, has emerged over the last twenty years or so. This section focuses largely on one case, the United Kingdom, where the process began in the early 1980s, a time when the kinds of economic pressures which in Austrian higher education were not finally brought to a head until the mid-1990s (Chapter 9) had already begun to bite.

New forms of managerial government have not sprung unaided from the local cultures of any of these countries. They are the outcome of policy measures on the part of specific governments, reinforced by a corporate community which gives them international credibility. For these outcomes have involved the deliberate promotion of key concepts and thus, as a matter of policy, deliberate attempts to modify people's cultural outlooks. The reader is referred to an earlier volume in the EASA series, edited by Shore and Wright (1997), which argues that 'policy' should be of great interest to anthropological enquiry as an arena where governments re-invent society and promote cultural change. Thus they point to a cluster of 'keywords' developed in the UK – but not restricted to it – during the New Right discourses of the 1980s.[13] It embedded certain conceptualizations of the 'individual' (person) in a nexus including 'freedom', 'market', 'enterprise' and 'family' (1997: 19–29). The constellation was quite deliberately put together, in Marquand's (1992: 69) words, as part of the Thatcherite project to limit the role of the state: 'Neo-liberals hold that the market is the realm of freedom, and the state the realm of coercion'.[14] 'Enterprise culture' summed it up at the time.[15]

In this constellation of values, the 'individual', understood as an individual person, was a political invention, or re-invention (cf.

Roberts 1996). Shore and Wright remind us that it incorporated a particular vision of the way in which people relate to the state. It was a relationship which could be mediated by, or translated into, ideas of how people would relate, as individuals and family members, to 'the market'. So new consumers, 'customers', were invented.[16] Now alongside 'customers', but with much less fanfare, new producers also appeared. They were the inevitable consequence of the way in which idioms of customer service moved into state-funded arenas of all kinds, so that the providers of services for the state were now regarded as producing services for individual customers – as doctors might be imagined in relation to patients or university teachers in relation to students (see, for example, Clarke 1996). Of course the state which purchased the services on behalf of these customers remained an interested party. Goverment defined the state's role as guardian or guarantor of value.

The new producers did not have a name, but what was everywhere being scrutinized was 'performance'. Against the background of purported constraints on public funding, 'selectivity' (between instutitions, for funding) seemed essential, and 'measures' of performance could be used as a bureaucratic yardstick.[17] At the same time the public was told it needed reassurance that 'quality' would not be devalued. For instance, the UK Audit Commission (see Chapter 2) set up to scrutinize local government for 'value for money' rapidly moved from its primary concern with finance to a general concern for efficiency and well-being. In fact the two kinds of performance were held to reinforce each other: good practice and good financial management were bracketed together in a consultative document put out in 1987 by the then UK Department of Education and Science, *Accounting and Auditing in Higher Education*.

Following from this, one can intepret the feedback loop (Power 1994: 36–7; 1996: 293) through which auditors and auditees create their own reality, not as some by-product of but as stemming from/contributing to a political doctrine of reinforcement. Auditing becomes an example to add to all the myriad ways in which people govern themselves (Rose 1992, 1993), and the social state gives way to the enabling state (Rose 1999: 142).[18] As I have noted, Mode I knowledge (see above) pressed into this kind of political service encourages measurements of what institutions produce by looking at what individuals produce. In promoting value for money and economic efficiency, persons and organizations are being assisted to provide public reassurance of their viability. When, as in higher education, 'individuals' become conscious of themselves as 'performers', seemingly 'in control' of their performance (Munro 1999), the bureaucratic reflexivity involved is part of their relationship to the enabling state.

It is thus no surprise that 'auditors' can be shown to be 'us' (cf. Brenneis 1994). In the ways in which academics are drawn into auditing practices, this is true at many levels. Peer reviews co-opt colleagues, willingly or otherwise. Those who devise and administer monitoring schemes are likely to come from the same kind of professional background as those whose performance they scrutinize. Lastly, academics supply thought, not just information about but also reflections upon conditions of life. Writing of Foucault's concept of governmentality,[19] Rose (1999: 7, my emphasis) adds:

> Once political power takes as its object the conduct of its subjects in relation to particular moral or secular standards, and takes the well-being of those subjects as its guiding principle, it is required to rationalize itself in particular ways. . . . [R]uling becomes a 'reflexive' activity: those who would rule must ask themselves who should govern. . . . Hence 'modern' governmental rationalities, modern ways of exercising rule, inescapably entail a certain investment of *thought* . . .

Among thinkers who have been developing their skills in the UK over the last two decades, when these policies have been taking effect, are those working in the fields of financial management and accounting, including 'critical accounting'[20] – a tiny handful of whom I have been citing.[21] This work may be informed by colleagues from sociology, including those with an investment in ethnography and thus in the relationship between descriptive practices (e.g. Law 1996).[22] For the common interests I have in mind arise from the point I have been reiterating, that organizations subject to audit have to be able to *describe* themselves. If auditing elicits skill, as Power remarks (1997: 21), in operational understanding, so does policy. What about ethnographic understanding?

Social anthropologists might learn about their own practices in asking whether policy-makers could ever or would never count as ethnographers, amateur or otherwise. For we (anthropologists, social scientists) have only begun to sketch out the significance of open-ended research. What is at stake (once again) is what is to count as knowledge, or at least as 'productive' knowledge. We encountered this in Chapter 3, and the way in which knowledge understood as expertise is pressed into the service of policy. Gefou-Madianou (Chapter 10) has some salutory comments on the limitations of policy-inspired (anthropological) ethnography when it redefines the anthropological project as most suitably applicable to 'home'. On a different tack, I have argued, along with Battaglia, that it is precisely in an imagined state – as open-ended and ambiguous enquiry in the most serious sense – that ethnography is good to think.

Contra bureaucratic assumptions about expert knowledge, however, it does not necessarily follow that the methods of ethnography are appropriate to all situations. Indeed, these studies suggest that it is by no means clear that more investment of time and energy into *understanding*, say, the process of policy-making is the obvious response (Chapter 8). 'Better' or 'more' ethnography is not necessarily going to help. One reason is precisely bureaucracy's iterative capacity for absorbing and turning knowledge to ends of its own. The question of how then we differentiate such iteration from the kind of transparency and moral responsibility (Chapters 6 and 7) social anthropologists and others might wish to nurture for themselves, in relation to others whom they value, could hold some interest. Giri (Chapter 6) opens with some critical observations here.

Ethics: codes of conduct

I do not propose to add much more about ethics; the chapters in Part III will have made their own impact. However, I expand on the connections which led the original EASA panel and workshop to set 'audit' and 'ethics' side by side.

Audit and ethics ricochet off one another.[23] We may readily accede that where monitoring extends to the conduct of research, there may a direct effect on the kind of work which social scientists are able to carry out. However, there is more to it than this. The ethos of accountability which underlies these new forms of managerial government is one which anthropologists and others have in a certain manner taken on board (Chapter 7) in their own disciplinary practices; from this point of view, Chapter 5 gives a Euro-American history of the changing character of ethics in professional life. An audit regime in turn complicates already existing practices of ethical accountability with its own set of protocols.[24]

There is a sense in which ethics, especially when it is codified ('ethical codes'), could be thought of as an enlarged or magnified version of audit: it specifically relates 'good practice' to individual conduct. It is not, of course, only individual persons who may be judged; ethical standards may apply to an institutions (collective individuals). Now audit endorses transparency as one of its own aims, for making procedures visible includes taking into account the aims of the institution. Auditing thus reinforces the requirement that administrators in all kinds of professions become more managerial and accountable.[25] Insofar as these roles are regarded as carrying the values of good practice,[26] the more people fulfill them, the more visibly an institution is seen to be ethical, to be taking good practice seriously. Being transparent about means and methods is regarded as generally 'ethical', then, insofar as it makes the practices of the institution available to outside enquiry. For institutions as organizations this has managerial consequences in terms of the demands for performance laid on its personnel. As a meta-performance, institutions must make their aims articulate, through, say, the 'mission statements' which universities among others feel compelled to produce.

However, whereas auditing re-shapes the way institutions describe themselves, formal procedures of ethical practice often become attached to professional status. In recent years there has been a spreading concern with public codes as a mark of professionalism; in Britain this contributes to a new explicitness about the quality of service which customers can expect from facilities such as health and education. There is a further distinctive dimension to ethics. Ethics re-describes accountability as a matter of responsibility towards those who will be affected by the outcome of certain actions.

Ethical practices refer to the interests of third parties, which are at once the reason for and lie outside the loop through which professionals demonstrate (to other professionals) their adherence to standards. By this very definition, the good practices which come under scrutiny concern relations with others. At the same time, applying ethical canons to behaviour summons a personal point of reference. So although the others may be corporate bodies, they are frequently understood as other persons; 'ethics' may thus be phrased in terms of 'personal' responsibilities, rights and liabilities. From this perspective, there is a crucial social difference between the evaluation of individual performance in audit and the scrutiny of personal conduct introduced by the concept of ethics. Where higher education audits create the performing individual who contributes to the productivity of academic enterprise, ethical codes create the responsible practitioner who does not want his or her actions to bring harm to others. Here, as Fillitz (n.d.) has shown, ethics draws on more general social sensibilities embedded in all kinds of human interactions or moralities. Obvious candidates for ethical codes and protocols are the social sciences whose very discipline involves other persons.

When Rose (1999: 188) coins the phrase 'ethico-politics' for a new game of power[27] concerned with 'the self-techniques necessary for responsible self-government', he adds its further concern with 'the relations between one's obligations to oneself and one's obligations to others'. Ethico-politics is thus also about one's conduct in the course of other duties. So the ends of ethical conduct do not divert means from other ends, but ensure that as means (to another end) they meet certain criteria in themselves. Audit, it was suggested, has been promoted by policies interested in refashioning the relationship between individual and state; beyond the loop between auditor and auditee, the state is the interested third party. In the case of the kind of ethics which flourish under the same governmental regimes, auditable ethics one might say (Chapter 5), a significant third party is the party who needs protection from the individual who acts with his or her own ends in mind. At this juncture we encounter the potential for 'ethics', with its current connotations, to refashion the peoples with whom ethnographers work. Not surprising perhaps that there is suddenly a new category of research practices, namely those which entail 'research with human subjects', and a new definition of the anthropologist's informants and respondents as 'human subjects'.[28] And here we should not forget that side by side with 'ethical codes' go 'ethics committees'. Codes and committees may come to co-define each other.

Paradigmatic ethics committees are found in clinical medicine. They were developed to protect patients from invasion of liberty and to protect practitioners from charges of abuse: each party was seen to have its own interests. 'Research' is a crucial instance where the ends of the medical researcher are obviously separable from the welfare of an individual patient. The kinds of approaches adopted by ethics committees have since expanded to become the template for scrutinizing all kinds of research involving material collected from people. This in turn has expanded the significant role already given to informed consent in the protocols of medical ethics (where the law has endeavoured to protect individuals from abuse and abrogation of autonomy).[29] When, as in research contexts, the issue is (informed) consent to a flow of information something happens to the idea of passing on information. For the protocols axiomatically define people as having an interest in material collected from them; extended to information, this presumes them to be in some sense owners, or at least the originators, of it.[30] The question of protection may thus hover between notions about keeping confidences and respecting privacy on the one hand and an idea that ownership rights need defending on the other. The question arises especially when interaction is initiated by the researcher. The subjects of research are thereby created as at once the recipients of the actions of others, and as having interests vulnerable to those of the researcher.

Let me repeat the point (and see Grey 1996: 604) that ethico-politics mobilizes (exploits) already existing values in the conduct of relations – people's sensibilities towards one another – that lie beyond the political (Chapter 6), in the same way as disciplinary ethical codes may mobilize a professional's stance towards others derived from practices already in place (Chapter 7). I have wanted to underline one implication for the relationship between the ethnographer and those informants crucial to his or her enquiries, the ethographer's third party (see above). This lies precisely in the fact that research which calls forth ethical guidelines may in turn be defined as research on or into human subjects. And here there is a further potential for slippage. The revised Code of Ethics of the AAA (*Anthropology Newsletter*, September 1998) is careful to state that its concern is with the protection of 'people with whom they [anthropologists] work', in research projects with 'persons studied *or providing information*' (my emphasis). In other words, it recognizes the fact that human subjects, the ethnographer's third party, are not necessarily the subject of the research. That subject is the manifold products of people's interactions. Hence socio-cultural anthropologists have generally summarized their enquiries as enquiry into the nature of 'society' and 'culture'. We begin to see how (auditable) ethics might indeed introduce displacements:

in the place of the study of society and culture, recasting social science research as 'research *on* human subjects' would at once subtly and crudely change the terrain.

A crude example was a further impetus for this book: Amit's (n.d.) exposition at an earlier EASA conference of the way in which her research had been moulded by her Canadian university's expectation of what constituted fieldwork. Her concern was with what we might call anticipatory audit. Ethics clearance bodies, charged with ensuring that research does no harm to people, in effect define the anthropologist's informants not as autonomous persons engaged with the ethnographer in acts of interpretation and narration about the nature of social and cultural life,[31] but as so many individual 'human subjects' whose consent can and must be given in an informed way. The implicit model of research is that of the interview or survey with respondents. Amit notes among other things that scrutiny has brought with it an explicit intolerance for open-ended research procedures.

This could, I suggest, hold a new way of being demeaning to informants. It pushes the exploratory, indeterminate and unpredictable nature of social relations (between ethnographer and his or her third party) back onto a 'point of production', with the ethnographer as initiator. However much talk there is of collaboration or of conserving the autonomy of subjects or recognizing their input into the research or taking power into account, this aspect of ethics in advance, of anticipated negotiations, belittles the creative power of social relations.

Caveat

The contributors to *Audit Cultures* have different ideas about what social anthropologists should be doing. They may argue for greater political sensibility or for going beyond the political, may appeal to deeper self-knowledge about what drives a discipline – an honesty that has nothing to do with audit – or conversely what the particular way forward seems to be in pressing local circumstances. They may deploy ethnography, advocate ethnographic awareness, suggest that ethnography is not the answer one thought it was, or see in the very duplexity of the ethnographic method the germs of a more generally applicable moral practice. The debates are still open. The academy can only be one of their fields, but they would all agree that we cannot isolate the goals of the discipline from the institutions through which they are reproduced.

Institutions have been taken as in the first case referring to universities; here anthropologists have their greatest professional presence. It is clear that change is ahead. The increasing diversification of 'knowledge production' and of locations from which Gibbons *et al.*'s Mode 2 knowledge practices are emerging will have their effect on universities. Perhaps in the process the worst excesses of the 'new accountabilities' will be swept away, as (Alsop hints as much) not so new after all. But I want to enter a caveat about the way the idea of – indeed the very description of – Mode 2 knowledge production has been taken up.

I suggested that perhaps part of the answer as to whether audit/policy/ethics really forms a convergent triad will depend on how divergent the responses are. One can imagine circumstances under which each may elicit its own specific response from social anthropologists.[32] However, my brief excursus has uncovered a commonalty of a kind. In asking questions about ethnography, I have found myself defending the idea of self-driven, multi-stranded, open-ended enquiry, just the kind which Mode 2 apparently enables, and describes, so well. Yet there is more to the anthropologist's 'open endedness' than the starting conditions for free enquiry. Anthropologists often strive to repeat that open-endeness in the preparation of their final product: 'the [written] ethnography'. More significantly, the anthropologist, and most so when in fieldwork dialogue, is open *to* others and their interpretations and descriptions. This is a question of disciplinary stance (in personal terms individual anthropologists manage particular situations with greater or lesser effectiveness). We could say that audit, policy and ethics are also 'open' to one another. But in the anthropologist's case these others invariably belong to institutions – formal and informal – 'outside' those where anthropologists work. Attending to people, relationships, circumstances that could not be predicted in advance but required absolute concentration of effort on what these people, relationships and circumstances were like in the past always brought its own, important, closure.

Now this kind of openness and closure obviously did not have to wait for the emergence of new institutions of the kind which generate what is now described as Mode 2 knowledge. So while it has been useful to hang my remarks about the nature of ethnographic research onto the delineation of Mode 2 knowledge production, it has also been disingenuous. Perhaps, rather, we should be paying attention to Fillitz's observation (pers. comm.)

that Mode 2 is no more politically innocent than Mode 1. It serves the powerful rhetoric of 'flexibility' and 'change' through which new policies acquire a value because they are new, promoting, among other things, a climate in which people are ready to change their jobs more often, as Gibbons and his colleagues themselves point out (1994: 74).

After decades of appeal to innovation, 'innovation' seems to gain rather that decrease in strength as a policy keyword. It is when Mode 2 practices are regarded as innovatory in this political sense, at once reinforcing the ideology of the new through a new kind of expertise (knowledge systems which comment on their own conditions for the production of knowledge) and summoning yet more bureaucratic reflexivity (how to press this expertise into service), that the ethographer should be most culturally alert.

Acknowledgements

Many have contributed to this piece, and the stimulus of some of them at least should be evident. Here I mention the pains which in addition Rolland Munro took with my text: I am most grateful.

Notes

1 In other contexts one might stress the distinctive nature of *anthropological* over other practices of ethnography.
2 One can proliferate parallels. Pels's (1999: 103) reference to MacIntyre's 1984 observation about the modern reduction of *ethics* to a 'simulacrum', a copy without an original, echoes Power's observation (1994: 56) that *audit* 'may be a narcissistic practice which feeds off its own representations. It is a simulacrum in Baudrillard's sense'.
3 In Chapter 5, Pels connects them as discrete yet overlapping technologies of the self, e.g. the exhortation to be open to public scrutiny changes character when it moves from the promotion of the professional self to the audited self. An ethical code can serve different technologies of the self. For further debate see the discussion in Munro's contribution to Parker 1998 [next note].
4 The loop back has already been anticipated in a volume on *Ethics and Organizations* (ed. Parker 1998), by writers in the fields of management science and organizational theory, which appeared in 1998. A future resource rather than a past reference point: my thanks to Rolland Munro for drawing it to my attention.
5 Objectives matter, observes Jeremy Mynott, Managing Director of Cambridge University Press (pers. comm.) – their debasement as mission-statement type 'aims and objectives' is no laughing matter. Practitioners may become cynical about the way they 'dress up' a

research proposal or package their teaching in order to meet outside expectations of how aims and objectives should be presented, but cynicism is a half-way house to self-alienation. The phrase 'self-alienation' I draw from Gledhill's (1994: 92–3) summary of how Mexican estate workers, with contempt for the administrators and foremen, claimed that they were the real base of the enterprise; what dignified their work under otherwise intolerable conditions was also their own appropriation of their objectives in life as work for the estate. What about social scientists who, apparently *against* the straitjacket of policy expectations, might claim that they are in fact producing the 'real' social knowledge that society needs?

6 I leave this reference to reflexivity deliberately open-ended and ambiguous; it may be read ironically (as intended in Strathern 1997) or as an invitation to think about the realpolitik role for a critical or political reflexivity advanced by Shore and Wright (1999) and in Chapter 2.

7 'Only the expert knowledge of private economic interest groups in the field of "business" is superior to the expert knowledge of the bureaucracy [because it is vital to survival – they have to get it right]' (Weber 1948: 235).

8 Although in the UK the Higher Education Funding Council's 1998/9 Teaching and Learning Initiative has sought out disciplinary responses; for a comment see Chapter 2.

9 As in anthropological fieldwork. More generally, see Woolgar 1997: by contrast with the tendency of UK research councils to buttress linearity through what he calls a supermarket model of research (making it attractive in the hopes of selling it), the selling of new computers – in one industrial/commercial instance – depended on a complex set of interactive and non-linear relations between company and potential customers. As a social category, such customers are of course relatively easy to define. But his general point is that systems of acountability fail to attend to the contingent and variable character of cultural artefacts.

10 In a positive sense Gibbons *et al.* (1994: 3) point to knowledge production through Mode 2 as [really] 'more socially acceptable' and 'reflexive' than through Mode 1. They have a complex model of accountability: apropos research, 'individuals themselves cannot function effectively without reflecting – trying to operate from the standpoint of – all the actors involved. The deepening understanding that this brings has an effect on . . . the structure of the research itself' (1994: 7).

11 I cite Tsoukas, among other management critics of management orthodoxies, to underline the point that there is enormous diversity in this field (management theory), and the practices which inform government-driven policy are drawn from only a very particular part of it. Note that the IMF team described in Chapter 1 were fully aware of the unpredictable. (Tsoukas [pers. comm.] draws attention to Weick's classic text, *The Social Psychology of Organization*, which argues for the recognition of contradiction and ambiguity in organizational creativity and in handling the unknown.)

12 And as far as the first sentence goes did: with the qualification that the same meanings can also be carried across contexts, this was Radcliffe-Brown's 1914 epiphany on the Andaman Islands.

13 However, Woolgar (1997) points to studies that show that the value-for-money ethos and public service reforms so evident in the Thatcher years substantially pre-date them, certainly in the US. See Davis, Sullivan and Yeatman (1997) on the new contractualism – and the new fashioning of individual subjects – under changing varieties of 'liberalism' over this period in New Zealand and Australia.

14 He points to the paradox that the cultural revolution implied by deliberately creating an enterprise culture can only be carried out by a strong and intrusive state able to change the mix of incentives and disincentives. 'If an enterprise culture is to come into existence, *universities must be remodelled*, the freedom of action of local authorities must be much more tightly curtailed, the self-governing professions must be "marketized" and the trade unions must lose power' . . . (1992: 70, my emphasis).

15 Delineated for example in the collection edited by Heelas and Morris (1992), which includes anthropological contributions. On the rise of 'accountable management' in the UK during the 1980s, see Humphrey, Miller and Scapens 1993.

16 Heelas and Morris (1992: 13–14) record, from among many, one pertinent criticism made at the time (1980s) of the new vocabulary and all it entailed: that the exercise of traditional enterprise virtues of responsibility and discipline had been eclipsed by the runaway success of promoting consumerism and the ethic of wealth creation. We might observe that 'responsibility' and 'discipline' were in the meanwhile being made visible in the development of separate organs dedicated to accountability and quality control (for an anthropological comment, see Shore and Selwyn 1998: 167).

17 Apropos the UK's Research Assessment Exercise (see Chapter 2), a HEFCE representative has recently observed: ' [in part the RAE is] to help improve the quality of research and to provide a degree of accountability. However, its main purpose is to provide information about the quality of research in different subjects, to enable us to implement our policy of selective funding . . . [S]ome instrument is needed to distinguish between the quality of different institutions' (Bekhradnia, 1999: 113).

18 The essays in Wright 1994 point to the emergence of ideas of 'empowerment' (in development practices, for example, which have moved towards building institutional capacity through encouraging local self-reliance [Marsden 1994: 4]) over the last twenty years, across a range of organizational situations, within Britain and beyond.

19 'Governmentality' in Foucault's works presupposes the freedom of the governed (whose wills and desires are co-opted). I would add that 'governance' is used in the present chapter with Shore and Wright's (1997: 5–6) conotations, that is, presupposing people's capacity to act as agents. The authors offer a resumé of recent sociological commentary on the 'techniques of the self' by which neo-liberal rationalities

create governable subjects with a sense of liberty (e.g. as consumers) and motivated through self-activation (after, for example, Miller and Rose 1990; Burchell 1991, 1993; Rose's 1992 inaugural lecture to Goldsmiths' College, University of London).

20 I owe a very belated debt to former colleagues from the Department of Accounting and Finance at Manchester University. Let me mention again Maryon McDonald's input; she has long traversed much of the same ground.

21 And do not pretend to have even scratched the surface. In the present context, however, see further Miller and O'Leary 1987; Miller 1992; Hopwood & Miller 1994; Roberts 1996.

22 Law analyses two sets of differences (a) in modes of representation and accounting which arise from managers shifting from being empiricists to being instrumentalists in their approach to the world (not unlike the doubling of the liberal self posited in Chapter 5); (b) in the distinctive subjectivities which discretionary management accounting systems and legal-bureaucratic processes each mobilize in organizations.

23 The title of Munro's essay in *Ethics and Organizations* (Parker 1998) is 'Ethics and accounting: the dual technologies of self'. Needless to say, the following remarks of mine can be problematized in various ways.

24 See Wright 1994 on 'indigenous' forms of organization as they work either for or against management-designed ones.

25 Rose (1990; and cf. Power 1994: 35) notes the new interventions from intermediaries in the persons of 'accountants, managements and consultants, lawyers, industrial relations specialists' and so forth 'to transform people into customers who can choose between products'. Since the 1980s a host of other professionals have become defined as, so to speak, quasi-managers only to find another intermediary layer – the auditors.

26 'Good practice' has become a bundled-together phrase of the kind Riles (1998) has analysed.

27 Rose (1999: 188) observes from a British vantage point that 'it is likely to be on the terrain of ethics that our most important political disputes will have to be fought for the foreseeable future'.

28 Especially in the field of bioethics, research potentially dubious on other grounds may be classified as research on human subjects in order to justify it on the specific grounds that safeguards in this arena are already in place. (No new ethical practices need be invented.)

29 My particular phrasing comes from an unpublished paper by Janet Dolgin (Hofstra Law School, 1999), on 'Choice, tradition and the new genetics', which includes a discussion about American views on informed consent in the context of the transmission of genetic knowledge beween family members. I am grateful for permisson to cite it.

30 Usually regarded as so 'natural' a connection it does not have to be spelled out. We may note (from Dolgin, see n. 29) that in the USA some legal commentators have proposed that the doctrine of 'informed consent' could work as an *alternative* to ownership rules and thus allow the law to avoid tackling questions about the ownership of knowledge.

31 One may of course question with Chapter 6 the extent to which anthropologists have failed to treat informants as 'true' collaborators or colleagues, the subject of extensive critical discussion in recent years. (One may also observe the extent to which current ethico-politics mobilizes a vocabulary which serves numerous local purposes.) In larger terms, Giri (1998a, 1998b) would ask what is needed for a person's self-preparation towards an outward orientation.

32 One could point to some possible differences in 'specific responses'. If Shore and Wright (1997) argue that one may pursue anthropology through treating policy as a field of research, I understand them to mean that the ramifications of policy itself forms a domain of activity with its own interconnections; but anthropologists do not, as it were, need a policy – they need tools of research. In the case of ethics, however, anthropologist practitioners need to take into account growing calls for ethics codes of practices, and will have to take an ethical stance themselves in their approach to these. Audit is different again: towards its insistence on visibility the only viable stance may be (as here) ironic.

References

Alsop, A. (1999) 'The RAE and the Production of Knowledge', *History of the Human Sciences* 12: 116–20, in special section, 'Knowledge for What? The Intellectual Consequences of the Research Assessment Exercise', edited by I. Velody.

Amit, V. (n.d.) 'The Insidiousness of Bureaucratic Banalities: Some Implications for Anthropological Fieldwork', paper presented to IV EASA conference workshop, Barcelona, 1996.

Battaglia, D. (1999) 'Towards an Ethics of the Open Subject: Writing Culture in Good Conscience', in H. Moore (ed.) *Anthropological Theory Today*, Cambridge: Polity Press.

Bekhradnia, B. (1999) 'The Research Assessment Exercise and its Intellectual Consequences', *History of the Human Sciences* 12: 113–16, in special section, 'Knowledge for What? The Intellectual Consequences of the Research Assessment Exercise', edited by I. Velody.

Brenneis, D. (1994) 'Discourse and Discipline at the National Research Council: a Bureaucratic *bildungsroman*', *Cultural Anthropology* 1: 23–36.

Burchell, G. (1991) 'Peculiar Interests: Civil Society and Governing "the System of Natural Liberty"', in G Burchell, C. Gordon and P. Miller (eds) *The Foucault Effect*, Hemel Hemspstead: Harvester Wheatsheaf.

—— (1993) 'Liberal Government and Techniques of the Self', *Economy & Society* 22: 267–82.

Clarke, J. (1996) 'Public Nightmares and Communitarian Dreams: the Crisis of the Social in Social Welfare', in S. Edgell, K. Hetherington and A. Warde (eds) *Consumption Matters*, Oxford: Blackwell Publishers/ Sociological Review.

Davis, G., Sullivan, B. and Yeatman, A. (eds) (1997) *The New Contract-ualism?*, Melbourne: Macmillan Educational Australia.

Filltiz, T. (n.d.) 'Morality Between Political Power and Altruism', paper delivered to workshop on *Ideology and Morality*, EASA conference, Oslo, 1994.

Gibbons, M., Limoges, C., Nowotny, H., Schwartzman, S., Scott, P. and Trow, M. (1994) *The New Production of Knowledge: the Dynamics of Science and Research in Contemporary Societies*, London: Sage Publications Ltd.

Giri, A. (1998a) 'Transcending Disciplinary Boundaries: Creative Experiments and Critiques of Modernity', *Critique of Anthropology* 18: 379–404.

—— (1998b) 'Social Criticism, Cultural Creativity and the Contemporary Dialectics of Transformation', *Dialectical Anthropology* 23: 215–46.

Gledhill, J. (1994) *Power and its Disguises: Anthropological Perspectives on Politics*, London: Pluto Presss.

Grey, C. (1996) 'Towards a Critique of Managerialism: the Contribution of Simone Weil', *Journal of Management Studies* 33: 591–611.

Heelas, P. and Morris, P. (eds) (1992) *The Values of the Enterprise Culture: the Moral Debate*, London: Routledge.

Hopwood, A. and Miller, P. (eds) (1994) *Accounting as Social and Insitutional Practice*, Cambridge; Cambridge University Press.

Humphrey C., Miller, P. and Scapens, R. (1993) 'Accountability and Accountable Management in the UK Public Sector', *Accounting, Auditing & Accountability Journal* 3: 7–29.

Law, J. (1996) 'Organizing Accountabilities: Ontology and the Mode of Accounting', in R. Munro and J. Mouritsen (eds) *Accountability: Power, Ethos and the Technologies of Managing*, London: International Thomson Business Press.

Marquand, D. (1992) 'The Enterprise Culture: Old Wine in New Bottles?' in P. Heelas and P. Morris (eds), *The Values of the Enterprise Culture: the Moral Debate*, London: Routledge.

Marsden, D. (1994) 'Indigenous Management and the Management of Indigenous Knowledge', in S. Wright (ed), *Anthropology of Organisations*, London: Routledge.

Miller, P. (1992) 'Accounting and Objectivity: the Invention of Calculable Selves and Calculable Spaces', *Annals of Scholarship* 9: 61–86.

Miller, P. and O'Leary, T. (1987) 'Accounting and the Construction of the Governable Person', *Accounting, Organization and Society* 12: 235–65.

Miller, P. and Rose, N. (1990) 'Governing Economic Life', *Economy & Society* 19: 1–31.

Moore, H. (1996) 'The Changing Nature of Anthropological Knowledge: an Introduction', in H. Moore (ed) *The Future of Anthropological Knowledge*, London: Routledge.

Munro, R. (1999) 'The Cultural Performance of Control', *Organization Studies* 20: 619–40.

Parker, M. (ed.) (1998) *Ethics and Organizations*, London: Sage Publications.

Pels, P. (1996) 'EASA Ethics Network', *EASA Newsletter* 18, October 1996: 18–19.

—— (1999) 'Professions of Duplexity: a Prehistory of Ethical Codes in Anthropology', *Current Anthropology* (with comments) 40: 101–36.

Power, M. (1994) *The Audit Explosion*, London : Demos.

—— (1996) 'Making Things Auditable', *Accounting, Organizations and Society* 21: 289–315.

Riles, A. (1998) 'Infinity within the Brackets', *American Ethnologist* 25: 378–98.

Riles, A. (2000) *The Network Inside Out*, Ann Arbor: Michigan University Press.

Roberts, J. (1996) 'From Discipline to Dialogue: Individualizing and Socializing Forms of Accountability', in R. Munro and J. Mouritsen (eds) *Accountability: Power, Ethos and the Technologies of Managing*, London: International Thomson Business Press.

Rose, N. (1990) *Governing the Soul: the Shaping of the Private Self*, London: Routledge.

—— (1992) 'Governing the Enterprising Self', in P. Heelas and P. Morris (eds) *The Values of the Enterprise Culture: the Moral Debate*, London: Routledge.

—— (1993) 'Government, Authority and Expertise in Advanced Liberalism', *Economy & Society* 22: 283–99.

—— (1999) *Powers of Freedom: Reframing Political Thought*, Cambridge : Cambridge University Press.

Shore, C. and Wright, S. (eds) (1997) *Anthropology of Policy: Critical Perspectives on Governance and Power*, EASA series, London: Routledge.

—— (1999) 'Audit Culture and Anthropology: Neo-liberalism in British Higher Education', *Journal of the Royal Anthropological Institute*, 5 (4): 557–75.

Shore, C. and Selwyn, T. (1998) 'The Marketisation of Higher Education: Management, Discourse and the Politics of Performance', in D. Jary and M. Parker (eds) *The New Higher Education: Issues and Directions for the post-Dearing University*, Stoke-on-Trent: Staffordshire University Press.

Strathern, M. (1997) ' "Improving Ratings": Audit in the British University System', *European Review* 5(3): 305–21.

Strathern, M. (1999) *Property, Substance and Effect: Anthropological Essays on Persons and Things*, London: Athlone Press.

Tsoukas, H. (1994) ' Introduction' to H. Tsoukas (ed.) *New Thinking in Organizational Behaviour: from Social Engineering to Reflective Action*, Oxford: Butterworth/Heinemann.

—— (1997) 'The Tyranny of Light: the Temptations and the Paradoxes of the Information Society', *Futures* 9: 827–43.

Tsoukas, H. and Papoulias, D. B. (1996) 'Understanding Social Reforms: a Conceptual Analysis', *Journal of the Operational Research Society* 47: 853–63.

Weber, M. (1948) 'Bureacracy', Part III chapter 6 of *Wirtschaft und Gesselschaft*, in H. H. Gerth and C. W. Mills (trans. & ed.) *From Max Weber: Essays in Sociology*, London: Routledge and Kegan Paul Ltd.

Woolgar, S. (1997) 'Accountability and Identity in the Age of UABs', CRICT (Centre for Research into Innovation, Culture and Technology, Brunel University) Discussion Paper no. 6.

Wright, S. (1994) ' "Culture" in Anthropology and Organizational Studies', in S. Wright (ed.) *Anthropology of Organizations*, London: Routledge.

Index

Printed in the United States
51295LVS00002B/139-195